The cliffs near Dipper Cove
glow pink in the setting sun
on Bowdoin conservation land
(hike 11).

COASTAL TRAILS
OF MAINE

INCLUDING ACADIA NATIONAL PARK

Dolores Kong and Dan Ring

FALCONGUIDES

GUILFORD, CONNECTICUT

D0920768

FALCONGUIDES®

An imprint of The Rowman & Littlefield Publishing Group, Inc.
4501 Forbes Blvd., Ste. 200
Lanham, MD 20706
www.rowman.com

Falcon, FalconGuides, and Outfit Your Mind are registered trademarks of Rowman & Littlefield.

Distributed by NATIONAL BOOK NETWORK

British Library Cataloguing-in-Publication Information available

Library of Congress Control Number: 2020934689

ISBN 978-1-4930-3737-7 (paper: alk. paper)
ISBN 978-1-4930-3738-4 (electronic)

♾™ The paper used in this publication meets the minimum requirements of American National
Standard for Information Sciences—Permanence of Paper for Printed Library Materials, ANSI/
NISO Z39.48-1992.

CONTENTS

THE HIKES

Acadia National Park and Bar Harbor   *135*

Overview

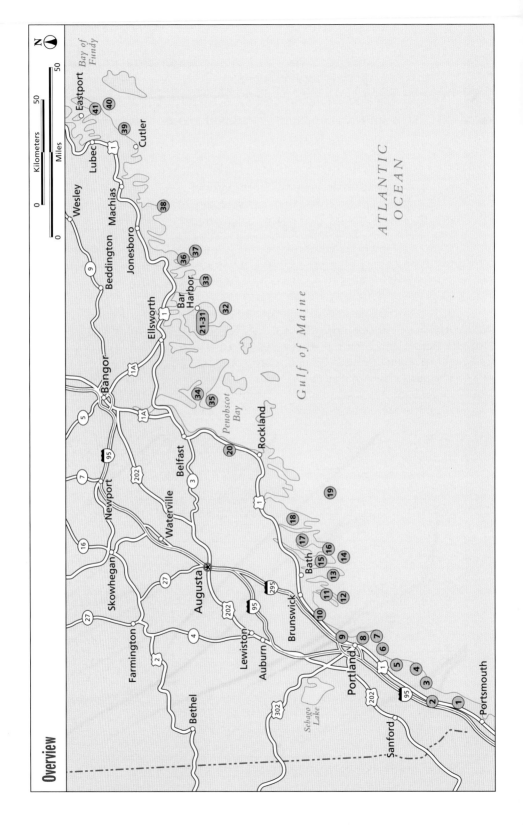

N

Kilometers
0   50   50

Miles
0   50

Bay of Fundy

Eastport

(41)

(40)

Lubec

(39)

Cutler

Wesley

Beddington   Machias

Jonesboro

(38)

9

Ellsworth

Bar Harbor

(36) (37)

(33)

(11)

(32)

(21-31)

Bangor

1A

1A

(34)

(35)

5

Penobscot Bay

7

95

202

Newport

Rockland

Waterville

Belfast

(20)

3

16

Skowhegan

(19)

Gulf of Maine

27

Augusta

(18)

(17)

27

Farmington

4

202

95

295

Brunswick

Bath

(15) (13)

(16)

(14)

(11)

(12)

2

Lewiston

Auburn

(10)

(9)

(8)

(7)

302

Sebago Lake

Portland

1

(6)

(5)

(4)

Sanford

202

95

(3)

ATLANTIC OCEAN

(2)

(1)

Portsmouth

MEET YOUR GUIDES

Dolores Kong and Dan Ring have backpacked all of the more than 270 miles of the Appalachian Trail in Maine and have climbed virtually all the peaks that are 4,000 feet and higher in the Northeast. They are members of the White Mountains Four Thousand Footer, the New England Four Thousand Footer, the Adirondack 46Rs, the Northeast 111ers, and the New England Hundred Highest Clubs.

Dolores is a Certified Financial Planner™ professional and senior vice president with Winslow, Evans & Crocker, Inc. (member of FINRA/SIPC), in Boston. A Barnard College graduate, she is also a Pulitzer Prize finalist in public service from her previous career as a staff writer at the *Boston Globe*.

Dan is an operations professional with Winslow, Evans & Crocker, Inc., in Boston and a writer who has been a Massachusetts Statehouse bureau chief for a variety of newspapers. He graduated from Boston College with a bachelor's degree in English. Dan and Dolores are married and live outside Boston. They write a blog: acadiaonmymind.com.

The third edition of their *Hiking Acadia National Park* guide won the 2016 National Outdoor Book Award in the outdoor adventure guidebook category and the 2018 Independent Publisher Book Award gold medal in the travel guidebook category.

Coauthors Dan Ring and Dolores Kong in Acadia National Park

ACKNOWLEDGMENTS

We want to thank some key people who provided important help and guidance and always responded to our questions about the coastal trails of Maine: Gary Stellpflug, trails foreman at Acadia National Park; Charlie Jacobi, retired ranger and natural resource specialist at Acadia National Park; Michael J. Good, a registered Maine guide and owner of Down East Nature Tours in Bar Harbor, who identified most of the scores of wild birds we photographed on the coastal trails of Maine; Jill E. Weber, consulting botanist at Acadia National Park, who identified many of the flowers and other plants we photographed at the coast; Tom and Susan Hayward of Mount Desert, guides during the Acadia Birding Festival who later identified photos of birds and plants; Michele L. Brann, reference librarian at the Maine State Library, who provided invaluable research for this book; and Sam Smith, journalist, author, and also a board member of the Wolfe's Neck Center for Agriculture & the Environment.

We owe a lot to the managers, staff, directors, and others of the municipal, state, federal, private, and nonprofit conserved lands that provide public access to the coastal trails of Maine, including Dick Cough of the Bar Harbor Village Improvement Association; Laura Sewall of the Bates–Morse Mountain Conservation Area; Nicholas J. Ullo of Boothbay Region Land Trust; Steven Allen of the Bowdoin College Schiller Coastal Studies Center; Bill Elliot of Camden Hills State Park; Billy Claflin and Carolyn Shubert of Coastal Rivers Conservation Trust; Kurt Shoener of Crescent Beach and Kettle Cove State Parks; Jon Southern of Downeast Coastal Conservancy; Cornelia J. Cesari of Keepers of Baker Island; Tom Bradbury of Kennebunkport Conservation Trust; Charles Cannon of Holbrook Island Sanctuary; Daniel Grenier, Doug Radziewicz, and Nancy Sferra of The Nature Conservancy; Nicholas Lund and Jenn Schmitt of Maine Audubon; Brian Benedict of Maine Coastal Islands National Wildlife Refuge and Northeast Canyons and Seamounts Marine National Monument; Caleb Jackson, Jane Arbuckle, and Melissa Lee of Maine Coast Heritage Trust; Gary Best of Maine Bureau of Parks and Lands; Jeanne Roche of the Marginal Way Preservation Fund; Rebecca FitzPatrick, Frederick Faller, and Rick Cameron, all of Monhegan Associates, Inc.; Sean M. Vaillancourt of Popham Beach State Park; Shawn Goggin of Quoddy Head State Park; Kimberly Ashby and Larry Conrad of the visitor center at Quoddy Head State Park; Steve Norris and Sue Keefer of Rachel Carson National Wildlife Refuge; Samantha Wilkinson of Reid State Park; Tom Blake of South Portland Land Trust; Scott Richardson, Sue Bickford, and Paul Dest of Wells Reserve at Laudholm; and Andy Hutchinson of Wolfe's Neck Woods State Park.

We are also grateful to the following people from Maine (unless otherwise noted), including Christie Denzel Anastasia, John T. Kelly, Maureen Fournier, and Anne Warner, all of Acadia National Park; John McKee of Bowdoin College; Ed and Deb Hawkes of Bar Harbor; Deborah Dyer of the Bar Harbor Historical Society; Tim Henderson of Castine; Reta Farnham Hunter of Brooksville; Ann Simonelli of The Conservation

Fund in Arlington, VA; Teresa M. Bragg of the Town of Cutler; David MacDonald, Jim Linnane, Gerry Fournier, and Jack Russell, all of Friends of Acadia; Robin Emery of Lamoine; Barbara Hopp Linton of Sullivan; Shannon Knight, owner of County Road Cuts, and Tara Matthews, both of Trescott, for giving us a much-needed ride; Eleody Libby of Lubec; Charles Legris of Lubec; Jennifer Multhopp, librarian at the Town of Lubec; Steve Spencer, retired from the Maine Bureau of Public Reserved Lands; Claire L. Enterline of the Maine Coastal Program, Department of Marine Resources; Janet Parker of the Maine Department of Agriculture, Conservation and Forestry; Carl Tugend and Colin Shankland, both of the Maine Department of Inland Fisheries and Wildlife; Sean Birkel and Shane Moeykens of the University of Maine; Timothy J. Dugan of the US Army Corps of Engineers, New England District in Concord, MA; Teri Frady of the National Oceanic and Atmospheric Administration Northeast Fisheries Science Center in Woods Hole, MA; Darriel Swatts of the US Environmental Protection Agency in Boston; Rachel Holland of Steuben; Mildred Dinsmore and Sean Billings of the Steuben Historical Society; Judy East of the Washington County Council of Governments; Angi King Johnston, naturalist, of Mount Desert; and staff at the Maine Geological Survey.

HOW TO USE THIS GUIDE

This guide is designed to be simple and easy to use.

It's divided into four sections: Southern Coast and Greater Portland, Midcoast, Acadia National Park and Bar Harbor, and Downeast. Hikes in the same geographic area are grouped together.

At the back of each section is a sampling of regional points of interest, from craft brewers to lighthouses, historic sites to museums. Also included in the back of each section is a roundup of places to get a lobster roll or other fare, nearby campgrounds and lodging, and other coastal attractions. The lists aren't exhaustive or definitive—this is a hiking guide and not a general travel guide. The coastal trails are the star attraction; the breweries, places to eat or sleep, and other points of interest are the supporting cast.

The **Trail Finder** highlights some of the special features of the hikes, whether they are particularly picturesque, are family- or dog-friendly, provide beach access, or offer solitude.

The **Top 5 Hikes** are among our favorites, but every trail has its attractions, and it's hard to choose just five.

Before You Hit the Trail gives an overview of what makes the Maine coast special, its history and challenges, the role philanthropy has played in preserving it, and who has been drawn to it, whether writers, artists, millionaires, or celebrities.

It also includes information about the weather and tides (as some of the hikes are low-tide walks) and general rules about land use.

The meat of this guide is the coastal trails. Each hike description includes a map and summary information that delivers the trail's vital statistics, including length, difficulty, and canine compatibility.

Directions to the trailhead are provided. Trailhead GPS coordinates are based on data collected by us, provided by land agencies, or gathered from other reliable sources, such as the website of the US Board on Geographic Names: usgs.gov/core-science-systems/ngp/board-on-geographic-names. If your GPS uses a different notation than the one used here, you can convert data here: fcc.gov/media/radio/dms-decimal.

But as with any GPS data provided for recreational use, there are no warranties, expressed or implied, about data accuracy, completeness, reliability, or suitability. The data should *not* be used for primary navigation. Readers of this guide assume the entire risk as to the quality and use of the data.

Officials advise that visitors obey posted signs and land use regulations, use common sense, and avoid accidentally traveling on private lands while using a GPS unit.

Following the overview for each hike, you'll find the following information:

Start tells you where the hike begins.

Elevation gain gives you an idea of how much climbing is involved.

Distance is the round-trip length, whether it is a loop, an out-and-back, or a circuit hike.

Difficulty rates hikes from easy to strenuous, from the short and flat, taking no more than 1 to 2 hours to complete, to the steepest and longest, taking as many as 5 hours to finish. Although these ratings are subjective, bear in mind that even the most strenuous routes can be made easier by hiking within your limits and resting when needed or by cutting short the hike. What is easy depends on your fitness and adequacy of your gear. If you are hiking with a group, select a hike with a rating that's appropriate for the least fit and prepared in your party.

Hiking time assumes that on flat ground, most walkers average 2 miles per hour. Adjust that rate by the steepness of the terrain and your level of fitness, and you have a ballpark hiking duration. Be sure to add more time if you plan to picnic or take part in other activities like birding or photography.

Seasons/schedule tells you when the trail is open and the best time to visit, whether for optimum weather, sightseeing and access, or fewer crowds.

Fees and permits describes day-use or parking fees or any special permits needed.

Trail contact gives you the name, mailing address, phone number, and website or e-mail for the agencies that can provide more information.

Dog-friendly lets you know whether dogs are permitted, and under what conditions.

Trail surface indicates the footing to expect, whether well-graded gravel that might be accessible for visitors with wheelchairs or strollers, forest floor with exposed roots and rocks, sandy or cobble beach, or rock ledges. Even for easy trails, it's recommended that you wear shoes with rubber soles and ankle support to minimize the risk of injury.

Land status tells you who owns or manages the land.

Nearest town helps orient you geographically, but don't assume there will be full services, or any services, as some of the towns are quite small. Don't let your gas tank approach empty as you're heading to the trailhead or expect you can find a public restroom and a convenience store nearby.

Maps lists USGS topo, trail agency, and commercial maps that may be a helpful supplement to this guide's maps. Don't rely on Google Maps, which often doesn't show hiking trails and may require mobile data access.

Other trail users alerts you to others you may encounter on a trail.

Special considerations is a catchall category for things to note, from restrooms near the trailhead to beach wheelchair availability; where to find a tide chart to plan a low-tide walk to whether there is overflow parking; and specific prohibitions on use of drones and other rules highlighted by the trail agency to whether picnic areas, showers, and other facilities are available.

Finding the trailhead provides specific directions from a major road, intersection, or town and includes trailhead GPS coordinates.

What to See tells you what makes each hike special, from lighthouses and islands in the distance to the birds, wildlife, and plants you can spot up close; from the history of the place and its preservation to the literary, artistic, or geologic significance.

Miles and Directions gives you turn-by-turn instructions and key junctions and landmarks along the hike.

At the back of each of the four sections of coastal hike descriptions, you'll find the following listings—by no means definitive or exhaustive—to give you a flavor of what's available nearby. For more complete listings, you can check out mainebrewersguild.org to find out more about the Maine Beer Trail, as well as websites for chambers of commerce, such as the statewide visitmaine.com and mainetourism.com.

Breweries, Eats, and Sleeps highlights some craft brewers, lobster shacks, and other dining experiences, along with a sample of lodging options.

Camping lists nearby public or private campgrounds, with such basic information as address, phone number, website, and operating season and whether they accommodate RVs or dogs and offer waterfront sites or other amenities.

Lighthouses, Museums, and Historic Sites rounds up some historic and cultural resources that are part of the true Maine experience.

Coastal Attractions is a grab bag of events, places, and other trails that can provide reasons to come back to coastal Maine again and again to see how the state lives up to the title "Vacationland" and the sayings "The Way Life Should Be," and "Worth a Visit, Worth a Lifetime."

TRAIL FINDER

The forty-one coastal trails in this book represent a wide diversity:

- Two have features so distinctive they have been named National Natural Landmarks by the National Park Service: Monhegan Island and Carrying Place Bog, which is part of Quoddy Head State Park.

- Three are included on Maine's Ice Age Trail, which highlights aspects of the landscape carved by glaciers: Cadillac Summit Loop Trail, Quoddy Head State Park, and Mowry Beach Preserve.

- Five of them are among the Maine Natural Areas Program's Natural Heritage Hikes, with brochures describing what makes them special: Ferry Beach State Park, Camden Hills State Park, Wonderland Trail in Acadia National Park, Cutler Coast Public Reserved Land, and Quoddy Head State Park.

- Six are low-tide walks or include a side trail accessible only at low tide: Vaughn Island, Timber Point Trail, Bowdoin College Schiller Coastal Studies Center, Popham Beach State Park, Bar Island Trail in Acadia, and the Birch Point Trail in Petit Manan National Wildlife Refuge.

- Two include "reversing falls," a phenomenon special to Maine along the US Atlantic seaboard, formed by the ebbing tide, bedrock just below the surface of the water, and a narrow, constricting channel: Josephine Newman Audubon Sanctuary and Holbrook Island Sanctuary.

HIKE NO.	HIKE NAME	BEST PHOTOS	FAMILY FRIENDLY	BEACH ACCESS	DOG FRIENDLY	FINDING SOLITUDE
SOUTHERN COAST AND GREATER PORTLAND						
1	Marginal Way	●	●			
2	Wells Reserve at Laudholm	●	●	●		
3	Vaughn Island	●			●	
4	Timber Point Trail	●				
5	Ferry Beach State Park		●	●		
6	Crescent Beach and Kettle Cove State Parks		●	●		
7	Fort Williams Park	●	●		●	
8	Spring Point Shoreway	●		●	●	

HIKE NO.	HIKE NAME	BEST PHOTOS	FAMILY FRIENDLY	BEACH ACCESS	DOG FRIENDLY	FINDING SOLITUDE
9	Mackworth Island	•				
10	Wolfe's Neck Woods State Park	•	•		•	
MIDCOAST						
11	Bowdoin College Schiller Coastal Studies Center				•	
12	Giant's Stairs	•	•		•	
13	Bates-Morse Mountain Conservation Area	•		•		•
14	Popham Beach State Park	•	•	•		
15	Josephine Newman Audubon Sanctuary					•
16	Reid State Park	•	•	•		
17	Ovens Mouth Preserve				•	•
18	LaVerna Preserve	•			•	•
19	Monhegan Island	•			•	•
20	Camden Hills State Park	•			•	
ACADIA NATIONAL PARK AND BAR HARBOR						
21	Indian Point Blagden Preserve (Bar Harbor)	•				•
22	The Shore Path (Bar Harbor)	•	•		•	
23	Bar Island Trail	•	•		•	
24	Compass Harbor Trail	•	•		•	
25	Sand Beach and Great Head Trail	•	•	•		
26	Ocean Path	•	•		•	
27	Gorham Mountain and Cadillac Cliffs Trails	•				
28	Cadillac Summit Loop Trail	•			•	
29	Flying Mountain Trail	•	•			
30	Wonderland		•	•	•	
31	Ship Harbor Trail	•	•		•	
32	Baker Island (Acadia—Cranberry Isles)	•				
33	Sundew Trail (Acadia—Schoodic Peninsula)	•	•		•	•

HIKE NO.	HIKE NAME	BEST PHOTOS	FAMILY FRIENDLY	BEACH ACCESS	DOG FRIENDLY	FINDING SOLITUDE
DOWNEAST						
34	Witherle Woods Preserve				•	
35	Holbrook Island Sanctuary				•	•
36	Petit Manan National Wildlife Refuge—Birch Point	•			•	
37	Petit Manan National Wildlife Refuge—Hollingsworth	•		•	•	
38	Great Wass Island Preserve	•				•
39	Cutler Coast Public Reserved Land	•			•	
40	Quoddy Head State Park	•			•	
41	Mowry Beach Preserve		•	•	•	•

TOP FIVE HIKES

SPRING POINT SHOREWAY.
This hike lacks majestic cliffs
and deep forests, but it features
just about everything else for a
memorable and fun trek: views
of islands and Casco Bay, two
lighthouses, a historic exhibit
of Maine's importance during
World War II, a sandy public
beach, a walk through a large
marina and college campus, and
old military forts on land and
sea.

Bug Light stands above Portland Harbor, with Fort
Gorges, an old military fort, on a ledge in front of
Hog Island (hike 8).

A rainbow appears after a
rainstorm at Popham Beach
State Park (hike 14).

POPHAM BEACH STATE PARK. At low tide over a limitless expanse of beach,
you can hike a sandbar to Fox Island, get closeup views of islands and offshore lighthouses, or trek northeast all the way to the Kennebec River and
southwest to the Morse River.

MONHEGAN ISLAND. Head here by boat for a magical experience with tremendous ocean vistas from the highest cliffs along the Maine coast and rewarding stops at quiet coves and headlands after some rugged up-and-down hiking.

The ocean views toward Black Head are striking as you stand on the Cliff Trail on Monhegan Island (hike 19).

A beaver bares its teeth, tinted orange from the iron in its tooth enamel (hike 38).

GREAT WASS ISLAND PRESERVE. Explore the myriad wonders, including some challenging hiking through one of the largest jack pine stands in coastal Maine and along a stretch of pink-and-white granite shoreline with some cobble beaches and the chance to see harbor seals hauled out on offshore ledges, or maybe a beaver or snowshoe hare.

CADILLAC SUMMIT LOOP TRAIL. Acadia National Park inspires a lot of passion and could easily fill an entire list of top-five hikes in coastal Maine, but to be balanced, only one—the summit loop on Cadillac Mountain—makes the cut. At 1,530 feet, Cadillac is the highest point on the US East Coast, with an unrivaled panorama of ocean, islands, and mountain peaks.

Bar Island and the four Porcupine Islands—Sheep, Burnt, Long, and Bald—form a quintessential view from the top of Cadillac Mountain (hike 28).

BEFORE YOU HIT THE TRAIL

With its soaring seaside cliffs, expansive sand beaches, and views of islands and open ocean, the long Maine coastline offers tremendous opportunities for enjoying some of the best coastal trails in the nation.

It's nearly impossible to understate the appeal of Maine's coastline. Adding to its rugged and genuine beauty, the coast is also laden with lighthouses, forts, and other maritime history dating back to the 1600s and is dotted with lobster boats, wild blueberry fields, small fishing villages, and Main Streets.

"We just have that unique Maine feel," said Jon Southern, executive director of the Downeast Coastal Conservancy in Machias, a nonprofit land trust. "It's like time is frozen on the coast of Maine in many places."

You can visit Acadia National Park's Cadillac Mountain, the highest peak on the US Atlantic coast, and look out over a massive bay with dozens of islands; go up and down the cliffs of Monhegan Island or Quoddy Head State Park; take a low-tide walk to rocky islands; or hike in awe along the infinite beaches of southern and central Maine, the pink granite and boulders of Ocean Path in Acadia, or the long shoreline of Great Wass Island.

Maine is also noted for being the most forested state in the nation; spruce, pine, birch, and other trees often grow right next to the coast.

From Washington County in Downeast Maine to Bar Harbor on Mount Desert Island, from Georgetown Island in the Midcoast to Ogunquit and Kennebunkport in the south, the coastline is vital and irreplaceable.

The coast supports recreational boating and commercial fishing, including the nation's leading lobster and soft-shell clam fisheries. It provides a big portion of local real estate taxes and is a pillar of tourism and economic development.

CHALLENGES FACING THE MAINE COAST

The coast is also changing amid fears of climate change. Some shorelines are expanding, but others are eroding and shifting because of winter storms, more intense rainstorms, and rising sea levels, which can scrape away dunes, bluffs, and sand.

Increased use of the coast is another issue. Record-breaking crowds at Acadia prompted the National Park Service to plan a new reservation system for motorists, scheduled to run in 2021, at popular destinations such as the summit of Cadillac Mountain and the Ocean Drive section of the Park Loop Road.

Private development is also accelerating in Maine, including the coastline, making the land too pricey for local people, and the state generally is not buying new conservation lands. New private owners often block access to big parcels of land that locals had used for generations.

People are attracted to Maine partly because it has so much coastline. In fact, according to the National Oceanic and Atmospheric Administration (NOAA), Maine has more coastline than California and is ranked No. 4 in the United States for shoreline mileage.

Draw a straight line from border to border, and the Maine coast is 228 miles. But if you count all the tidal shoreline, including tidal rivers up to the head of tide, as well as more than 3,000 islands, the Maine coastline is 5,408 miles according to 2019 statistics provided by Claire L. Enterline, research coordinator, Maine Coastal Program, Department of Marine Resources.

Unfortunately, only a small percent is publicly owned.

Of the total coastline, 16 percent, or 573 square miles, is categorized as Maine Conserved Lands, including easements and lands owned by federal, state, municipal, and private nonprofit organizations. That 573 square miles includes conserved lands in communities that touch the coast, as well as conserved lands that border other conserved lands touching the coast.

To preserve land on the coast for public use and provide coastal trails, Maine heavily depends on more than eighty land trusts, or nonprofit conservation organizations, such as Downeast Coastal Conservancy, the private Monhegan Associates, Inc., The Nature Conservancy, and Maine Coast Heritage Trust. Maine has more land trusts per capita than any other state, according to the Maine Land Trust Network.

People can become members of land trusts and have a greater say in how the land is managed and used. More than 85 percent of all the state land trusts' boards of directors consist primarily of Maine residents.

PHILANTHROPY AND PUBLIC ACCESS

Ironically, while wealthy homeowners face criticism for fencing off parts of the coast, the preservation of Maine's coastline and forests owes much to some exceptionally large land donations from out-of-state wealth and philanthropy, starting with the creation of Acadia National Park and continuing to this day.

Leaders of two big families of twentieth-century US capitalism—the Rockefellers and the Mellons—saved critical parts of the Maine coastline that otherwise would likely have been bulldozed for vacation homes.

Financier and conservationist John D. Rockefeller Jr., the only son of a founder of Standard Oil, donated millions of dollars and about 10,000 acres to Acadia and paid for the construction of 45 miles of carriage roads and sixteen intricate stone bridges.

To help create Acadia, George B. Dorr, known as the "father of Acadia," inherited and then spent his family's fortune, which was built in Massachusetts.

David Rockefeller Sr., a son of John D. Rockefeller Jr., was noted for donating coastal properties and conservation easements in Maine and making major financial contributions to conservation organizations. His wife, Peggy, was a founder of Maine Coast Heritage Trust in 1970.

Anita K. Harris, daughter of a wealthy Massachusetts businessman, donated virtually all the land for the estimated 1,350-acre Holbrook Island Sanctuary state park.

The eponymous foundation created by Richard King Mellon, an heir to the Mellon bank fortune, financed the preservation of critical parts of the Bold Coast in Downeast

Maine, including conveying the beautiful 2,174-acre coastal lands in Cutler and donating another 10,724 acres just north of the Cutler coast, both to the state.

Working with nonprofit groups, the Mellon Foundation has spent millions of dollars to finance the purchase of tens of thousands of acres in coastal and inland Maine, including helping Maine Coast Heritage Trust buy 2,655 acres for a preserve on the Bold Coast, Bog Brook Cove Preserve.

A husband and wife from old wealth in Philadelphia, Lawrence M. C. Smith and Eleanor Houston Smith, were passionate environmentalists who quietly purchased Popham Beach in the early 1960s. The Smiths held the beach behind the scenes for several years to save it from developers and then sold it to the state at cost when the state legislature finally appropriated money for the purchase after years of refusal.

The Smiths lived in Freeport and later donated land that became Wolfe's Neck Woods State Park on Casco Bay and the Maine Audubon Society's Mast Landing Sanctuary.

Public access to the coast could be even more limited if not for the work of these and many other activists.

The Smiths, for example, helped fund a groundbreaking photo exhibit that more than fifty years ago raised public awareness about abuse of the coast and the paucity of public access.

Titled "As Maine Goes," the fifty-plus photographs in the Bowdoin College Museum of Art exhibit, taken during a 1965 survey of the Maine coast by John McKee, now emeritus professor of art at Bowdoin, helped spark environmental support in Maine. The exhibit included photos that revealed some shocking and distressing instances of schlock and strip commercialism, pollution, debris, industrial contamination and wastewater from homes and businesses, and rampant subdivision.

All the photos raised the issue: What about public access to an untrammeled coast?

An important result of the exhibit was a three-day symposium that included a presentation by noted iconoclast, writer, and planner William H. Whyte, who advocated for conservation easements for preserving open space. Just three years after Whyte's speech, Maine became one of the first states to approve a law enabling the use—now widespread—of conservation easements, a mechanism by which the owner agrees to limits on future development, sometimes allowing public access, while leaving the land in private ownership.

Land trusts hold hundreds of easements on the coast today.

In 1987, another turning point in conservation occurred when Maine voters approved a ballot measure for $35 million in bonds to leverage federal and private matching money to buy land for public access. That led to the establishment of the Land for Maine's Future, the primary funding vehicle for conserving land for its natural and recreational value. Voters subsequently approved five additional land bonds.

Public access to the coast is a longstanding issue in Maine. Some private oceanfront owners have deeded rights to the mean low-tide mark, but the courts have ruled that the public has rights to "fish, fowl, and navigate" within the intertidal zone.

In a victory for public access, in October 2019 the Maine Supreme Court upheld a trial court's decision that the town of Kennebunkport owns the popular Goose Rocks Beach and that the public has a right to use it between the high- and low-water marks.

The latest edition of a Maine citizen's guide says the public is permitted to use privately owned coastal areas below the mean high-tide mark, unless an owner explicitly exercises a right to restrict access. Fortunately, many private land owners do not attempt to prevent access.

FROM SANDY BEACH TO RUGGED CLIFFS

The Maine coast may be one of the most diverse in the country.

Only about 2 percent, or 70 miles, of Maine's coast is sand and cobble beach. About 1 percent, or 35 miles, is sandy beach, and most of that is located between Kittery and Portland.

From almost every coastal trail, you can see a lighthouse on the mainland or on an island. Maine's sixty-five or so lighthouses, the second most in the United States, are a powerful and alluring part of the state's seafaring history; and while there are no more lighthouse keepers, many of the towers are automated and still operating as Coast Guard aids to navigation.

The coast can be broken down into roughly four sections.

In southern Maine—from Kittery to Cape Elizabeth, just south of Portland—the coast is home to most of the state's famous sandy beaches and comparatively few islands. This region includes most of Maine's 19,500 acres of salt marsh, more than any other North Atlantic state.

From Cape Elizabeth to the Penobscot River, the coast is renowned for numerous islands and major bays such as Casco, Sheepscot, Boothbay, Muscongus, and Western Penobscot. Long, narrow rivers meet the sea in this region and often become tidal as the ocean cuts deep into the coastal lowlands.

From East Penobscot Bay to around Great Wass Island off Jonesport, including Mount Desert Island, the shore is noted for its pink and white granites and more big bays, such as Blue Hill, Frenchman, Eastern, and Western Bays. This could be the most dramatic section of the coast, with its round and dome-like islands, the high coastal peaks of Acadia National Park, and Somes Sound, the only fjord-like feature on the US Atlantic coast.

Farther Downeast, the shore is marked by volcanic rocks and wider bays, as well as dark and deep green cliffs, spruce forests right next to the water, and bigger tides, such as those at Quoddy Head State Park.

A MAGNET FOR WRITERS, ARTISTS, AND CELEBRITIES

The coastline is so spectacular that it has inspired native Maine poets like Henry Wadsworth Longfellow and Edna St. Vincent Millay and painters, including nineteenth-century artists Thomas Cole and Frederic E. Church, who depicted the scenery of Mount Desert Island, and Winslow Homer, who produced some of his best paintings while living in Prouts Neck in southern Maine.

Edward Hopper is noted for oil paintings of the Two Lights lighthouse at Cape Elizabeth and watercolors of Ogunquit and Monhegan Island.

Andrew Wyeth spent summers in Cushing and is noted not only for *Christina's World* but also for paintings of sweeping grasslands on the coast and other seascapes. His son and fellow artist Jamie Wyeth owns a Monhegan Island home that previously belonged to Rockwell Kent.

And inspired by the sea around her, Rachel Carson worked on *The Edge of the Sea* and *Silent Spring* in the 1950s and 1960s in her summer cottage on the island of Southport, in the Boothbay Harbor region.

Myron Avery, the driving force behind extending the Appalachian Trail into Maine, and the first to walk its entire 2,000-plus-mile length, grew up in North Lubec and often wrote about the coastal fishing community.

These days, the rich and famous are still attracted to the Maine coast, often as a way to get away and relax in the summer. *Saturday Night Live* producer Lorne Michaels has a house in Downeast Maine and owns a wild blueberry farm in Whiting.

Historian David McCullough has a home in Camden. Actors Chris O'Donnell, costar of *NCIS: Los Angeles*, and John Travolta of *Pulp Fiction* and *Saturday Night Fever* fame and his late wife, Kelly Preston, who starred in *Jerry Maguire*, have homes on Islesboro; former *Grey's Anatomy* star Patrick Dempsey has one in Kennebunkport.

Martha Stewart long has summered in "Skylands" in Seal Harbor on Mount Desert island. She is a longtime hiker in Acadia and a big donor to Friends of Acadia.

Horror writer Stephen King, a longtime Bangor resident, sometimes uses the coast as a setting for dark tales of life in Maine towns. The hardscrabble existence of people in one King story, "The Reach," seems a lot like that of the family that settled Baker Island in Acadia.

Like us, you will likely find a storybook setting around almost every corner on the coastal trails of Maine.

WEATHER AND TIDES

Often inconsistent and difficult to predict, the weather may be the biggest factor when it comes to enjoying the coastal trails of Maine. While a foggy and damp day on the coast may offer a certain mystique, the ocean views are a lot more rewarding and the walking much easier and engaging if the weather is sunny and pleasant.

A sunny day in June—known as a June gem—is the best time for hiking on the Maine coast. The leaves on the trees are turning deep green, flowers are blooming, and lots of birds are active. You might not see a cloud in the sky, and sandy beaches can be nearly empty, especially on a weekday, because it is generally too cool to swim or sunbathe and too early for summer vacationers. The daily temperatures will be about 63°F to 73°F in June, falling to about 50°F to 55°F at night.

July and August are the warmest months and can be first-rate for hiking along the coast; maximum normal temperatures are about 78°F, with occasional heat waves of three to four days above 90°F. Late July and August can also see humidity spikes for stretches. These are also the busiest months.

Early to mid-September is another great time to hike the coast of Maine. The temperatures hover about 65°F and the days are still long; the mosquitoes, ticks, and greenhead flies that can bedevil hikers during the late spring to midsummer months are largely out of the picture.

Some beautiful days for hiking can occur in May and October, but those months can also be rainy and foggy. Fall foliage peaks on the Downeast coast the first week in October, possibly the last week in September, and the colors will continue to the south until about the middle of October.

Winter temperatures average between 20°F and 30°F. Snow on the coast of Maine, even Downeast, can be significantly less than inland, though the ground will often be frozen and icy.

Be careful hiking along the coast during a storm. On August 23, 2009, a hurricane passed just offshore of Maine and a large wave crashed over a crowd of people near the viewing platform of Thunder Hole, along Ocean Path in Acadia National Park; seven people were swept out to sea, including a 7-year-old girl, who drowned.

If you're planning on hiking trails that are accessible only at low tide, you'll want to check the tide tables for the closest harbor at usharbors.com/harbor/maine/; it's safest to cross only within 1.5 hours of either side of low tide.

Two high and two low tides occur in Maine each day, with just about 6 hours between each peak and trough and just over 12 hours between one high tide and the next and one low tide and the next. The tidal range—the difference between high and low—can be 8 to 10 feet on the southern Maine coast and as much as 18 to 20 feet Downeast.

LAND USE RULES AND REGULATIONS

Each land use agency has its own set of rules and regulations, whether for different properties or the same property at different times of year. For example, at Maine state park beaches, no pets are allowed between April 1 and September 30, but they are welcome—as long as they are leashed and under physical control—October 1 through March 31.

Each hike description covers some of the rules in the **Dog-friendly** and **Special considerations** sections, but you should check the land agency's website and any information kiosks near trailheads to learn more and keep up to date on any changes.

No matter what a land agency's particular rules may be, you can't go wrong by observing the following Leave No Trace Seven Principles (© 1999 by the Leave No Trace Center for Outdoor Ethics: www.LNT.org):

1. Plan Ahead and Prepare

2. Travel and Camp on Durable Surfaces

3. Dispose of Waste Properly

4. Leave What You Find

5. Minimize Campfire Impacts

6. Respect Wildlife

7. Be Considerate of Other Visitors

Note: This copyrighted information has been reprinted with permission from the Leave No Trace Center for Outdoor Ethics: www.lnt.org.

PANDEMIC POSTSCRIPT

The 2020 pandemic led Acadia National Park to delay opening to vehicles, cancel its fare-free shuttle, and close campgrounds. Maine shut ten coastal parks, including Crescent, Popham, and Reid, for two months and then limited capacity to 50 percent when parks reopened.

Yet in August, visits to Acadia were down only about 10 percent from August 2019. While the 2021 outlook was uncertain, Acadia Superintendent Kevin Schneider echoed the hope of others in Maine. "People are going to feel safe getting in their cars and going to a predominantly outdoor destination," Schneider said during an online panel. "I am bullish on our future."

As of this book's writing, it was unclear if Maine's strict travel restrictions would continue in 2021. For updates, go to maine.gov/covid19/. The Maine coast is a powerful magnet for visitors. As the pandemic wore on, that attraction proved resilient.

Map Legend

Municipal

≡⟨95⟩≡ Interstate Highway

≡⟨202⟩≡ US Highway

≡⟨16⟩≡ State Road

Local/County Road

Unpaved Road

State Boundary

Trails

Featured Trail

Trail or Fire Road

Water Features

Body of Water

River/Creek

Waterfall

Land Management

National Park

State/County/Misc. Park

Symbols

⟨20⟩ Trailhead

⊛ Capital

○ Town

▪ Building/Point of Interest

☍ Bridge

▲ Campsite

🄿 Parking

▲ Peak

Scenic View

❓ Visitor/Information Center

●—● Gate

Lighthouse

Tower

Lodge

☏ Telephone

Boat Launch

Bench

✕ Airport

Picnic Area

† Cemetery

SOUTHERN COAST AND GREATER PORTLAND

Southern Maine's shoreline offers just about everything desired in coastal trails.

Hikers can enjoy spectacular views of islands; visit lighthouses, old military forts, and other historical sites; and walk along major bays, peninsulas, coves, or the Atlantic Ocean. The trails are fantastic for viewing such birds as plovers, terns, herons, sea ducks, and ospreys.

The hikes in southern Maine comprise a wide variety of habitat and terrain. Some follow sand beaches and epic low-tide flats or traverse rock, crushed-shell, and pebble beaches; others are high atop cliffs with ocean views that seem to extend forever. Sometimes you will need to step carefully along boulders and granite and volcanic ledges while the surf crashes or gently laps the shore. Some trails go past salt marshes and tidal creeks, or through forests with pitch pine, hardwoods, insect-threatened hemlock, or tupelo.

The inlet called Devil's Kitchen on Marginal Way is part of the Kittery Formation on the Maine coast.

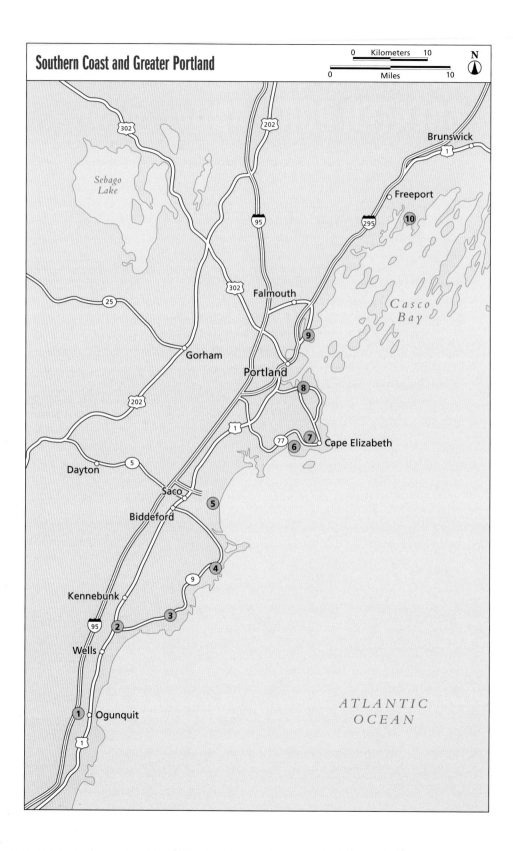

0   Kilometers   10

0   Miles   10

N

Brunswick

Sebago Lake

Freeport

10

Falmouth

Casco Bay

Gorham

Portland

9

8

Dayton

Cape Elizabeth

77

7

6

Saco

5

Biddeford

4

9

Kennebunk

3

2

Wells

1   Ogunquit

ATLANTIC OCEAN

The southernmost featured trail, Marginal Way in Ogunquit, gives visitors panoramic views of the Atlantic Ocean and Ogunquit Beach.

The most northerly, Wolfe's Neck Woods State Park in Freeport, offers a program for watching raptors such as ospreys and bald eagles.

If you are looking for a sand beach, consider Laudholm Beach in Wells, part of the 2,250-acre Wells National Estuarine Research Reserve; Ferry Beach State Park in Saco, adjacent to City of Saco beaches; and Crescent Beach State Park, a pocket beach on Seal Cove in Cape Elizabeth. Each offers almost otherworldly walks at low tide on long, wide sand flats backed by grassy dunes and forest.

Southern Maine also includes some offbeat ways to visit the Atlantic coast.

The Spring Point Shoreway, an urban hike in South Portland, is among the more diverse and fascinating walks.

In Fort Williams Park, you can visit one of Maine's more noted lighthouses, Portland Head Light.

For a couple of trails that are more out of the way, consider low-tide hikes to Timber Island in Biddeford and Vaughn Island in Kennebunkport, both of which can only be accessed within 1.5 hours on either side of low tide or you risk becoming stranded.

You can drive over a causeway to a third island in southern Maine, Mackworth Island, a state park in Falmouth. A loop hike around the perimeter includes sweeping views of islands and at least two lighthouses, as well as the chance to visit the unusual pet cemetery of the man who donated the island, former governor Percival Baxter, who also gifted Mount Katahdin to the state.

Baxter is only one example of the people who helped preserve some of the beautiful coastal places in southern Maine that lure visitors back to the region year after year.

1 MARGINAL WAY

Perhaps the most iconic coastal trail in Maine, the estimated mile-long Marginal Way starts in a quintessential seaport community and takes you high above the Atlantic surf, with optional treks down stairs to ledges and small beaches. The trail features such sights as the "Devil's Kitchen" gorge and a replica lighthouse and passes by resorts and private estates.

Start: Marginal Way trailhead on Shore Road at the Sparhawk Oceanfront Resort, across from Obeds Lane
Elevation gain: 50 feet
Distance: 2.2 miles out and back
Difficulty: Easy
Hiking time: 1–1.5 hours
Seasons/schedule: Open year-round; best spring through fall, particularly early morning or late afternoon in summer to avoid the crowds
Fees and permits: No fees or permits
Trail contact: Marginal Way Committee, Town of Ogunquit, PO Box 875, Ogunquit 03907; (207) 646-5139; townofogunquit.org/marginalwaycommittee
   Marginal Way Preservation Fund, PO Box 1455, Ogunquit 03907; (207) 641-2200; marginalwayfund.org
Dog-friendly: Leashed dogs permitted Oct 1 through Mar 31; prohibited other times of year
Trail surface: Paved walkway

Land status: Owned by the Town of Ogunquit
Nearest town: Ogunquit
Maps: USGS York Beach; Marginal Way Preservation Fund trail map
Other trail users: Trail runners, wedding parties, local residents
Special considerations: There are public restrooms across from the Obeds Lane municipal parking lot, at the Dunaway Community Center, next to the Ogunquit Fire Department. While the path is accessible for visitors with wheelchairs or strollers, busy times can make it difficult to navigate through the crowds. A wheelchair can be borrowed from the fire department by leaving a driver's license. Paid public parking is also available at the south end of Marginal Way at Perkins Cove, and the town licenses a trolley service that runs from June through Columbus Day.

FINDING THE TRAILHEAD

Head north on US 1 to downtown Ogunquit and turn sharply right (southeast) onto Shore Road, just before Beach Street. In just over 0.1 mile, turn right onto Cottage Street and park in the Obeds Lane municipal parking lot. Cross over Shore Road and turn right (southeast) for 0.1 mile. Turn left (northeast) at the sign marked "Marginal Way Walkway Entrance" by the Sparhawk Oceanfront Resort. **GPS:** N43 14.46' / W70 35.50'

WHAT TO SEE

Marginal Way is one of the most popular coastal walks in Maine—and for good reason. The paved path offers captivating ocean views, a replica lighthouse, a craggy shoreline that ranks among the best in Maine, easy access, and thirty-nine benches located at key spots for enjoying the scenery.

Brilliant rugosa rose blooms near the blue ocean along Marginal Way.

Located in downtown Ogunquit, Marginal Way is owned by the town and attracted more than 400,000 walkers in a recent year.

If you want to check out the path ahead of your arrival, the website for the nonprofit Marginal Way Preservation Fund has a webcam that provides four views around the clock each day of the year: 72.45.186.34/local/viewer/camera.html.

The path, a little more than 1 mile long and overseen by the town's Marginal Way Committee, begins by the Sparhawk Oceanfront Resort in downtown Ogunquit at a sign marked "Marginal Way Walkway Entrance."

Head to the shore between tennis and shuffleboard courts on the left and resort parking on the right and turn right (southeast) as the path reaches the ocean.

Enjoy the bright pink rugosa rose, an ornamental plant that blooms all along the path in season, and then look behind you (north) for a panorama of Ogunquit Beach, with whitecaps spread along the coast.

A rocky shore, contrasting with the sand of Ogunquit Beach, looms to the south, along with a designated area that is being revegetated with native coastal plants such as bayberry and bush honeysuckle to replace invasive species.

Reach a stairway at 0.4 mile with twenty-three cement steps and railings for a visit to a cobblestone beach in a cove framed by impressive rock walls with red hues. Here, at what is known as Little Beach, you also get the first up-close views of layered brown rocks and volcanic granite, along with the constant waves that roll against ledges and shore, causing erosion or generating the sand for nearby beaches.

Keeping the vast rocky coast to your left, pass through a tunnel of hedgerows and then reach another stairway to the ocean with railings and eighteen steps down to Mother's Beach.

At 0.5 mile come to the Marginal Way Lighthouse, which has a slot for donations to the Marginal Way Town Fund for beautification and eradicating invasive species. Other donations can go into blue boxes at each end of the path for the Marginal Way Preservation Fund, which helps finance projects to prevent erosion and repair storm damage.

The lighthouse was built in 1948, and its top section was repaired and covered in fiberglass in 1993. Upgraded in 2009 to make it look more like a genuine lighthouse, it also functions as a pump station for the town's wastewater collection system.

Steps after the lighthouse, follow a distinctive U-shaped curve in the path and at 0.6 mile reach the Devil's Kitchen, the most stunning geological sight on Marginal Way. You can look down on a big gorge and some layers of granite and other massive rock formations that jut into the sea. Put on a geologist's cap and look for "dikes," layers of (maybe) white rock that cut into the walls of darker rock, or "sills," which are sheets of rock that run in the same direction as other veins of the bedrock.

This is a dreamy section of the path with some beautifully maintained wooden benches, some on stone patios, situated on either side of the Devil's Kitchen, affording unobstructed ocean views over ledges of bedrock. No matter how many other people might be on the path, you will likely find a bench for relaxing with the Atlantic before you.

Pass a plaque that recognizes Josiah Chase Jr., a former state lawmaker who donated the first lands of Marginal Way in 1925. You will then get the chance to stop and read a couple of wayside exhibits, one about the common eiders, harlequin ducks, and bald eagles that can be spotted off the path.

Bear right at a junction at 0.8 mile for a side path to·view another exhibit about the geology of the Kittery Formation, caused by the collision of continents hundreds of millions of years ago. To avoid missing any of the coastal geology you just read about, circle back to the junction and turn right, back onto the main path. For a shortcut, you can continue straight on the side trail back onto the main trail.

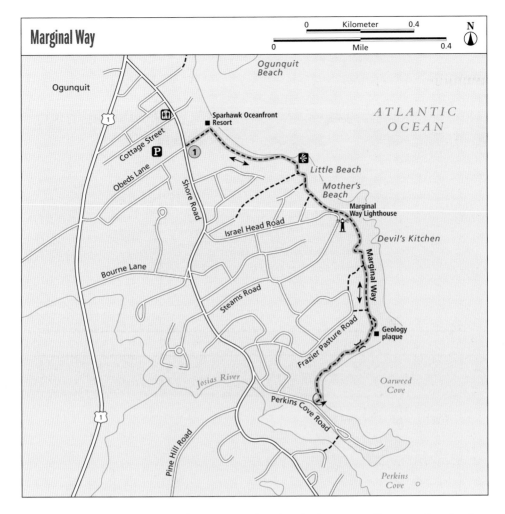

Marginal Way

Ogunquit

Ogunquit Beach

Sparhawk Oceanfront Resort

ATLANTIC OCEAN

Cottage Street

Obeds Lane

Shore Road

Israel Head Road

Little Beach

Mother's Beach

Marginal Way Lighthouse

Devil's Kitchen

Bourne Lane

Steams Road

Marginal Way

Frazier Pasture Road

Geology plaque

Josias River

Perkins Cove Road

Oarweed Cove

Pine Hill Road

Perkins Cove

At 0.9 mile cross a wooden footbridge with 5-foot-high cement pillars at each end and metal railings as you begin rounding Oarweed Cove. The bridge spans a gorge, and you can see Perkins Cove to the south.

At 1.0 mile the trail enters a cedar grove and, if you hike at the right time of year, becomes fragrant with honeysuckle. The path descends slightly and at 1.1 miles terminates at Perkins Cove, which hosts a small fleet of fishing boats as well as shops and restaurants.

Return the way you came.

MILES AND DIRECTIONS

0.0 Start at the Marginal Way trailhead by the Sparhawk Oceanfront Resort; turn right (southeast) as the path begins following the shore.

0.4 Walk by Little Beach then Mother's Beach, both of which can be accessed by a series of steps.

Marginal Way is a good spot to watch for seabirds such as this common eider floating just offshore.

0.5 Reach Marginal Way Lighthouse, which has a slot to accept donations for preserving the footpath.

0.6 Walk by a geologic formation known as Devil's Kitchen.

0.8 Bear right (south) at a junction for a side path to a wayside exhibit about geology. Circle back and turn right (southeast), back onto the main path, to avoid missing any coastal views. (**Option:** Stay straight on the side path for a shortcut back to the main trail.)

0.9 Cross a wooden footbridge as the trail begins rounding Oarweed Cove; follow the path through a cedar grove.

1.1 Reach Perkins Cove. Return the way you came.

2.2 Arrive back at the trailhead.

2 WELLS RESERVE AT LAUDHOLM

This circuit hike, most enjoyable at low tide, takes you on a round-trip along Laudholm Beach and later through meadows and forests and to boardwalks and observation decks with views of the Little River estuary, as well as numerous exhibits for learning about the reserve and its plants and wildlife. The beach boasts boundless stretches of sand flats at low tide. You may see least terns, ospreys, and great black-backed gulls, the largest gull in the world.

Start: Knight trailhead, kitty-corner (southeast) from the Wells Reserve at Laudholm Visitor Center
Elevation gain: 41 feet
Distance: 3.1-mile circuit loop
Difficulty: Easy to moderate
Hiking time: 1.5–2 hours
Seasons/schedule: Trails open year-round 7 a.m. to sunset; best spring through fall and at low tide. Visitor center is open Apr through Nov from 10 a.m. to 4 p.m. daily during peak season (Memorial Day weekend to mid-Oct), Mon to Fri during shoulder seasons.
Fees and permits: Free year-round for members of the nonprofit Laudholm Trust; day-use fee for nonmembers from Memorial Day weekend to mid-Oct
Trail contact: Wells National Estuarine Research Reserve, 342 Laudholm Farm Rd., Wells 04090; (207) 646-1555; wellsreserve.org
Dog-friendly: No dogs allowed

Trail surface: Field, beach, forest floor, graded dirt paths, boardwalks
Land status: 2,250-acre Wells Reserve composed of lands owned and managed by the Rachel Carson National Wildlife Refuge, Maine Bureau of Parks and Lands, Town of Wells, and Wells Reserve Management Authority
Nearest town: Wells
Maps: USGS Wells; Wells Reserve at Laudholm trail map
Other trail users: Trail runners, birders, festival- and concertgoers, workshop attendees, researchers, wedding parties; snowshoers and cross-country skiers in winter
Special considerations: No smoking, camping, bicycling, or drones allowed; exhibits about nature and history, picnic tables, and restrooms at the Laudholm Farm campus; benches and observation decks along trails

FINDING THE TRAILHEAD

Heading north on I-95, take exit 19 (Wells) and follow ME 109 / ME 9 east to US 1; turn left to follow US 1 north for 1.5 miles. Turn right (east) on Laudholm Farm Road then left on Skinner Mill Road, following the signs to the Wells Reserve at Laudholm parking lot, about 0.5 mile off US 1. From the parking lot, walk past the entrance booth toward the farmhouse, which serves as the seasonal Wells Reserve at Laudholm Visitor Center. Start on the Knight Trail, located kitty-corner (southeast) of the farmhouse.

If heading south on I-95, take exit 25 (Kennebunk) to US 1; follow that south for 3.5 miles and turn left (east) on Laudholm Farm Road. **GPS:** N43 20.13' / W70 33.00'

Note: From late June through Labor Day, you can take the Shoreline Explorer BLUE 4B trolley from the Wells Regional Transportation Center to Wells Reserve at Laudholm, about 20 minutes away.

WHAT TO SEE

Laudholm Beach is a striking barrier spit on the Gulf of Maine with a massive tidal river and salt marsh and plenty of space to walk along the shore at low tide. With the Little River between them, Laudholm and Crescent Surf Beaches create a double barrier sandy spit and marsh system that is exceptional in Maine.

Laudholm Beach is part of the 2,250-acre Wells National Estuarine Research Reserve, a refuge in a busy and built-up part of southern Maine. "Thank goodness this is preserved," said Eileen Willard, a volunteer at the reserve and instructor in dendrology at the University of New Hampshire. "It's a wonderful oasis of nature in a rapidly developed area."

One of only twenty-nine estuaries in a national system established for long-term research, education, and conservation, Wells Reserve focuses on salt marsh habitat and restoration; fish, shellfish, and birds; and the impact of rising sea levels. Funded largely by donations to the nonprofit Laudholm Trust and grants from the National Oceanic and Atmospheric Administration, the reserve also hosts festivals, concerts, charity fundraisers, workshops, guided walks, and kayak tours.

The 3.1-mile circuit loop hike described here takes you on a round-trip along the beach and later through meadows and forests and to observation points with great views of the Little River estuary and myriad exhibits for learning more about the reserve and its plants and wildlife.

The hike starts at the Knight trailhead outside the Wells Reserve at Laudholm Visitor Center, where you go right (southeast) to Laudholm Beach. First off, you get an expansive view over grasslands with Mount Agamenticus in the distance. A brown thrasher, among more than 270 birds documented over the years on the reserve, scooted in front of us during our walk on a gem of a June day.

At 0.3 mile turn right (south) on the Barrier Beach Trail, an old road at this point, to head toward Laudholm Beach. Pass a junction with the Laird-Norton Trail (which you'll be taking on the return) and the Pilger Trail, and stay straight on the Barrier Beach Trail as it takes you by a swampy wetland.

Pass stone pillars marking the entrance to Drakes Island and follow a dirt road past private drives to a boardwalk that takes you to the main attraction at 0.6 mile—Laudholm Beach, acquired by the state in 1968 as part of 199 acres sold by a member of the family that had farmed the land mainly between 1890 and 1955.

A sweeping vista looms at the platform at the end of the boardwalk, with an immediate look at the beach's incredible variety of cobblestones, pebbles, and tide pools amid long sandy stretches at low tide and crashing surf.

Turn left (northeast) on the beach, past low dunes fronted by sloping sand in some areas and boulders in others. A giant lone pitch pine and then a thick stand of two to three dozen pitch pines tower above beach heather, beach pea, and beach grass in the wooded area behind the dunes.

If you're here at low tide, pause at the vast expanse of sand and tide pools, which are separated in some spots from the upland sand by fields of cobblestones. High tide leaves little beach for walking.

All along the beach, opportunities for birding abound. Along the tidal flats we saw a great black-backed gull—the largest gull in the world—feeding on a fish, while a herring gull stayed out of its way. Overhead, we saw an osprey soar.

A couple walks along part of the massive beach exposed at low tide at Laudholm Beach in Wells.

At nearly 1.0 mile reach the mouth of the flowing waters of the Little River, a spit tidal river with Crescent Surf Beach on the other side. During our visit, the sharp calls of at least twenty-five to thirty least terns filled the air; we watched as the black-crowned birds lined the shores and often flew and dived into the river for food. Turn around and return the way you came.

At 1.4 miles reach the boardwalk again and turn right (northwest) to retrace your steps via the Barrier Beach Trail to the junction with the Laird-Norton and Pilger Trails at 1.6 miles. Turn right (northeast) onto the Laird-Norton Trail. Pass cinnamon fern, skunk cabbage, and honeysuckle and reach a junction with a spur to the Barrier Beach Overlook to the right (southeast) at 1.8 miles. The overlook, lined with wooden benches, offers a different perspective on the beach, with a view of a high and low salt marsh and mudflats near the Little River as it enters the Gulf of Maine. Education and research are primary at the reserve, and the overlook includes two wayside exhibits, entitled "Why are estuaries important to people?" and "What is a salt marsh?"

Return to the junction and bear right (north) on the Laird-Norton Trail, past signs identifying different types of ferns and eastern white pine, red spruce, and white birch. Reach an intersection with the Farley Trail on the right and Cart Path on the left at 2.1 miles. Turn right (northeast) on the Farley Trail to visit two other scenic overlooks. (**Option:** If you are pressed for time, the fastest way to the visitor center is to turn left on Cart Path.)

At 2.2 miles bear right (east) to the first overlook of the Little River, crossing a boardwalk and passing a restricted kayak ramp to the river. Two more wayside exhibits here explain how wildlife use the estuary and how birds such as sharp-tailed sparrows, great blue herons, herring gulls, and northern harriers eat other living things to survive in the marsh. We watched a large, stocky shorebird known as a willet spread its wings from this overlook and saw families of Canada geese feeding along the marsh.

Return to the Farley Trail at 2.3 miles and bear right (northwest) to continue to the next overlook. Reach a junction at 2.4 miles with the Farley Connector Trail (which you will be coming back to, to return to the visitor center via the Laird-Norton and

A great black-backed gull, the largest gull in the world, carries a meal in its beak as a herring gull heads in the other direction.

Saw-whet Owl Trails); bear right (northwest) to stay on the Farley Trail. At 2.5 miles reach the second overlook, with views of the Little River winding through marsh and woods.

Retrace your steps to the junction with the Farley Connector Trail at 2.6 miles and turn right (west) onto the connector to return to the visitor center via the Laird-Norton and Saw-whet Owl Trails. Turn right (northwest) at 2.7 miles onto the Laird-Norton Trail then left (southwest) at 2.8 miles onto the Saw-whet Owl Trail, named for Maine's smallest owl. At 3.0 miles reach the end of the trail; turn left (southeast) at the paved entrance road to the visitor center. Return to the parking lot at 3.1 miles.

MILES AND DIRECTIONS

- 0.0 Start at the Knight trailhead, kitty-corner (southeast) from the Laudholm farmhouse that serves as a seasonal visitor center, following signs to Laudholm Beach.
- 0.3 Turn right (south) at the end of the Knight Trail onto the Barrier Beach Trail (an old road) to Laudholm Beach.
- 0.4 Pass the junction with the Laird-Norton Trail (which will be your return) and the Pilger Trail; stay straight on the Barrier Beach Trail, passing signs showing where rising sea levels would put the edge of high tide.
- 0.5 Pass stone pillars marking Drakes Island; follow a dirt road past private drives and take the boardwalk to Laudholm Beach.
- 0.6 Turn left (northeast) and explore the beach.
- 1.0 Reach the mouth of the Little River; turn around.
- 1.4 Turn right (northwest), back onto the boardwalk, and follow the Barrier Beach Trail back to the junction with the Laird-Norton and Pilger Trails.

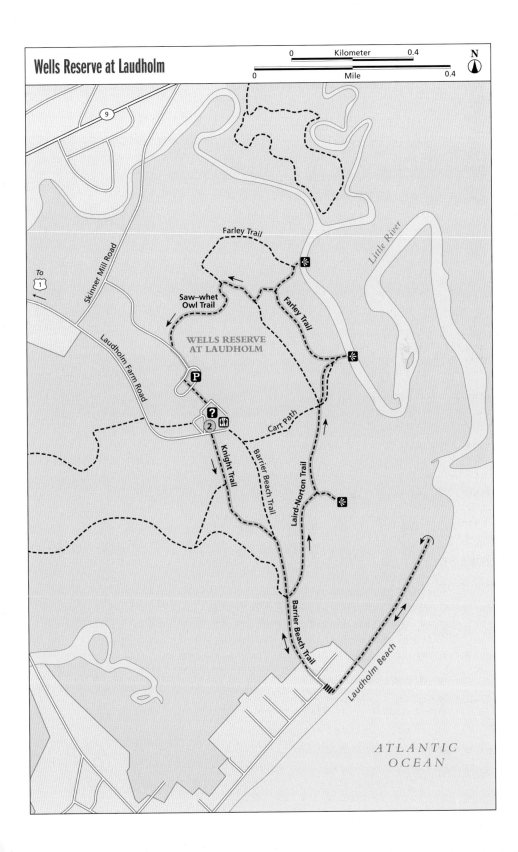

Low ridges of sand, shaped like tiny dunes, line up in a pattern at low tide on Laudholm Beach in Wells.

1.6 Turn right (northeast) onto the Laird-Norton Trail.

1.8 Reach a junction with a spur to the Barrier Beach Overlook on the right (southeast). Take the short spur for a different perspective on the beach you already walked.

1.9 Return to the junction and bear right (north) to continue on the Laird-Norton Trail.

2.1 Reach an intersection with the Farley Trail on the right and Cart Path on the left. Turn right (northeast) onto the Farley Trail to visit more scenic overlooks. (**Option:** If you are pressed for time, turn left on Cart Path, the shortest way back to the visitor center.)

2.2 Bear right (east) at a junction with the first of two overlooks of the Little River, crossing a boardwalk and passing a restricted kayak ramp access to the river.

2.3 Return to the Farley Trail and bear right (northwest) to continue to the next overlook.

2.4 Reach a junction on the left with the Farley Connector Trail. Bear right (northwest) to continue on the Farley Trail to the second Little River overlook.

2.5 Bear right (east) at a junction for the overlook, where there are benches and wayside exhibits.

2.6 Return to the junction with the Farley Trail and backtrack to the junction with the Farley Connector Trail; turn right (west) to return to the visitor center via the Laird-Norton and Saw-whet Owl Trails.

2.7 Turn right (northwest) onto the Laird-Norton Trail.

2.8 Reach the junction with the Saw-whet Owl Trail; turn left (southwest).

3.0 Reach the end of the trail at the paved entrance road to the visitor center; turn left (southeast).

3.1 Arrive back at the parking lot.

3 VAUGHN ISLAND

A short walk over mudflats at low tide takes you to a place that is unusual and can seem isolated. Vaughn Island offers just about everything in a coastal trail: the surging waves of the Atlantic; views of nearby islands, including one with a lighthouse; the spectacular seasonal colors of rugosa rose and other wildflowers; tide pools; beaches; and some big rock hopping.

Start: End of Turbats Creek Road
Elevation gain: None
Distance: 2.0 miles out and back
Difficulty: Moderate
Hiking time: 1.5–2 hours
Seasons/schedule: Passable only within 1.5 hours on either side of low tide; best in summer if you need to wade across
Fees and permits: No fees, but fire and camping permits required from the Kennebunkport Police; membership in the nonprofit Kennebunkport Conservation Trust appreciated
Trail contact: Kennebunkport Conservation Trust, 57 Gravelly Brook Rd., Kennebunkport 04046 (mailing address: PO Box 7004, Cape Porpoise 04104); (207) 967-3465; kporttrust.org
   Kennebunkport Police (for fire and camping permits), 101 Main St., Kennebunkport 04046; (207) 967-2454; kennebunkportme.gov/police
Dog-friendly: Dogs allowed off-leash but must be under voice control

Trail surface: Creek crossing, rocky and sandy coast, granite ledges, forest floor
Land status: 48-acre island owned and maintained by the nonprofit Kennebunkport Conservation Trust
Nearest town: Kennebunkport
Maps: USGS Kennebunkport; Kennebunkport Conservation Trust Vaughn Island map
Other trail users: Canoeists and kayakers camping by permit, birders, licensed hunters in season, local seaweed harvesters, local residents
Special considerations: Very limited parking at the end of Turbats Creek Road; check with police about other parking options. No restrooms or other facilities. Bring a change of shoes and socks in case your feet get wet, and be mindful that the creek can be crossed safely only within 1.5 hours on either side of low tide; see tide chart here: usharbors .com/harbor/maine/cape-porpoise-me/tides/. If hiking during hunting season, it's recommended that you wear blaze orange.

FINDING THE TRAILHEAD

From ME 9 heading east into downtown Kennebunkport, turn right (south-east) onto Maine Street. Stay straight on Maine instead of making a quick left to continue east on ME 9; at the three-way intersection with South Main Street and Wildes District Road, bear left to follow Wildes District Road for 0.7 mile to Turbats Creek Road. Turn right (southeast) onto Turbats Creek Road and follow that 0.7 mile to the dead end with very limited parking. Cross the creek at low tide to the southwestern shore of Vaughn Island. **GPS:** N43 21.26' / W70 26.44'

WHAT TO SEE

With wide-open views of the Atlantic and nearby islands and an enormous and diverse shoreline, Vaughn Island in Kennebunkport is an incomparable low-tide walk in southern Maine. One of the islands of Cape Porpoise Harbor, Vaughn Island is among fourteen

The wooded interior of Vaughn Island looms across Turbats Creek in Kennebunkport.

islands, including a half dozen or so barely visible at high tide, owned and protected by the Kennebunkport Conservation Trust.

Tom Bradbury, executive director of the nonprofit trust, described Vaughn Island as a different world with a rich history and unusual opportunities for experiencing solitude and beauty. "It always amazes me that such a short walk across the flats can lead to such a remote and special place," he said. "It's a lovely piece of coastal Maine."

A visit to the island leaves you with a sense of respect for the power and expanse of the ocean—and for the people who worked to preserve Vaughn Island. The island was actually developed during the Gilded Age of the late nineteenth century, with a bridge across the creek and several buildings and cottages owned by Biddeford's mayor.

While the bridge and buildings eventually were torn down, or collapsed from disrepair, the island faced new development pressures in the fast-growing 1960s. In 1968 the late Sterling Dow III, an early leader in Maine conservation of open space, discovered that the longtime owner of the island was preparing to sell to a subdivision builder and helped launch an effort to save the land. In a major grassroots victory, a nonprofit community group raised $90,000 to buy the island. After a period of ownership by The Nature Conservancy, the island was donated to the Kennebunkport Conservation Trust in 1982.

The hike, done only at low tide, begins at the end of Turbats Creek Road in Kennebunkport, where the thick central forest of Vaughn Island comes into view across tidal waters on the west side of the island.

Goat Island, with its automated lighthouse, sits in the distance offshore Vaughn Island.

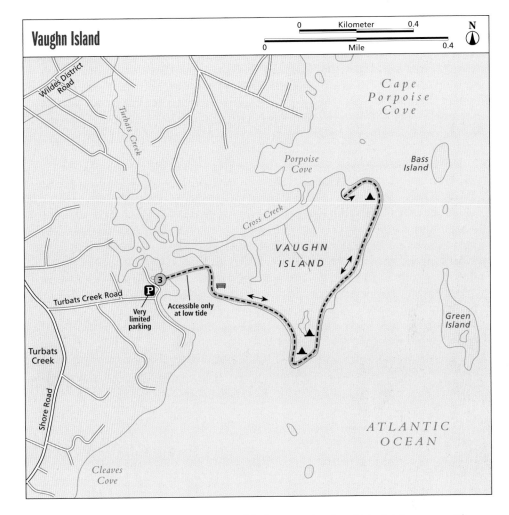

Turbats Creek and the mudflats can safely be crossed only within 1.5 hours on either side of low tide. Be sure to stay within those parameters—the waters rise fast, and you don't want to be stranded or forced to swim or wade in deep waters.

Once onto the 48-acre island, at 0.1 mile, bear right to follow the southwestern shore. Walk along wide sandy flats and past dunes, with the tidal waters swishing and the coast of the Kennebunkport mainland behind you to the southwest.

At 0.2 mile climb the small bluff on the left (north) for a day-use area shaded by hardwood trees including aspen and featuring seating and a fire ring. Near the site, beach pea and wild geranium were blooming during our hike in June.

Continue along the southwestern shore and pass a wide area of exposed ledges and tide pools with a lot of periwinkles, mussels, and broken shells. Walk next to a vast area of grass and look eastward to see Green Island and 3.5-acre Goat Island, with the automated Goat Island Lighthouse, also owned and maintained by the Kennebunkport Conservation Trust. Walk by a jetty jutting out into the ocean, where you may hear the sound of a bell buoy and see a lobster boat out at sea.

Round a point at 0.5 mile, where there are a couple of campsites rimmed in season by the dark pink and white blooms of rugosa rose, native to Asia but well established in New England after being introduced more than a century ago. Continue along the eastern shore and walk a sandy area with dunes before reaching brown-and-white bedrock. You can stand on the rocks and get a great view of Goat Island, with the double forested hills of Green Island just to the south. The eastern shore is noticeably rockier than the southwestern shore. During our visit, snowy egrets, one of some sixty species of birds that have been identified on the island, appeared to be feeding while perched amid seaweed just offshore.

The tan and dark granite and other rocks are examples of the metamorphic rock of the Kittery Formation. It's amazing to stand on the shore here and gaze back at the big blocks of rocks that rim the sand and forested eastern shore of Vaughn Island and are in such contrast to the southwest shore. There is a third campsite along this stretch of Vaughn—part of the 375-mile Maine Island Trail, with more than 200 sites accessible by canoe, kayak, or other small watercraft for day use or camping.

At 1.0 mile come to a huge oak tree, which marks a good point to turn around. Beyond are a tidal marsh and the thickly wooded interior of the island, which is nearly impassable and brimming with poison ivy in season. From here, to the north you can see boats motoring through Cape Porpoise Harbor to the pier, a water tower, and the small tidal channel known as Cross Creek separating Vaughn Island from the mainland. To the northeast look for bigger Trott Island and then Redin Island.

The walk along the shores of Vaughn Island is an unforgettable experience that will leave you with an intense appreciation of just about all the features available along the Maine coast.

Return the way you came.

MILES AND DIRECTIONS

0.0 Start at the end of Turbats Creek Road and cross the creek at low tide.

0.1 Reach Vaughn Island; bear right to follow the southwestern shore.

0.2 Climb a small bluff on the left (north) to reach a day-use area with seating and a fire ring. Continue along the southwestern shore.

0.5 Pass a cobble jetty and round a point past two campsites to the noticeably rockier eastern shore.

1.0 Reach the end of the trail at an oak tree. Return the way you came, crossing back over Turbats Creek. (**Note:** If the tide has started coming in, the shallowest place to wade is at the wider mouth of the channel.)

2.0 Arrive back at Turbats Creek Road.

4 TIMBER POINT TRAIL

At low tide, walk over a natural bridge to Timber Island and enjoy the dramatic shoreline on the Atlantic Ocean while circling the island. Timber Point and the island offer more types of habitat than any other area in Maine's Rachel Carson National Wildlife Refuge.

Start: Timber Point trailhead at the end of Granite Point Road, heading southwest from the small parking area

Elevation gain: 40 feet

Distance: 2.4-mile circuit loop

Difficulty: Easy to moderate

Hiking time: 1.5–2 hours

Seasons/schedule: Open year-round sunrise to sunset; best from spring through fall (be mindful of fall hunting season). Access to the island is only within 1.5 hours on either side of low tide; best in summer if you need to wade across.

Fees and permits: No fees or permits

Trail contact: Rachel Carson National Wildlife Refuge, 321 Port Rd., Wells 04090; (207) 646-9226; fws.gov/refuge/rachel_carson/

Dog-friendly: No dogs allowed

Trail surface: Gravel road, boardwalks, forest floor, grassy field, rocky coastline

Land status: 157-acre tract, including island, owned and maintained by the US Fish and Wildlife Service (The Town of Biddeford maintains the small parking lot and road leading to the tract.)

Nearest town: Biddeford

Maps: USGS Biddeford; Rachel Carson National Wildlife Refuge trail map

Other trail users: Trail runners, birders, local residents

Special considerations: Very limited parking. No facilities; no camping, fires, or bicycling allowed. Trail partly accessible to visitors with wheelchairs or strollers up to the observation deck. Canoes and kayaks can be launched along the Little River near the trailhead. Sandy beach near the start. Tide chart at end of Timber Point, across from Timber Island. Fall hunting (archery) by refuge permit. Check the refuge's online calendar for seasonal guided walks.

FINDING THE TRAILHEAD

From I-95 take exit 32 (Biddeford); turn left (north) onto ME 111 (Alfred Street) and continue 1.3 miles to the junction of US 1 and West Street. Go straight across the intersection onto West Street, and follow that for 5.7 miles to the end. Turn left (east) onto ME 9 (Pool Street) for 0.4 mile then right (south) onto Granite Point Road; continue 1.6 miles to the end, where there is parking for 6 cars. The Timber Point Trail heads southwest from the parking area, along a dirt road. **GPS:** N43 24.26' / W70 23.44'

WHAT TO SEE

Hikers on the Timber Point Trail can take a spectacular low tide walk to 13-acre Timber Island, view a tidal river and several distant islands, and experience up to seven different habitats packed into a small area.

Timber Island is the most outstanding feature of this 2.4-mile loop hike in one of the most beautiful areas of southern Maine. To reach Timber Island, schedule your visit for low tide, when a natural bridge, or rocky bar, is exposed between the Timber Point peninsula and the island. The bridge is safely accessible only within 1.5 hours on either

A weathered log marks the boundary between Goose Rocks Beach in Kennebunkport and the Timber Point refuge in Biddeford.

side of low tide—be careful to restrict your time on the island to avoid getting stranded by the high tide that envelops the rocky bridge.

Timber Point and Island offer an enormous amount of biodiversity in a small space. No other area in the Rachel Carson National Wildlife Refuge can match it for variety of plants and animals. The refuge, renamed in 1970 for the noted scientist and writer who lived much of her life in Maine, is owned by the US Fish and Wildlife Service. Several conservation groups worked together to raise $2 million in private money to help add this 157-acre tract to the refuge in December 2011, preserving what was then one of the last large, relatively undeveloped properties under private ownership on the southern Maine coast.

Habitats include salt marsh and saltwater beach; a freshwater wetland; a forest of mixed oak, maple, and other hardwoods; a forest of evergreens, including pine and spruce; then a rocky coast and open ocean.

More than 200 species of birds use Timber Point, both seasonally and permanently, including land birds like warblers and catbirds, shorebirds including plovers and sandpipers, and waterfowl such as common eiders and scoters, as well as gulls and loons.

Aim for an early start; there are only six parking spaces for the Timber Point Trail at the end of Granite Point Road in Biddeford, and beachgoers and people putting in canoes and kayaks may also park here. From the trailhead, walk along a gravel road with a sandy beach to your left on Curtis Cove, named for the family that owned the peninsula in the 1700s and 1800s; bear right behind a gate and down a dirt path. Pass a marsh on your left and walk through a deciduous forest to an observation deck at the mouth of the Little River. Up to the observation deck, the trail is accessible for visitors with wheelchairs or strollers. The observation deck includes a helpful exhibit that points out great views of the 7.6-mile-long Little River, which ends at Goosefare Bay, as well as mudflats at low tide and salt marshes that are vital to the wildlife and shorebirds that inhabit the area.

Across the river to the west from the observation deck is the popular Goose Rocks Beach, where at low tide people can cross over the river to the Timber Point refuge.

Off the observation deck, a red maple swamp is to your left as you continue on the trail. Soon take a right at a junction; go through a hardwood forest and follow a bog-walk—a series of boards taking you across wet sections of the trail—toward the coast.

At 0.65 mile reach a junction with a nice bench to the right over-looking Goose Rocks Beach and a side trail that leads left to a his-toric estate, including a fourteen-

Timber Point includes the historic 1930s-era estate of architect Charles Ewing and his family.

bedroom, 6,500-square-foot main house, built in 1931 by architect Charles Ewing and his family. Stay straight to get to the shore and soon see Timber Island, which is exciting to view in the distance with its green interior and exposed bedrock around the shore. The rock bar itself is fascinating, with the bay to the west and the Atlantic Ocean to the east.

Once on the island, bear right and begin to savor a 0.3-mile loop completely around the islet. It's amazing to look back and see Goose Rocks Beach, the Timber Point pen-insula, and other parts of the mainland. Timber Island is a relatively small island close to shore, but the crashing surf and ocean horizon make it feel vast and isolated, especially if you visit on a weekday in the early morning or late afternoon, when fewer people will be around.

Cross the bar back to the mainland and bear right to an exhibit on Maine's rocky coast. Here you can see Cape Island farthest to the southwest of Kennebunkport then, closer, Stage Island, West Goose Rocks, and East Goose Rocks.

Return to the junction for the historic buildings and turn right to explore the Colo-nial Revival–style main house and other properties at 1.5 miles. You can explore the buildings from the outside and then follow the sign to the parking lot to return via a gravel drive. Pass the observation deck again and return to the trailhead.

MILES AND DIRECTIONS

- **0.0** Start at the Timber Point trailhead.
- **0.2** Bear right (southwest) behind a gate and down a dirt path.
- **0.3** Reach an observation deck with a wayside exhibit describing habitats along the trail and a view across to Goose Rocks Beach and private homes.
- **0.5** Turn right (west) off the dirt path at a sign marked "Trail" and continue through a hardwood forest.

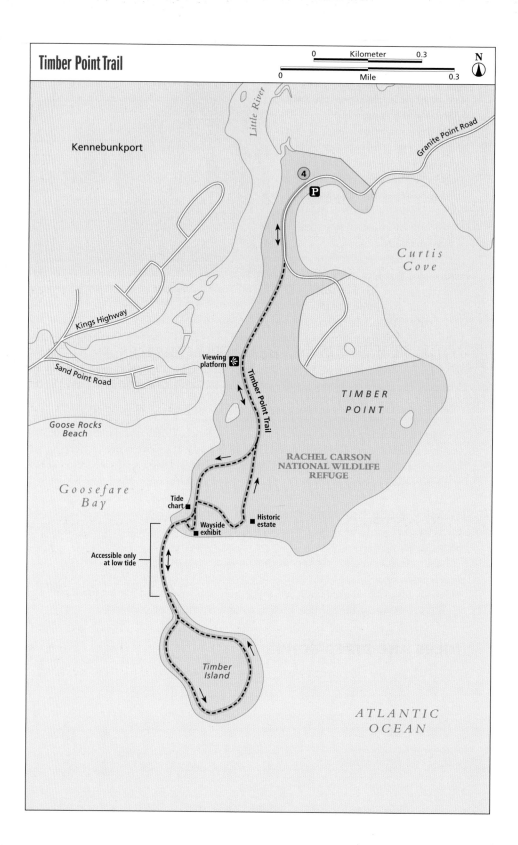

Timber Point Trail

0   Kilometer   0.3

0   Mile   0.3

N

Little River

Kennebunkport

Granite Point Road

4

P

Curtis Cove

Kings Highway

Sand Point Road

Viewing platform

Timber Point Trail

TIMBER POINT

Goose Rocks Beach

RACHEL CARSON NATIONAL WILDLIFE REFUGE

Goosefare Bay

Tide chart

Wayside exhibit

Historic estate

Accessible only at low tide

Timber Island

ATLANTIC OCEAN

Hikers enjoy a bench at Timber Point that overlooks Goose Rocks Beach.

0.6 Pass a bench overlooking Goose Rocks Beach on the right. Stay straight at the next junction, bypassing the turnoff to the left to historic buildings, to head toward Timber Island.

0.7 Reach a grassy loop at the shore and bear right (west) around the loop to the bulletin board with a tide chart at the access point to Timber Island. If you arrive within 1.5 hours on either side of low tide, it is safe to cross to the island on the exposed rocky bar. If not, just enjoy the views and pick up the trail description below after the Timber Island loop (milepoint 1.6).

0.9 Reach Timber Island, where you are greeted by a Rachel Carson Wildlife Refuge sign. Bear right (west) to go counterclockwise along the shore of the rocky island.

1.4 Complete the Timber Island loop and cross back to Timber Point on the exposed rocky bar.

1.6 Back on Timber Point, continue southeast along the grassy loop to read a wayside exhibit about Maine's rocky coast and return to the junction with the turnoff for the historic buildings.

1.7 Turn right (southeast) at the junction to head toward the historic buildings.

1.8 Explore the historic site and read the wayside exhibit about the Ewing House, which is not open to the public. Follow the sign back to the parking lot via the dirt path, heading north and passing the "Trail" sign that had pointed west through a hardwood forest on the way in.

2.0 Pass the observation deck again.

2.4 Arrive back at the trailhead.

5 FERRY BEACH STATE PARK

You can walk next to a magnificent stand of tupelo trees, rare for Maine, and then sink your feet into sand flats along a state beach and two adjoining municipal beaches. Along the way, you can see offshore islands and a lighthouse in the distance. The walk ends at a majestic tidal stream that rushes from a salt marsh into the great Saco Bay.

Start: Tupelo trailhead, at the northeast corner of the state beach parking lot, farthest from the entrance station
Elevation gain: 36 feet
Distance: 4.3-mile circuit loop
Difficulty: Easy
Hiking time: 2.5–3 hours
Seasons/schedule: State beach parking lot and facilities open 9 a.m. to sunset Memorial Day to Sept 30; off-season visitors can park outside the gate and walk in during the same hours. The beach is best at low tide.
Fees and permits: Day-use fee at the state park
Trail contact: Ferry Beach State Park, 95 Bayview Rd., Saco 04072; (207) 283-0067 Memorial Day to Sept 30, (207) 624-6070 off-season; maine.gov/ferrybeach
 City of Saco Beach Manager, 300 Main St., Saco 04072; (207) 283-3139, x812; sacomaine.org/departments/parks_and_recreation/beaches.php
Dog-friendly: Dogs not allowed on the state park beach Apr 1 to Sept 30, but leashed dogs permitted during that time on Saco beaches and at other times on the state beach; leashed dogs permitted year-round on the state park's inland trails

Trail surface: Forest floor, gravel path, boardwalks, sandy beach
Land status: 117-acre Ferry Beach State Park is owned and maintained by the State of Maine. The 0.5-mile-long Bay View and 0.4-mile-long Kinney Shores beaches are owned and maintained by the City of Saco. About 500 acres of salt marsh estuary along Goosefare Brook are owned by the Rachel Carson National Wildlife Refuge.
Nearest town: Saco
Maps: USGS Biddeford; Maine Natural Heritage Hikes map for Ferry Beach State Park
Other trail users: Beachgoers, local residents
Special considerations: State seasonal facilities include a nature center, picnic tables, chemical toilets, outdoor shower, water fountain, and beach changing area. Check the state park's calendar of events at maine.gov/dacf/parks/discover_history_explore_nature/activities/index.shtml. Inland state park hiking trails are generally accessible to visitors using wheelchairs or strollers, and the state beach is accessible with assistance (beach wheelchair available). Bay View Beach restrooms with flush toilets open Memorial Day to Labor Day.

FINDING THE TRAILHEAD

From I-95 take exit 36 (Saco / Old Orchard Beach) and follow I-195 East until it becomes ME 5. Stay straight for 0.3 mile, and instead of following ME 3 as it bears left toward Old Orchard Beach at the 7-Eleven, stay straight toward Ocean Park and onto Temple Road. Stay on Temple Road for 1.3 miles and then turn right onto ME 9 (Seaside Avenue) for 1.1 miles. Turn right onto Bayview Road at the sign for Ferry Beach State Park, and in about 0.3 mile turn left onto the park entrance road. Head to the northeast corner of the parking lot, farthest from the entrance station, and follow the signs to the Tupelo trailhead. **GPS:** N43 28.33' / W70 23.15'

WHAT TO SEE

Combining Ferry Beach State Park with two City of Saco beaches, this hike contains a lot of variety, led off by a long stretch of giant sand flats and dunes on a wide bay and a 1-mile inland walk that includes a rare stand of medium-size tupelo trees. During this 4.3-mile trek, you can also visit a freshwater beach and the riveting Goosefare Brook tidal stream, which creates big sandy banks before it spills into the Atlantic Ocean.

Like other coastal hikes, Ferry Beach is best done at low tide, when the sand flats are most dramatic and provide the greatest space for walking or searching for shells such as periwinkles, moon snails, and razor clams.

The name of the 117-acre state park derives from an earlier era, when people would take a ferry across the Saco River to get to the beach. The history also includes the "Dummy Railroad," possibly named for its relatively quiet engine, which ran between Old Orchard Beach, Ferry Beach, and Camp Ellis Beach from 1880 to 1923. While there are no locomotives at Ferry Beach State Park these days, a nearby gun training club in Saco can be distracting in certain spots. The intermittent gunfire can be easily heard on the nature trails, but not on the beach itself.

Begin the hike by following the sign for the nature trails at the northeast corner of the parking lot; cross a wooden footbridge and immediately bear right (northeast) onto the Tupelo Trail. Soon follow a boardwalk for the "famous tupelo swamp," to view a tree species, rare in Maine, that thrives in deep wet soils near streams or swamps. During a stop, the rich green leaves and light brown bark of the tupelos appeared particularly stunning against the bright blue sky of early June. Black tupelo trees, maybe about 40 feet high, rose right next to the boardwalk for some eye-level views of the hallmark "breaks" in the bark, resembling alligator hide.

While the tree is common in eastern North America, Ferry Beach hosts one of a limited number of significant stands of tupelo in Maine, helping to make this one of thirty-one "Natural Heritage Hikes" highlighted by the Maine Natural Areas Program. Related to the tupelo honey trees of the southeastern United States, the trees are among the longest-lived deciduous trees, with brilliant fall foliage, and in the coldest part of their range here.

A tupelo tree soars into the blue sky, showing bark that looks like the rough skin of an alligator.

Stay straight on the Tupelo Trail past junctions with the Greenbriar and Witch Hazel Trails until you reach the Red Oak Trail at 0.4 mile. Turn right (southeast) onto a spur marked "Trail End," then at 0.5 mile bear right (south) to explore the sandy north shore of 5-acre Long Pond.

Return to the junction with the Red Oak Trail at 0.6 mile and stay straight (northwest) on that trail. At 0.7 mile, at a junction with the White Oak Trail, turn left (southeast) and

pass cinnamon fern, seasonally noted for the brown fronds in the center, and hemlock trees. Stay on the White Oak Trail past three side trails until you reach a junction with the Tupelo Trail at 1.0 mile; bear right (southeast) to get back to the parking lot and complete a loop at 1.1 miles.

From the parking lot turn left (east) to aim for the beach by going through a tunnel under ME 9 and along a boardwalk past some older pitch pine trees. Turn left (north) on Ferry Beach, the centerpiece of the hike on Saco Bay and part of the longest stretch of sandy shoreline in the state. You get your first look at the waves tumbling onto the shore; Eagle Island is prominent over the ocean to the east and, later, Bluff and Stratton Islands to the northeast.

Look south and you can see the developed shoreline of the Camp Ellis beach. North on Ferry Beach are some spectacular dunes backed by grasses, shrubs, and trees. Farther north you can see heavily developed Old Orchard Beach, located beyond Goosefare Brook.

Ferry Beach ends at Bayview Road, and at 1.8 miles the hike seamlessly transitions to Bay View Beach, the first of two City of Saco beaches. Just north, jagged gray rocks stretch into the ocean at low tide. Standing north of this ledge, you can look northeast over the ocean to see the 71-foot-tall light station on Wood Island. You can also find newer City of Saco public bathrooms off Bayview Road. The unisex bathrooms are accessible from the beach and open to the public between Memorial Day and Labor Day.

At 2.3 miles reach Kinney Shores, the second city beach, which begins just south of the corner of Outlook Avenue and Oceanside Drive, a more developed stretch. Along the way you might see a fenced area for nesting piping plovers. Please keep your distance from these rare shorebirds, which nest from April 1 to October 1.

At about 2.5 miles come to sand dunes and shoreline owned by the Rachel Carson National Wildlife Refuge where Goosefare Brook meets the ocean. The federal refuge owns about 500 acres in the salt marsh estuary for protecting migratory bird habitat and coastal wetlands. Look out over the brook and you can see a vast expanse of sand flats at low tide and the stream draining through sandy banks into Saco Bay. If the tide permits, round the sand dunes to view remnants of the trestle for the Dummy Railroad at 2.7 miles.

Spend some time here and then return the way you came, reaching the parking lot at 4.3 miles.

MILES AND DIRECTIONS

0.0 Start at the trailhead, cross a wooden footbridge, and immediately bear right (northeast) onto the Tupelo Trail.

0.2 Walk along a boardwalk through the "famous tupelo swamp."

0.3 Bear right at the next two junctions, past the Greenbriar and Witch Hazel Trails, to stay on the Tupelo Trail.

0.4 At the junction with the Red Oak Trail, turn right (southeast) onto a spur marked "Trail End" to head to the northern shore of Long Pond.

0.5 Bear right (south) to reach the sandy north shore of Long Pond.

0.6 Return to the junction with the Red Oak Trail and stay straight (northwest) on that trail.

Endangered piping plovers display an orange bill with a black tip, a black collar, and a black line on the forehead during breeding season.

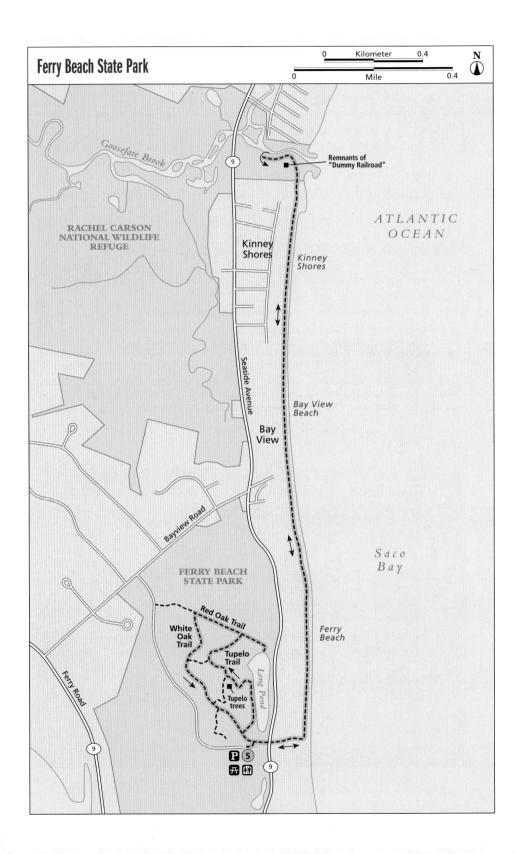

Ferry Beach State Park

0 Kilometer 0.4

0 Mile 0.4

N

Goosefare Brook

9

RACHEL CARSON
NATIONAL WILDLIFE
REFUGE

Kinney
Shores

Kinney
Shores

*ATLANTIC
OCEAN*

Remnants of
"Dummy Railroad"

Seaside Avenue

Bay View
Beach

Bay
View

Bayview Road

FERRY BEACH
STATE PARK

*Saco
Bay*

Red Oak Trail

White
Oak
Trail

Tupelo
Trail

Tupelo
trees

Long Pond

Ferry
Beach

Ferry Road

9

9

P 5

🅰 🚻

Old pilings, perhaps remnants of the Dummy Railroad, are unearthed at the mouth of Goosefare Brook on shorefront owned by the Rachel Carson National Wildlife Refuge.

0.7   Turn left (southeast) at the junction with the White Oak Trail; stay straight on that trail past three side trails.

1.0   Reach the junction with the Tupelo Trail; bear right (south) across the footbridge to return to the parking lot.

1.1   From the parking lot, turn left (east) to head toward the beach, walking past a water fountain and outdoor shower then heading through a tunnel under the road and along a boardwalk.

1.2   At the end of the boardwalk, turn left (north) to explore Ferry Beach.

1.8   Reach the City of Saco's Bay View Beach, where there is a lifeguard station and restrooms with flush toilets open in season.

2.3   Reach Kinney Shores, another City of Saco beach, staffed by lifeguards in season.

2.5   Reach sand dunes and the mouth of Goosefare Brook, part of about 500 acres of salt marsh estuary owned by the Rachel Carson National Wildlife Refuge.

2.7   If the tide permits, round the sand dunes to view remnants of the trestle for the Dummy Railroad, being careful to stay outside the protected nesting area for terns and plovers. Return the way you came.

4.3   Arrive back at the parking lot.

6 CRESCENT BEACH AND KETTLE COVE STATE PARKS

You stay on the beach and next to dunes and the sea on this 2.6-mile hike along Crescent and Kettle Cove State Parks in Cape Elizabeth. Aim to visit at low tide when massive sandy stretches are exposed and you might be enchanted by migrating shorebirds flittering on the flats and sea ducks close to shore.

Start: Crescent Beach access to the right (west) of the bathhouse, at the southeastern corner of the parking lot

Elevation gain: 3 feet

Distance: 2.6-mile round-trip

Difficulty: Easy to moderate

Hiking time: 1.5–2 hours

Seasons/schedule: Open year-round 9 a.m. to sunset; best at low tide, spring through fall

Fees and permits: Day-use fee

Trail contact: Crescent Beach and Kettle Cove State Parks, 7 Tower Dr., Cape Elizabeth 04107; (207) 799-5871; maine.gov/crescentbeach

Dog-friendly: Dogs not allowed on state park beaches Apr 1 to Sept 30; must be leashed at other times

Trail surface: Sandy beach, rock ledges, boardwalks, forest floor

Land status: 1-mile-long Crescent Beach and the smaller Kettle Cove are owned and maintained by the State of Maine.

Nearest town: Cape Elizabeth

Maps: USGS Cape Elizabeth

Other trail users: Beachgoers, local residents, birders

Special considerations: Seasonal snack bar and food trucks, restrooms, bathhouse with cold-water showers, playground, picnic tables, and grills at Crescent Beach. Inland trails are generally accessible to visitors using wheelchairs or strollers, and the beach is accessible with assistance (beach wheelchair available). Bring extra shoes, socks, and a towel in case your feet get wet while crossing the tidal flats. Seasonal kayak and paddleboard rentals with online reservation at portlandpaddle.net. Off-season visitors can park outside the gate at Crescent Beach State Park or at the smaller Kettle Cove State Park lot, which is plowed in winter.

FINDING THE TRAILHEAD

From I-95 take exit 45 (US 1 / ME 114 / Maine Mall Road / Payne Road) and turn right on US 1, heading south for 0.6 mile. Turn left (southeast) onto Pleasant Hill Road for 3.3 miles then left onto ME 77, heading north for 2.9 miles. Turn right at the sign for Crescent Beach State Park and head to the southeastern corner of the parking lot. Access Crescent Beach to the right (west) of the bathhouse, and turn right (southwest) on the beach to start the hike. **GPS:** N43 33.51' / W70 13.48'

WHAT TO SEE

Crescent and Kettle Cove state beaches join to provide a long round-trip hike on a sandy shore and enormous sand flats next to a roaring ocean with views of a big island and dramatic outcrops and possible sightings of beautiful shorebirds and large sea ducks.

The 2.6-mile hike, the majority on sickle-shaped Crescent Beach, is designed to stay entirely adjacent to the water and is best done at low tide and in early morning or

evening, when wildlife and the natural surroundings can be more dazzling with fewer people around. More than 1,000 people can pack the beaches on a nice summer day, sometimes filling or nearly filling the 750-space Crescent Beach parking lot.

Kurt Shoener, manager of Crescent Beach and Kettle Cove State Parks, said the two beaches together create a special place. "It is an impressive wide-open expanse of beach with unlimited ocean views," said Shoener, also manager of nearby Two Lights State Park, which has a more rugged and rocky coast and is a short drive away—an option to tag onto the hike on Crescent and Kettle Cove. Shoener said seals can also be spotted either hauled out on the ledges off Crescent Beach or bobbing in the surf. Early morning at low tide, you may get a special sighting of deer on the beach.

Crescent Beach is a pocket beach on Seal Cove in Cape Elizabeth and is named for its shape; the adjacent Kettle Cove is a smaller pocket beach. While there are loop options and inland trails and a service road paralleling much of the coastline that can provide more solitude during the busy season, the hike described here stays mostly on the scenic shore.

Access Crescent Beach to the right (west) of the bathhouse, at the southeastern corner of the parking lot, and turn right (west) toward rocky Jordan Point. Keep the 4- to 5-foot-tall grass-covered dunes to the right (north); do not walk on them—they are easily eroded and damaged.

At 0.2 mile cross a small inlet that emerges from a forest and almost immediately see Richmond Island, with a 2,000-foot-long breakwater exposed at low tide, and a big offshore ledge. The breakwater, completed in 1881 by the US Army Corps of Engineers,

A lone piping plover is spotted at low tide at Crescent Beach State Park.

provides refuge for boats in either Richmond Island Harbor to the west or Seal Cove to the east, depending on the direction of the storm.

Jordan Point, reached at 0.4 mile, is part of the Scarboro Formation and includes a 10-foot-high sea cliff and about 30 feet of gray limestone with folds, joints, and quartz veins. Just east of Jordan Point, during an early evening hike in mid-June at low tide, a couple broods of common eiders dived and swam quickly across the sea just offshore, entertaining us with their hallmark *coo* sounds and throaty calls.

Backtrack from Jordan Point, pass the bathhouse, and head northeast along Crescent Beach toward Kettle Cove. Here the dunes become steeper, maybe 6 feet tall. In the uplands behind the dunes is critical habitat for one of the largest groups of state-endangered New England cottontail rabbits—inspiration for the children's book *The Adventures of Peter Cottontail*—protected through the efforts of conservation officials and staff at the nearby Inn by the Sea.

Soon, at low tide, the flats stretch away from the dunes and offer a huge amount of space for walking. In the early-evening light, tiny shorebirds flittered on the massive sand flats and often flew tight together just over the ocean, providing a spectacular show. The magical display included a congregation of semipalmated plovers and state-endangered piping plovers and a group of semipalmated sandpipers, all of which regularly migrate through Maine. The semipalmated plover is distinguished from the piping plover by its darker back.

At 1.0 mile reach another small inlet, with a ledge offshore. During a hike in mid-October, a lone great blue heron waded in the shallow waters and then quickly flew away after a period of eating and searching for food. (**Note:** If you are visiting at high tide, walking beyond here may be difficult. You can turn around here, or you can find an access point up the bluff and turn right (east) onto the parallel service road then right again onto Kettle Cove Road to connect to Kettle Cove State Park.)

At 1.3 miles, or roughly 0.7 mile east of the bathhouse, see a sign for Kettle Cove State Park on the road up on the bluff and climb a rocky ledge topped by riprap to a grassy point and a parking lot with more than sixty spaces. Here, two wooden benches overlook

Crescent Beach and Kettle Cove State Parks

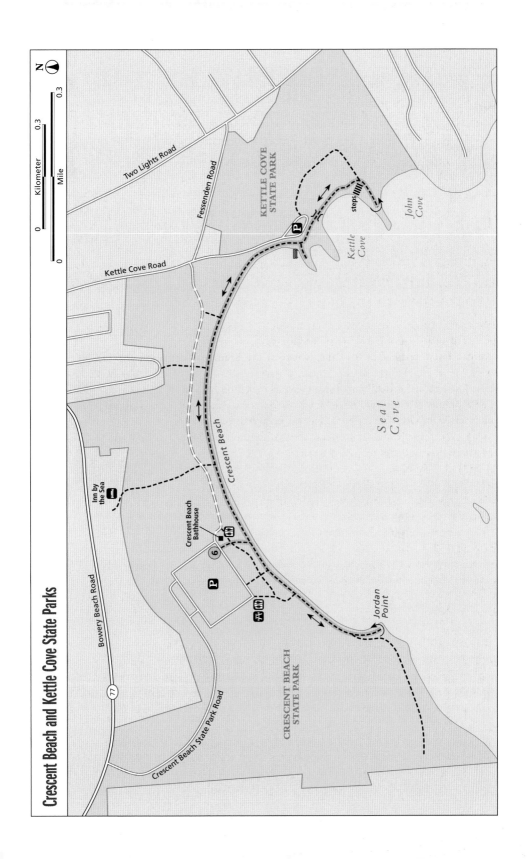

N

| 0 | Kilometer | 0.3 |
| 0 | Mile | 0.3 |

Bowery Beach Road

77

Two Lights Road

Fessenden Road

Kettle Cove Road

KETTLE COVE STATE PARK

P

Kettle Cove

steps

John Cove

Crescent Beach State Park Road

Inn by the Sea

Crescent Beach Bathhouse

6

P

CRESCENT BEACH STATE PARK

Crescent Beach

Seal Cove

Jordan Point

THE MAINE COAST IS A SUPERHIGHWAY FOR MIGRATING BIRDS

The coastal trails of Maine can be a paradise for watching wild birds.

The Maine shoreline is critical for migrating birds, acting as a superhighway for the 4 to 10 million birds that come and go at various times each year. The coastline, islands, and ledges provide shelter, nesting grounds, and the food reserves required to make their long journeys between north and south.

"Maine is great for certain birds," said Ed Hawkes, a master bird carver in Bar Harbor and volunteer with Acadia National Park's HawkWatch program. "It has a lot of habitat." Hawks migrate up and down the coast, but some red-tailed, sharp-shinned, and Cooper's hawks will stay for the winter if they can find food, he said.

Maine's bountiful birds make the state a magnet for birders.

Michael J. Good, a registered Maine guide and owner of Down East Nature Tours in Bar Harbor, founded a birdwatching festival on Mount Desert Island in 1997; today there are a half dozen in the state. "My hope is that the international passion for birding will translate to a desire to protect the birds' natural habitats and food sources, especially including the river fisheries," said Good, who founded what is now called the Acadia Birding Festival, usually held in late May or early June.

Many visitors are eager to see the iconic Atlantic puffin, which only breeds in Maine in the United States. Puffins cannot be viewed from the mainland; a boat tour is required to see the colorful birds nesting on or flying near the offshore islands. An easier sighting is Maine's official state bird, the black-capped chickadee. Since it does not migrate, the bird can be seen and heard almost everywhere in Maine at any time of year.

The chickadee, Maine's state bird, is often seen on all coastal trails. It uses both a distinctive *chickadee-dee-dee* call, with increasing *dee* notes when alarmed, and a melodic *fee-bee* song.

Along the coast, many species can be mesmerizing, such as the plovers and sandpipers that flitter in the sunlight at low tide on sandy beaches, including Crescent Beach State Park in June and Petit Manan Point in early October. The endangered piping plover also nests at beaches in the southern and middle coasts, including Laudholm Beach, Reid State Park, Popham Beach State Park, and Rachel Carson National Wildlife Refuge in Saco.

In May the coastal forests will often be filled with the call of the black-throated green warbler. Some birds, such as the yellow warbler and American redstart, can even be seen on the low shrubs bordering the sandy uplands of beaches.

Bald eagles, the largest bird of prey regularly in Maine, and peregrine falcons were decimated by DDT until the pesticide was banned by the US Environmental Protection Agency in 1972 in the wake of the publication of *Silent Spring* by Maine's Rachel Carson. The birds recovered so well that they were removed from federal lists of endangered and threatened species about a decade ago, but the breeding population of peregrine falcons remains on the Maine endangered list. Today there are more than 700 nesting pairs of bald eagles in Maine, up from 62 in 1968, according to the Maine Department of Inland Fisheries and Wildlife. Ospreys have also rebounded and can often be seen nesting or feeding along the coast or near rivers and ponds until they migrate south.

The mystical forces of nature are embodied in the snowy owl, a native of the Arctic that flies to the peaks of Acadia and other sections of the Maine coast some winters.

At times the tidal rivers on the coast teem with common terns, while the state-endangered least tern is more difficult to spot. Least terns are known to nest at Laudholm Beach in Wells and other beaches, but the nests are often decimated by predators such as foxes and coyotes.

An adult bald eagle is distinguished by its white head and tail, as opposed to the dark head and tail of an immature eagle.

Terns migrate and will generally head south by September.

Laughing gulls dive-bomb into the ocean waves for food, and the frenetic activity of herring gulls is constant. Watch for the giant black-backed gull, the largest gull on the planet, which rules the beaches year-round in Maine.

Some seabirds, such as common eiders, stay the winter on the Maine coast. Common loons migrate to the ocean for winter after nesting on freshwater during the warmer months, and the marshland along the Maine coast is often abundant with wading herons, egrets, willets, and even yellowlegs.

a tiny cove and a small sand and cobblestone beach framed by rocky ledges. You can also look back at the full length of Crescent Beach.

Continue southeast along the edge of the Kettle Cove parking lot; reach five more benches at 1.4 miles overlooking a larger sandy beach with flats at low tide. This beach, a "mini-Crescent," is bookmarked by rocky ledges. Pick up a trail on the left (east) that parallels the shore and cross a nice wooden footbridge with railings. At a trail junction at 1.5 miles, turn right (southwest) to round the mini pocket beach; stay straight past a set of steps that go down to the beach on the right.

At the next junction, at 1.6 miles, go straight (west) to head to a rocky point, where you can look back on Kettle Cove and Crescent Beach. Enjoy the views here before returning the way you came.

Complete the trip back to the Crescent Beach bathhouse at 2.6 miles.

MILES AND DIRECTIONS

0.0 Access Crescent Beach to the right (west) of the bathhouse, at the southeast corner of the parking lot; turn right (southwest) toward rocky Jordan Point.

0.2 Cross a small inlet.

0.4 Reach Jordan Point. Return the way you came.

0.8 Walk past the bathhouse and continue northeast on Crescent Beach toward Kettle Cove.

1.0 Cross a small inlet. (**Option:** If you are visiting at high tide and it's difficult to walk from Crescent Beach to Kettle Cove, look for an access point up the bluff and turn right [east] on the parallel service road and then right again onto Kettle Cove Road to access Kettle Cove State Park.)

A sunny late-June day at low tide is a good time to walk the aptly named Crescent Beach.

1.3   See the Kettle Cove State Park sign on the road up on the bluff; climb a rocky ledge to a grassy point with benches overlooking a small sandy and cobblestone beach and the Kettle Cove parking lot.

1.4   Continue southeast along the edge of the parking lot to a larger sandy beach and pick up a trail on the left (east) that parallels the beach.

1.5   At a trail junction, turn right (southwest) to round the beach; stay straight past a set of steps that go down to the beach on the right.

1.6   At the next junction, go straight (west) to head to a rocky point. Enjoy the views then return the way you came.

2.6   Arrive back at the Crescent Beach bathhouse.

7 FORT WILLIAMS PARK

Home to Portland Head Light, the oldest and one of the most photographed lighthouses in Maine, Fort Williams Park offers sweeping
coastal views, history, and links to well-known figures past and present, from Henry Wadsworth Longfellow to Joan Benoit Samuelson.
Maine's largest road race ends here. Park trails take you by the rocky
coast, an arboretum, and remnants of the old fort.

Start: Cliff Walk trailhead, to the right (east) and up a hill from the beach parking lot, on the far end of a pullout
Elevation gain: 52 feet
Distance: 1.2-mile circuit loop
Difficulty: Easy to moderate
Hiking time: 45 minutes–1 hour
Seasons/schedule: Open year-round sunrise to sunset; best spring through fall
Fees and permits: No fees or permits except for large groups; nonresident parking fee for premier spots May 1 through Nov 1; free parking at rear of park
Trail contact: Portland Head Light and Fort Williams Park, 1000 Shore Rd., Cape Elizabeth 04107; (207) 799-2661; portlandheadlight.com
   Fort Williams Park Foundation, PO Box 6260, Cape Elizabeth 04107; (207) 767-3707; fortwilliams.org

Dog-friendly: Dogs must be on-leash except in designated "off-leash" sections.
Trail surface: Graded gravel paths, paved walkways
Land status: 90-acre park owned and maintained by the Town of Cape Elizabeth; US Coast Guard keeps up the automated light and fog signal.
Nearest town: Cape Elizabeth
Maps: USGS Cape Elizabeth; Fort Williams Park Foundation trail map
Other trail users: Trail runners, dog walkers, wedding parties, tour bus passengers
Special considerations: Seasonal lighthouse museum and gift shop, seasonal snack bar and food trucks, beach, historic ruins, playgrounds, ballfields, tennis courts, picnic areas, restrooms

FINDING THE TRAILHEAD

From the blinking light at the intersection of ME 77 and Shore Road in Cape
Elizabeth, head east-northeast on Shore Road for 2.3 miles; turn right (east) at
the entrance into Fort Williams Park. Turn left (northwest) into the first parking lot, adjacent to the beach. Walk on the sidewalk to the right (east) of the beach,
heading uphill to a little pullout area on the left. Cross to the far (eastern) end of the
pullout to start on the Cliff Walk Trail, which heads left (northeast) on a gravel path
toward the rocky coast. **GPS:** N43 37.30' / W70 12.43'

WHAT TO SEE

For more than 200 years, Portland Head Light has served as a beacon, offering safe passage to mariners and inspiration to generations of artists, from Henry Wadsworth Longfellow to Edward Hopper. And over the four decades since Cape Elizabeth designated
the surrounding 90 acres as Fort Williams Park, the lighthouse has attracted visitors from
around the world, even serving as the endpoint of the internationally known TD Beach
to Beacon 10K, founded by Joan Benoit Samuelson, the Cape Elizabeth native who won
the first-ever women's Olympic Marathon.

Portland Head Light, Maine's oldest lighthouse, stands on a promontory near the entrance to Portland Harbor.

This 1.2-mile hike circles the base of Portland Head Light as its centerpiece and offers spectacular views of Casco Bay, Portland Harbor, and four other lighthouses: Spring Point Ledge Lighthouse, 2 miles north; Ram Island Ledge Light, 1 mile offshore; Halfway Rock Light, 10 miles out to sea; and Cape Elizabeth Light, 4 miles south.

From a pullout up the hill and to the right (east) of the beach parking lot, start on the north end of the Cliff Walk Trail on a gravel path, heading left (northeast) toward the shore. Bear left at each junction to hug the coastline, enjoying the arboretum plantings, benches, historic plaques, scenery, and perhaps the song of the northern mockingbird, as we heard one spring.

At 0.1 mile Portland Head Light comes into view at the top of the rise. At 0.2 mile, after passing a cobble beach at the base of the cliff, turn left (east) onto a short side trail to an overlook. From here, you not only get a good perspective of Portland Head Light but also see Ram Island Ledge Light directly across and Portland's boat traffic.

Return to the main trail at 0.3 mile; continue southeast to the end of the Cliff Walk Trail, then turn left (east) at the head of a circular drive onto the paved walk to the lighthouse. Walk around the base of the lighthouse and visit the seasonal museum and gift shop if open.

Towering nearly 100 feet above the rocky point known as Portland Head, the lighthouse was commissioned in 1790 by George Washington. First lit with whale oil lamps, the beacon is now automated. It is open to the public only during Maine Open Lighthouse Day in September. A plaque quotes Henry Wadsworth Longfellow's poem "The Lighthouse" and describes his walks from Portland to visit his friend the lighthouse keeper. A hand-painted rock memorializes the Christmas Eve 1886 wreck of the *Annie C. Maguire*, which hit a ledge so close to the lighthouse that everyone clambered to safety using a ladder as a gangplank.

From the base of the lighthouse, return on the paved walk to the edge of the circular drive at 0.4 mile; turn left (south) to continue on the path paralleling the coast. At 0.6 mile turn left (northeast) onto a short side trail to get another view of Portland Head Light. Continue on the main trail, going straight past another side trail, and head into a wooded area. At 0.7 mile turn right (northeast) onto a paved walkway to loop back toward the lighthouse, passing an old fortress remnant known as Battery Garesche and an off-leash section for dogs.

At 0.9 mile, beyond the chemical toilets behind a stockade fence, turn right on a gravel path toward the lighthouse; head counterclockwise three-quarters of the way around the circular drive to a seasonal snack bar. Signs near the snack bar mark the service of the Civilian Conservation Corps and the area's military beginnings in 1873. Formally named Fort Williams in 1899, the base's batteries were completed in time for the Spanish-American War but never used in combat. The base closed in 1964.

From the snack bar, follow a path that leads north and up a series of steps up a hill to the left (west), known as Battery Knoll. Wayside exhibits among the greenery here describe the Arboretum at Fort Williams Park, a long-range project to eradicate invasive plants and bring back native species in fourteen distinct sites, such as the garden area you're walking through now, known as Lighthouse View.

Climb the steps up Battery Knoll and at 1.0 mile you'll be at the top of the parapet of another old fortress remnant, Battery DeHart. Turn right (north) and follow a graded gravel path offering views of the Cliff Walk Trail below. Pass another fortress remnant, the southern part of Battery Sullivan, repurposed as a picnic area. Turn right (northeast) before the northern section of Battery Sullivan to head down a series of stone steps and walk along another arboretum site, Cliff Walk Landscape, still being developed when we visited.

Follow the path down the hill until it ends at the Cliff Walk Trail at 1.1 miles. Turn left (north) along the Cliff Walk Trail. At the next junction bear left (northwest) to stroll through Cliffside, the first arboretum site to have been completed.

Take your next left (south) to head up a series of stone steps to an overlook with another view of Portland Head Light. Turn right (southwest) and go down a series of steps to the road then right (northwest) to walk along the sidewalk. Pass an informational sign describing the Cliffside arboretum site you just explored. At 1.2 miles, arrive back at the trailhead.

If you have the time and inclination, you can grab a lobster roll at a seasonal food truck by the flagpole up the hill from the trailhead and then explore nearby wayside exhibits describing the views and area connections to such luminaries as Edward Hopper, whose 1927 watercolor of Portland Head Light is in the Museum of Fine Arts Boston's collection, and Bette Davis, who lived in a fourteen-room estate in Cape Elizabeth known as Witch Way from 1953 to 1960 with her then-husband actor Gary Merrill.

On your way back to the parking lot, you can explore rocky Ship Cove beach, where a scene from the 1960s TV series *Route 66* was filmed with guest star William Shatner, before his *Star Trek* fame.

MILES AND DIRECTIONS

0.0 Start at the Cliff Walk trailhead, on the far eastern end of a pullout, uphill from the beach parking lot; bear left toward the shore.

0.2 Pass a cobble beach at the base of a cliff and turn left (east) onto a short side trail to an overlook.

0.3 Continue to the end of the Cliff Walk Trail; turn left (east) at the head of a circular drive onto the paved walk to the lighthouse.

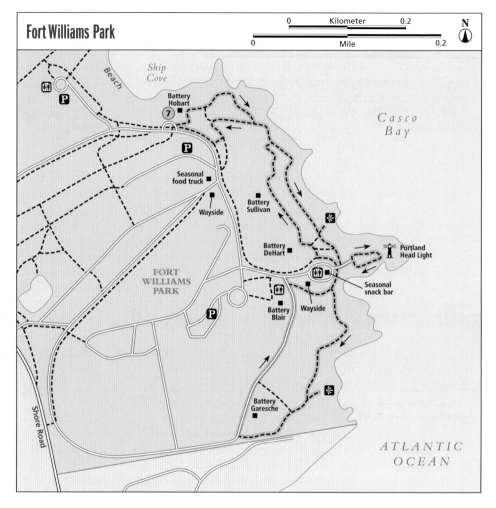

0   Kilometer   0.2

0   Mile   0.2

N

Ship Cove

Beach

Battery Hobart

7

Casco Bay

P

Seasonal food truck

Wayside

Battery Sullivan

Battery DeHart

Portland Head Light

FORT WILLIAMS PARK

Seasonal snack bar

P

Battery Blair

Wayside

Shore Road

Battery Garesche

ATLANTIC OCEAN

0.4 Walk around the base of the lighthouse and return to the edge of the circular drive. Turn left (south) to continue on the path that parallels the coast.

0.6 Turn left (northeast) onto a short side trail for a view back toward the lighthouse. Continue straight (southwest) on the main trail, bypass a second side trail on the right, and enter a wooded area.

0.7 Reach a junction with a paved walkway; turn right (northeast) to loop back to the lighthouse, passing an old fortress remnant known as Battery Garesche and an off-leash section for dogs.

0.9 Pass chemical toilets hidden behind a stockade fence and turn right (east) on a gravel path toward the lighthouse. Walk counterclockwise three-quarters around the circular drive toward the seasonal snack bar; follow a path north up a series of steps toward the bank on the left (west), Battery Knoll.

1.0 Turn right (north) at the top of the steps to follow a graded gravel path along the edge of the parapet of Battery DeHart. Pass another fortress remnant, the southern part of Battery Sullivan, repurposed as a picnic area. Just before the northern part of Battery Sullivan, turn right (northeast) to follow the path down a series of stone steps and toward the Cliff Walk Trail.

A hardy shrub of rugosa rose shows its colors in the foreground of the shore at Cape Elizabeth's Fort Williams Park.

1.1   At the junction with the Cliff Walk Trail, turn left along the coast then left again (northwest) at the next junction to stroll through part of the Cliffside arboretum site. Take your next left (south) and climb up stone steps to an overlook. Turn right (southwest) to go down steps to the road and then right again (northwest) to walk along the sidewalk.

1.2   Arrive back at the trailhead.

8 SPRING POINT SHOREWAY

The Spring Point Shoreway in South Portland delivers a lot for hikers. You can visit two historic lighthouses, including one via a 900-foot-long breakwater, a sandy beach; beautiful oceanfront city parks; exhibits on shipbuilding; and the ruins of Fort Preble. Along the way, you cut through a working boatyard and a college campus while enjoying wonderful views of islands, including several with old military forts.

Start: The northeastern edge of the Bug Light parking lot
Elevation gain: 27 feet
Distance: 4.0-mile circuit hike
Difficulty: Easy to moderate
Hiking time: 2–2.5 hours
Seasons/schedule: Open year-round 6 a.m. to 9 p.m.; best spring through fall
Fees and permits: No fees or permits
Trail contact: South Portland Parks Department, 21 Nelson Rd., South Portland 04106; (207) 767-7670; southportland.org/departments/parks-recreation-aquaticspool/parks-department/
    South Portland Land Trust, PO Box 2312, South Portland 04116; (207) 799-5723; southportlandlandtrust.org
Dog-friendly: Dogs not allowed on Willard Beach between May 1 and Sept 30 except 7–9 a.m. and 7–9 p.m.; dogs allowed at other times of the year but must be leashed or under immediate voice control at all times. Dogs must be leashed or under immediate voice control in Bug Light Park and must be leashed on public streets, sidewalks, parking lots, and other public throughways.

Trail surface: Pavement, sandy beach, riprap and breakwater, wood and stone steps
Land status: The City of South Portland manages the 1.6-mile Spring Port Shoreway in collaboration with the nonprofit South Portland Land Trust. The trail crosses city and state property, including city-owned Bug Light Park and Willard Beach and the state-owned Southern Maine Community College campus.
Nearest town: South Portland
Maps: USGS Portland East
Other trail users: Trail runners, dog walkers, bicyclists, festival- and beachgoers, community college students, local residents, history and lighthouse buffs, wedding parties, tour bus passengers
Special considerations: Seasonal restrooms and South Portland Historical Society and museum at Bug Light Park; seasonal gift shop across from Spring Point Ledge Lighthouse on the Southern Maine Community College campus; seasonal Willard Beach bathhouse with restrooms, snack bar, and showers

FINDING THE TRAILHEAD

From I-95 take exit 45 (US 1 / ME 114 / Maine Mall Road / Payne Road); turn left on US 1 and head north for 1 mile. Turn right (northeast) onto Broadway, heading toward ME 77. In 2 miles, at the junction with ME 77, turn right to continue on Broadway as it overlaps ME 77 South for 0.2 mile. Stay straight on Broadway (do not follow ME 77 South as it turns right onto Ocean Street), and travel about 1.5 miles to Breakwater Drive, at the entrance to Spring Point Marina. Turn left (northwest) onto Breakwater Drive for 0.1 mile, then turn right (northeast) onto Madison Street for 0.4 mile. Turn right (northeast) before the entrance to South Portland's Fore River boat facility to enter Bug Light Park. Head to the far northeast edge of the

Spring Point Ledge Lighthouse is situated at the end of a 900-foot-long stone breakwater.

parking lot to start the hike on the paved walkway to the lighthouse. **GPS:** N43 39.2' / W70 14.0'

WHAT TO SEE

Two spectacular lighthouses, close views of at least eight islands in Casco Bay, a big sandy public beach, and several smaller beaches are among the attractions packed into a short distance on South Portland's Spring Point Shoreway. In addition to those draws, the 1.6-mile-long shoreway goes across the oceanfront campus of the second-oldest community college in Maine and starts and ends at beautiful city parks. The shoreway, owned by the city and the state, offers history galore, including views of four old military forts, exhibits on shipbuilding, and Fisherman's Point, which juts into the Atlantic Ocean and boasts a long tradition of use by local fishermen. Tom Blake, board member of the South Portland Land Trust, said the shoreway is one of the first urban trails in New England, with construction funded by a state grant in the 1970s.

With lots of free parking at 9-acre Bug Light Park, we began the hike at the north end of the shoreway on a sunny June day. From the northeast edge of the parking lot, follow a paved walk in front of more than a dozen benches toward the lighthouse. Walk more than fifty large stone steps to get a close-up view of the restored tower of Portland Breakwater Lighthouse, also known as Bug Light, at 0.1 mile. "It is a busy walk, but it is gorgeous and outstanding," said Blake, former mayor of South Portland.

The interior of Bug Light is closed to the public. Owned by the City of South Portland, the lighthouse is no longer maintained by the US Coast Guard as a navigation aid, but it does have a solar-powered light that sparkles over the ocean.

From Bug Light, go back to the parking lot at 0.2 mile and continue straight (southeast) on the shoreway, which at this point overlaps the East Coast Greenway, a walking and biking path that will eventually stretch 3,000 miles from Florida to Maine, and the regional Greenbelt Walkway. Stop at the nostalgic "Liberty Ship Memorial" to learn about the vital roles of the cargo vessels during World War II. Yards in South Portland built 260 of the 441-foot-long Liberty Ships between 1941 and 1945 and employed 30,000 people at their peak.

Follow the paved walkway as it heads southwest and exits Bug Light Park at 0.4 mile. Bear left on the sidewalk along Madison Street, then turn left (southeast) onto Cushing Court at 0.5 mile. Turn right (southwest) at 0.6 mile and head onto the boardwalk that goes along Breakwater Marina; turn left (southeast) in front of the Breakwater Condos to continue around the marina.

At 0.7 mile pass the North 43 Bistro restaurant at the Spring Point Marina, Maine's largest full-service marina, which is owned by the City of South Portland and leased to an operator. Continue southeast along the edge of the marina and cut across a yard with yachts and other boats under repair. Walk around a boat lift and then straight through an opening in a chain-link fence at 0.8 mile.

Turn left (northeast) and follow the paved shoreway to a picnic area overlooking the marina at 0.9 mile. To the northeast, look for the white brick walls of the Spring Point Ledge Lighthouse, which is raised on an underwater cement foundation in a cast-iron tube. Turn right (east) to continue on the paved shoreway through the campus of Southern Maine Community College.

Walk by a pebble-and-sand beach, best at low tide, and look out to the ocean to the north for a stunning view of Fort Gorges, a Civil War–era fort that never hosted a soldier and stands by itself on a ledge in the middle of Casco Bay.

Continue straight (east) until the shoreway comes to a paved drive. Bear right past an art studio then left to head east through a campus parking lot toward the 77-foot-tall Spring Point Ledge Lighthouse. On the right at 1.1 miles, across from a small beach, reach a seasonal gift shop for the lighthouse, which is owned and preserved by the Spring Point Ledge Light Trust, a public charity. The US Coast Guard maintains the structure's automated light and fog signal, and volunteers with the trust lead public tours of the lighthouse on most Tuesdays and some Saturdays and Sundays between Memorial and Labor Day weekends. Check the lighthouse tour schedule at facebook.com/springpointledgelight/.

Spring Point Ledge Lighthouse is the only so-called caisson lighthouse in the United States that can be reached on foot from shore, with access provided by a 900-foot-long stone breakwater. A caisson is the cement and cast-iron tube the lighthouse is built on, giving it the appearance of a sparkplug. The US Army Corps of Engineers constructed the breakwater in 1950 and 1951, placing about 50,000 tons of stone from Spring Point to the lighthouse with the aim of creating a barrier to protect the wharves and facilities in South Portland, noted Corps spokesman Tim Dugan.

Continue east of the gift shop on the paved shoreway; climb steps and walk carefully over the breakwater to reach the lighthouse at 1.3 miles for sweeping views of islands and old military forts, including Fort Gorges to the north. Do not attempt crossing the breakwater in windy or stormy conditions.

From Spring Point Lighthouse, Bug Light is visible to the northwest. Little Diamond and Great Diamond Islands are to the northeast, then to the east is House Island, home to Fort Scammel, constructed as a deterrent in 1808. Farther out to sea to the east is Peaks Island, the most populated island in Casco Bay; to the southeast is Cushing Island,

home to Fort Levett, an old US Army fortification built at the turn of the twentieth century.

Return over the breakwater (the round-trip adds about 0.5 mile to the length of the shoreway), and at 1.5 miles turn left (south) just before the gift shop to take a stairway up to a paved path. Turn left (east) at 1.6 miles at the top of the steps and follow the paved path, which has benches and views overlooking the lighthouse and the ruins of Fort Preble. Constructed in the face of possible aggression from England or France in 1808 and active during four wars through World War II, Fort Preble was mothballed and sold to the State of Maine in 1952; it eventually became what is now the campus of Southern Maine Community College. Once beyond the Fort Preble ruins, turn left (southeast) down wooden steps, with stops to read exhibits about early settlements and Casco Bay. Continue southwest on the paved shoreway, paralleling the coastline and passing campus buildings.

At 1.9 miles, as the shoreway comes out onto a driveway behind the Hildreth Science Center, turn left (south) to continue paralleling the coastline and walk past the Old Settlers Cemetery. At 2.0 miles reach the end of the paved shoreway. Turn left (southeast) to get down to 4-acre Willard Beach. Turn right (south) to walk along this sand-and-pebble beach on Simonton Cove with wide flats during low tide, boats cruising at sea, and vibrant eiders and herring gulls feeding offshore.

Willard Beach is a favorite of dog owners because it is among the few public beaches in Maine to allow dogs during the summer season (May 1 to September 30), though only from 7 to 9 a.m. and 7 to 9 p.m. Dogs are welcome in the off-season (October 1 to April 30) any time from 6 a.m. to 9 p.m., when the beach is open.

The lone public beach in South Portland, Willard Beach is a longtime tourist attraction, starting in the 1800s, when people from Boston, New Haven, New York, and other cities would take a train and then a trolley to the beach and maybe stay in one of the three big hotels that once stood on its shores, said Blake.

We walked Willard Beach and enjoyed the wide sand and close views of House Island to the northeast and Cushing Island to the southeast.

Climb stairs at the end of the beach and turn left (northeast) at the top of the stairs to Fisherman's Point at 2.3 miles on the hike. The point provides panoramic views, including a look south to Portland Head Light, the state's oldest lighthouse, in Cape Elizabeth and north to the Spring Point Shore Shoreway, the city of Portland, islands, and lighthouses. The hillside at the point was resplendent with dense clusters of bright yellow mossy stonecrop, an herb that blooms in sunny areas from spring to summer.

Since prior to the Civil War, Fisherman's Point has been a base for shacks shared by fishermen for storage of nets, traps, equipment, and buoys. The City of South Portland honors the nearly two-century-old tradition and provides three nicely-maintained storage buildings at no cost to commercial fishermen on a first-come, first-served basis.

The park on the point is right next to the sea and includes an exhibit on the history of Willard Beach and Simonton Cove. You can relax on any of several benches on a grassy knob to soak in the incredible views of the Atlantic Ocean and Casco Bay before you turn around and return the way you came.

MILES AND DIRECTIONS

0.0   From the northeastern edge of the Bug Light parking lot, head toward the lighthouse on the paved walkway.

0.1   Reach Bug Light and walk around the lighthouse. Return the way you came.

0.2   Reach the edge of the parking lot again and continue straight (southeast) on the paved walkway.

0.3   Pass the Liberty Ship Memorial.

0.4   Exit Bug Light Park and bear left on the sidewalk along Madison Street.

0.5   Turn left (southeast) onto Cushing Court.

0.6   Turn right (southwest) to head onto the boardwalk to go around Breakwater Marina; turn left (southeast) in front of the Breakwater Condos to continue around the marina.

0.7   Pass the North 43 Bistro restaurant at Spring Point Marina and continue southeast along the edge of the marina, cutting straight across a boatyard and exiting through an opening in a chain-link fence.

0.8   Turn left (northeast) on the other side of the chain-link fence, following the paved shoreway.

0.9   Reach a brick patio with a picnic table and wayside exhibit about shipbuilding. Spring Point Ledge Lighthouse comes into view to the northeast. Turn right (east) to continue on the paved shoreway through the campus of Southern Maine Community College.

1.0   Pass a small beach and student parking lot. When the walkway reaches a paved drive, bear right past the art studio then left to head east across visitor and student parking toward Spring Point Ledge Lighthouse.

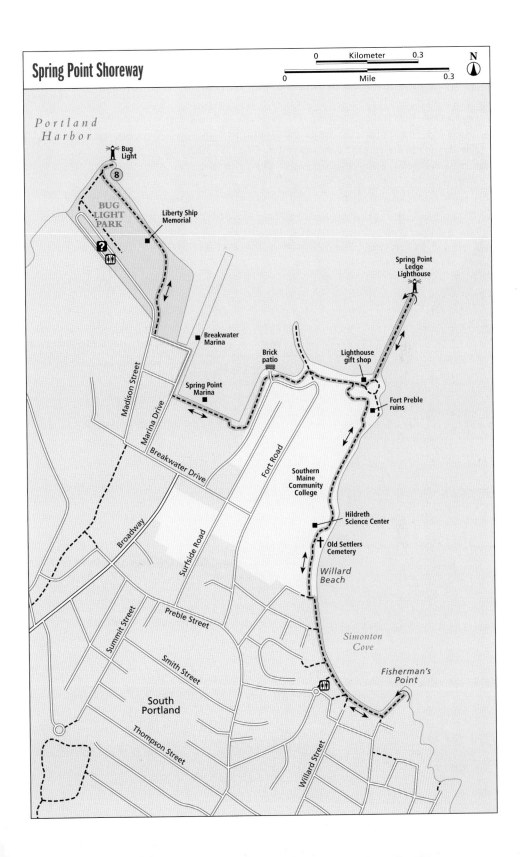

Spring Point Shoreway

0   Kilometer   0.3

0   Mile   0.3

N

Portland Harbor

Bug Light

8

BUG LIGHT PARK

Liberty Ship Memorial

?

Spring Point Ledge Lighthouse

Breakwater Marina

Brick patio

Lighthouse gift shop

Madison Street

Marina Drive

Spring Point Marina

Fort Preble ruins

Breakwater Drive

Fort Road

Southern Maine Community College

Broadway

Surfside Road

Hildreth Science Center

Old Settlers Cemetery

Willard Beach

Summit Street

Preble Street

Simonton Cove

Smith Street

South Portland

Fisherman's Point

Thompson Street

Willard Street

Looking north from Fisherman's Point in South Portland, hikers can see Spring Point Ledge Lighthouse and Fort Gorges.

1.1 Reach a small lighthouse gift shop, open seasonally, on the right, across from a small beach. Continue on the paved shoreway east of the gift shop; climb wood and granite steps to get over the seawall, and walk the breakwater to the lighthouse.

1.3 Reach the base of the lighthouse and walk around It. Head back toward the gift shop.

1.5 Turn left (south) just before the gift shop to take wooden steps up to a paved path.

1.6 Turn left (east) at the top of the steps and follow the paved path, which features benches and views overlooking the lighthouse and Fort Preble, as well as a distant view back toward Bug Light and the marina.

1.7 Once past the ruins of Fort Preble, take a left (east) down wooden steps and continue following the paved shoreway as it heads southwest, paralleling the coastline and passing campus buildings.

1.9 The paved shoreway comes out onto a driveway behind the Hildreth Science Center. Turn left (south) to continue paralleling the coastline, and walk past the Old Settlers Cemetery, founded in 1658.

2.0 Reach the end of the paved shoreway and turn left (southeast) to get down to Willard Beach. Turn right (south) and walk along the beach, passing a playground and seasonal bathhouse and restrooms.

2.3 Climb stairs at the end of the beach and turn left (northeast) at the top of the stairs to head to Fisherman's Point, where a wayside exhibit features some of the area's history. Return the way you came.

4.0 Arrive back at the Bug Light parking lot, saving about 0.7 mile on the round-trip if you don't explore either of the lighthouses on the return.

9 MACKWORTH ISLAND

Featuring a pet cemetery, fairy houses, and a dark history, Mackworth Island could almost be the setting for a Stephen King story. But once you sample the coastal views from this island near Portland, you'll understand why Governor Percival Baxter "spent the happiest days" of his life here and donated his family's summer home to the State of Maine "as a sanctuary for wild beasts and birds."

Start: Mackworth Island trailhead at the far (southwest) end of the main island parking lot
Elevation gain: None
Distance: 1.25-mile loop
Difficulty: Easy
Hiking time: 45 minutes–1 hour
Seasons/schedule: Open year-round 9 a.m. to sunset; best spring through fall
Fees and permits: Day-use fee
Trail contact: Maine Bureau of Parks and Lands, Mackworth Island State Park Trail, 528 Hallowell Rd., Pownal 04069; (207) 688-4712; maine.gov/mackworthisland
Dog-friendly: Dogs must be on-leash and are prohibited from beaches between Apr 1 and Sept 30
Trail surface: Packed soil
Land status: 100-acre island owned by the State of Maine. While the perimeter trail is open to the public, the Governor Baxter School for the Deaf is not unless arrangements are made.
Nearest town: Falmouth
Maps: USGS Portland (ME) East; Maine Bureau of Parks and Lands Mackworth Island trail map
Other trail users: Trail runners, dog walkers, anglers, swimmers and sunbathers, kayakers coming ashore
Special considerations: The trail is largely accessible to visitors with wheelchairs or strollers except for short side trails. There is limited parking, and you may be turned away if the lot Is full. There are benches, a couple of small beaches, side trails to a pet cemetery and fairy house village, and a chemical toilet near the trailhead. A self-guiding trail brochure by the Maine Department of Conservation may be available upon request at the entrance station. Bring insect repellent during black fly and mosquito season.

FINDING THE TRAILHEAD

From Portland take I-295 North to exit 9 for US 1 North to Falmouth. Follow US 1 for 1.3 miles and turn right (southeast) onto Andrews Avenue at the blue sign marked "The Maine Educational Center for the Deaf & Hard of Hearing." Follow the causeway to the Mackworth Island entrance station at 0.7 mile and turn right (southwest) into the main island parking lot. The Mackworth Island trailhead is on the far (southwest) side of the lot. **GPS:** N43 41.20' / W70 14.07'

WHAT TO SEE

The same conservation-minded Governor Percival Baxter who donated Mount Katahdin to the State of Maine also gave Mackworth Island to the public. But while Baxter State Park may seem a grander gift with its hundreds of thousands of acres in the North Woods and the highest peak in Maine, this 100-acre coastal island near Portland may have been a more deeply felt one.

"This island means everything to me," Baxter told the state legislature in 1943, "and I want the people of Maine to own and enjoy this island in the years to come."

Take in the views of Casco Bay, Portland, nearby islands and lighthouses; visit the pet cemetery for "Baxter's Best Friends"; and learn about his family's connection to Mackworth and you will understand why this place meant so much to the former governor. Baxter's father, James, who'd served as mayor of Portland, bought the island in 1885 and soon built a twenty-two-room summer "cottage," as mansions of the era were often called. A second mansion, built in 1916, is part of what the governor gave to the school for the deaf that now bears his name.

But there is also a dark side to the island's history. For decades up through the 1970s, hundreds of students at the Governor Baxter School for the Deaf and its predecessor, the Maine School for the Deaf, were sexually or physically abused, a state investigation found in the 1980s. To try to make amends, the state apologized and created the Baxter Compensation Authority, paying about $20 million to former students who were harmed. The old farmhouse where the unspeakable occurred was burned down, and today the school continues to provide needed services to families with deaf children, from infants to high school students, on the bucolic island campus.

As you walk the Mackworth Island Trail, remember the island's past, but also enjoy the pleasures of the present, as Baxter intended.

From the island's main parking lot, where there are steps down to a small sandy beach, take the trail at the far (southwest) end of the lot to circle the island. At 0.1 mile bear right at a fork to continue paralleling the shoreline. At 0.2 mile reach a spur to a swinging bench, where you can get a partial view toward Portland and glimpses of two lighthouses. The closer one is Spring Point Ledge Lighthouse in South Portland; the other is Portland Head Light at Fort Williams Park in Cape Elizabeth.

At 0.3 mile the buildings for the Governor Baxter School for the Deaf come into view on the left (north). Bear right, away from school grounds, to continue paralleling

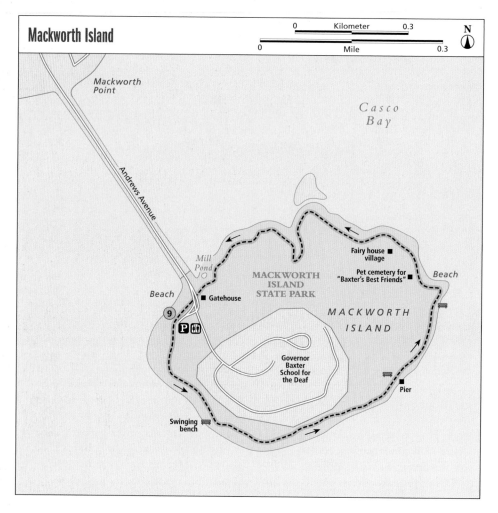

the shoreline. Off to the right (south) you'll see Fort Gorges in Casco Bay. Completed in 1864 but never used in defense, it's now the object of preservation efforts.

At 0.5 mile reach an ornate memorial wood bench on the left (north) and a pier on the right (south) that was built during the Civil War, when Mackworth Island served as Camp Berry, a Union Army facility.

As you begin rounding a point on the northeast corner of the island at 0.7 mile, sit at a bench under the tamarack trees and take in the view of some of the Calendar Islands, so named because it was once thought there were as many islands in Casco Bay as days in the year. The two closest islands straight ahead (north) are The Brothers; Cousins, with its smokestack, lies in the distance. Also visible are Sturdivant, Clapboard, Basket, Great Chebeague, Little Chebeague, Long, and Great Diamond Islands. Soon after rounding the point, you'll see a short side trail to the right (north) to a gravel beach. Then you'll see a short loop trail off to the left (south) that takes you by Baxter's pet cemetery, where fourteen Irish setters and his horse, Jerry Roan, are buried.

The State of Maine sets aside an area on Mackworth Island where people can use sticks to erect small "fairy houses," kind of a tradition in some places in the Pine Tree State.

WELCOME TO MACKWORTH ISLAND COMMUNITY VILLAGE

YOU MAY BUILD HOUSES SMALL AND HIDDEN FOR THE FAIRIES, BUT PLEASE DO NOT USE LIVING OR ARTIFICIAL MATERIALS.

THE BEST MATERIALS ARE FOUND IN THE LANDSCAPE OF THE VILLAGE ITSELF; BUT IF YOU CHOSE TO BRING IN NATURAL MATERIALS, PLEASE RETURN WITH THOSE THAT YOU DIDN'T USE.

THANK YOU FOR TREATING THE ISLAND WITH CARE AND RESPECT. THIS HELPS KEEP THE FAIRIES COMING BACK.

Governor Percival Baxter donated Mackworth Island to the State of Maine and also established his pet cemetery on the island, years before the Stephen King novel about a pet graveyard in Maine.

At 0.8 mile you'll reach the fairy house village on the left (south), marked by a sign that says, "Welcome to Mackworth Island Community Village" and spells out the use of natural materials in construction, which "helps keep the fairies coming back."

At 1.1 mile reach a small millpond that is one of the few spots in Maine where Columbia water-meal, the smallest of flowering plants, is known to grow. The Maine Natural Areas Program lists the aquatic plant as being of "special concern" and "imperiled" in the state, primarily as a result of its being at the northern limit of its range.

At 1.25 miles arrive at the island entrance station. Cross over to the main parking lot to return to your car.

MILES AND DIRECTIONS

0.0   Start at the Mackworth Island trailhead on the far (southwest) end of the main parking lot.

0.1   Bear right to continue paralleling the shoreline.

0.2   Pass a swinging bench with views south to Portland, Spring Point Ledge Lighthouse, and Portland Head Light.

0.3   Pass the buildings of the Governor Baxter School for the Deaf on the left (north); bear right to continue paralleling the shoreline.

0.5   Reach an ornate wooden bench and Civil War–era pier.

0.7   Sit on the bench under the tamarack trees to enjoy views north to some of the Calendar Islands. Follow the trail around the point and pass a short side trail on your right (north) to a gravel beach and a short loop trail on your left (south) to Baxter's pet cemetery.

0.8   Pass the fairy house village.

1.1   Reach a small millpond.

1.25 Arrive at the island entrance station. Cross to the main parking lot to reach your car.

10 WOLFE'S NECK WOODS STATE PARK

Wolfe's Neck Woods State Park offers an easily accessible shore that includes marshland, a gravel-and-sand beach, and rocky headlands along Casco Bay, as well as stunning views of islands and the Harraseeket River. The park is also distinguished by its interpretive exhibits and ranger-led nature programs such as Osprey Watch, Secrets of a Tide Pool, and Casco Bay Walk. You can also take advantage of a special Maine benefit and dig some soft-shell clams at low tide on the park's massive mudflats.

Start: White Pines trailhead at the northern edge of parking lot #2
Elevation gain: 322 feet
Distance: 2.3-mile circuit loop
Difficulty: Easy to moderate
Hiking time: 1.5–2 hours
Seasons/schedule: Open year-round 9 a.m. to sunset; best spring through fall, at low tide for shorebird viewing and clamming
Fees and permits: Day-use fee
Trail contact: Wolfe's Neck Woods State Park, 426 Wolfe's Neck Rd., Freeport 04032; (207) 865-4465; maine.gov/wolfesneckwoods
Dog-friendly: Leashed dogs permitted
Trail surface: Forest floor, rock ledges, footbridges, bogwalks, gravel path, sand-and-gravel beach, wood and rock steps, pavement
Land status: 245-acre park owned and maintained by the State of Maine

Nearest town: Freeport
Maps: USGS Freeport; Wolfe's Neck Woods State Park trail map
Other trail users: Trail runners, dog walkers, clammers, birders, local residents; snowshoers and cross-country skiers in winter
Special considerations: Facilities include picnic area and restrooms. Check the state park's calendar of events at maine.gov/dacf/parks/discover_history_explore_nature/activities/index.shtml. Site of annual "Feathers over Freeport" event the last weekend of April. White Pines Trail and osprey viewing area are generally accessible to visitors using wheelchairs or strollers. Benches, interpretive signs, and picnic areas with grills can be found along the trails.

FINDING THE TRAILHEAD

From US 1 in downtown Freeport, across from the flagship L.L.Bean store, head east on Bow Street for 1 mile; bear right (southeast) onto Flying Point Road for 1.3 miles. Turn right (southwest) onto Wolfe's Neck Road for 2.1 miles then left (southeast) onto a gravel road to enter Wolfe's Neck Woods State Park. Pass the entrance station and proceed to parking lot #2 to pick up the White Pines Trail at the northern edge of the lot. **GPS:** N43 49.20' / W70 04.59'

WHAT TO SEE

Situated near the center of a peninsula between Casco Bay and the long tidal Harraseeket River, Wolfe's Neck Woods State Park is a crown jewel in the Maine state park system, with a network of trails through forests and along the bay and river. Visitors can enjoy

An osprey lands in its nest at Googins Island in Wolfe's Neck Woods State Park.

close-up island views and easy access to a dramatic waterfront of granite ledges, marshland, small beaches, and tide pools. A visit between roughly April and early September means the opportunity to participate in the "osprey watch," when you can look through a spotting scope to see the raptors nesting on Googins Island and diving to catch fish in the bay.

Andy Hutchinson, who started as a park receptionist at Wolfe's Neck Woods in 1985 and has been park manager since 1990, said the park is a very special place with a wide variety of ecosystems. "Once people discover us, they know they have found a real gem and they usually come back," he said. "We have a lot of people who come back every year, even if they are from far away."

The park is a short distance from downtown Freeport, which hosts the corporate headquarters of L.L.Bean and its flagship store.

Of all Maine state parks, Wolfe's Neck Woods holds the most frequent and diverse ranger-led nature programs for the public and the most interpretive signs on the environment and history. The emphasis on education is a legacy of the donors of Wolfe's Neck, lawyer Lawrence M. C. Smith and his wife, Eleanor Houston Smith, who were both active environmentalists and came from families with deep roots in Philadelphia. The Smiths were trailblazers and innovators who bought up waterfront land in depressed post–World War II Maine and operated an organic beef farm on Wolfe's Neck some years before *Silent Spring* was published in 1962.

Lawrence Smith had quit a Philadelphia law firm to work as a lawyer for the federal government during the New Deal in Washington and also served in West Africa and Europe during World War II. The family farm, which borders the state park and is now the Wolfe's Neck Center for Agriculture and the Environment, was donated by Eleanor Smith after her husband's death and is operated as a nonprofit center for education and research on regenerative agriculture, a way of farming that is better for topsoil and the environment.

The Smiths required the park to be preserved for education, research, and limited recreation when they deeded the land to the state for $1 in 1969, clearing the way for the 245-acre Wolfe's Neck Woods State Park to open in 1972. The Smiths also mandated that 7-acre Googins Island be protected solely as a bird sanctuary and that snowmobiles, as well as paved parking lots and roads, be avoided.

The Smiths set up a trust that has helped finance the salaries of rangers at the park who specialize in interpretation and environmental education, including Patty Bailey, who was key in developing all the current exhibits and programs in the park before she retired in 2006. Rangers Kate LeRoyer and Pam Truesdale laid the groundwork for the interpretive programs and signs before Bailey.

The Smiths also deeded numerous other properties to organizations such as the Maine Audubon Society, assuring protection for significant amounts of land in Freeport and elsewhere in Maine. "It was their mind-set," said Sam Smith of Freeport, an author and journalist and one of the Smiths' six children, who serves as a liaison between the family and the park. "They just had charitable instincts."

The 2.3-mile loop hike described here goes through old pine and hardwood forests and along salt marsh, mudflats, ledges of granite and other rocks, tide pools, and sand beaches. Toward the end, you get a view of the Harraseeket River, a 3.2-mile-long tidal river on the west side of Wolfe's Neck Woods, a park named for the first permanent European family that settled there.

The hike starts at the White Pines trailhead and continues straight (north) at a junction at 0.1 mile, onto the North Loop Trail, which includes a view through the woods to the

A visitor digs for soft-shell clams on the flats at Wolfe's Neck.

southeast of a salt marsh and the Flying Point peninsula. The North Loop Trail is also the site of the first of many interpretive signs on this hike, called "From Field to Forest."

Circle around the North Loop Trail and back at the junction with the White Pines Trail at 0.5 mile; take a left (east) to continue on that trail, passing some giant white pines, Maine's official state tree. Soon you come to a thirty-six-step stairway, framed by balsam and leading to the mudflats at low tide, rocky ledges, and a view of Flying Point and Bustins Island, joined to the point by a natural causeway exposed at low tide.

As the White Pines Trail turns right away from the shore at 0.8 mile, continue straight until you are across from Googins Island and an osprey nest high on the island's treetops and built with telltale big sticks. The wingspan of a female osprey can be 6 feet, but the bird was concealed as it sat in the nest, one of four such aeries visible in the park, along with maybe three to four others in inaccessible areas.

In a June visit during a nature program, Park Ranger Michael Frey pointed to a pair of ospreys that were fending off a bald eagle high in the sky near Googins Island. Bald eagles will sometimes attack the nests of ospreys or torment or steal fish from the talons of their rival raptors.

Follow the path down to the intertidal area of Wolfe's Neck, which is tops among state parks for digging soft-shell clams—at no additional charge after paying the park admission fee. Maine is special in allowing people to harvest clams at state parks for free without a permit. Each person is allowed to dig a peck of clams with at least 2-inch-long shells (the legal minimum). Digging for clams is hard work. You need to go at low tide, and you might need a shovel, a metal ring for measuring the clams, and a peck-size wire basket.

Down on the shore, Frey talked about steamers and about how tide pools support a food chain in Casco Bay and could be considered where life begins. Frey crouched to the water to show examples of tiny sea anemones, which can be eaten by fish, and snails such as dog whelks, which use their radula, or minuscule teeth, to drill into clams, and periwinkles, which feed on algae that grow in the sunlight in the pools. Throughout, barnacles clung to exposed rocks, jockeying for space with rockweed, a type of seaweed. Spartina, a common marsh grass, held silt that ran from a ravine and accumulated in the marshy area.

The hike becomes spectacular as it continues beyond the White Pines Trail onto the Casco Bay Trail, with electrifying views of Googins and Bustins Islands to the east and ospreys soaring and plunging into the ocean. Outcrops of white granite and older ledges of black metamorphic rock cover the shore and are ideal for sitting and enjoying the waves lapping from Casco Bay.

At 0.9 mile there is a scenic overlook of the bay and a wooden bench near an interpretive sign about animals critical to the ecosystem, such as harbor seals, common eiders, and mackerel. A junction with the Casco Bay Connector here allows you to return inland to the parking lot if you are pressed for time or don't want to climb a steep ridge.

Continue on the Casco Bay Trail, paralleling the rocky shore, until it ends at 1.1 miles at the Harraseeket Trail, with an exhibit of all the islands in sight, including—north to south on the bay—Bustins and Little Bustins Islands, tiny French Island farther out to sea, Big Moshier and Little Moshier, part of Great Chebeague in the distance, and finally Littlejohn and Cousins, recognizable by its power plant. To the right (southwest) of the exhibit, descend thirty-one wooden stairs and some ledge to reach a tidal sand-and-gravel beach—a "rare gem" in Maine, Hutchinson said, because only 2 percent of the state's shoreline is sand beach. After a visit to the shore, climb back up the steps to the Harraseeket Trail and turn left (northwest) onto the trail as it heads inland; ascend rather steeply for a short distance to the top of a ridge.

At 1.2 miles pass the Ledge Trail on your right; at 1.3 miles pass the Old Woods Road Trail, also on your right, and look to cross part of an eighteenth-century stone wall, erected by the first Europeans to live on the peninsula. At 1.4 miles pass the Hemlock Ridge Trail on your right as you go through a dense forest of mature hemlock trees, which have long branches, very short needles, and a red tint to their bark. Unfortunately, many of these beautiful trees are dying because they are infested with the invasive hemlock woolly adelgid, a resistant pest that weakens and ultimately kills the tree.

At 1.5 miles cross paved Wolfe's Neck Road—watch for traffic both ways—and soon get some views of the Harraseeket River. To the northwest, at a couple of overlooks, you can

A girl enjoys digging with a toy bucket on the beach at Wolfe's Neck.

see a marina on the shore of South Freeport and the stone tower of "Casco Castle," once part of an old hotel that burned down in the early twentieth century. Follow the river's shore and then at 1.8 miles turn right (southeast) to switchback up the ridge away from the river.

At 2.0 miles cross back over the paved Wolfe's Neck Road and pass the Hemlock Ridge Trail and Power Line Trail on your right. Here we saw pink lady's slipper, a wildflower often seen at the park in late May or June, and listened to the poignant song of a hermit thrush.

Continue on the Harraseeket Trail past an intersection with the Old Woods Road Trail at 2.1 miles, and follow it as it ends at the Casco Bay Connector at 2.2 miles; turn left (north) to head back to the parking lot at 2.3 miles.

MILES AND DIRECTIONS

0.0 Start at the White Pines trailhead at the northern edge of parking lot #2.

0.1 Head straight (north) onto the North Loop Trail to circle along the marshland.

0.5 Back at the junction with the White Pines Trail, turn left (east) to continue on that trail.

0.8 As the White Pines Trail turns right away from the shore, head straight until you are across from the osprey nesting area on Googins Island; pick up the Casco Bay Trail.

0.9 Reach a scenic overlook at the junction with the Casco Bay Connector. (**Option:** Take the connector inland back to the parking lot if you are pressed for time or don't want to climb a steep ridge.)

Wolfe's Neck Woods State Park

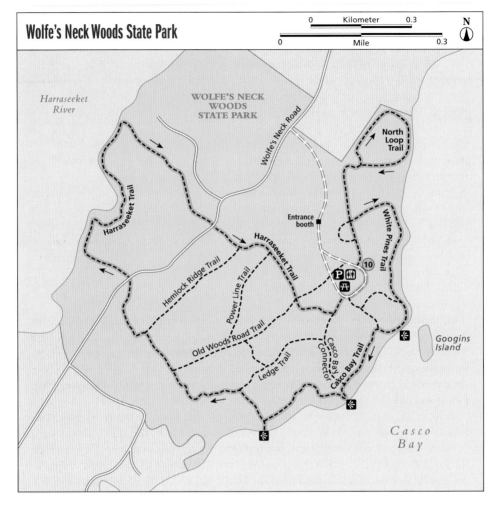

1.1 Continue paralleling the shore along the Casco Bay Trail until it ends at the Harraseeket Trail, where there is an exhibit about the islands that are in view. Descend wood steps to the right (southwest) to a sand-and-gravel beach that's best explored at low tide. Climb back up the steps and turn left (northwest) on the Harraseeket Trail to head inland and ascend the ridge.

1.2 Pass the Ledge Trail on the right.

1.3 Pass the Old Woods Road Trail on the right.

1.4 Pass the Hemlock Ridge Trail on the right; continue following the Harraseeket Trail down the ridge.

1.5 Cross Wolfe's Neck Road, watching out for traffic in both directions.

1.7 Enjoy the views of the Harraseeket River, the South Freeport marina, and the stone tower of "Casco Castle."

1.8 Follow the Harraseeket Trail as it turns right (southeast) to switchback up the ridge, away from the river.

2.0 Cross back over Wolfe's Neck Road; pass the Hemlock Ridge Trail and Power Line Trail on the right.

2.1 Pass the Old Woods Road Trail on the right.

2.2 The Harraseeket Trail ends at the Casco Bay Connector. Turn left (north) on the connector to head to the parking area.

2.3 Turn right (east) upon reaching parking lot #1 to arrive back at parking lot #2.

MORE IN SOUTHERN COAST AND GREATER PORTLAND

BREWERIES, EATS, AND SLEEPS

Sebago Brewing Co. has three brewpubs in coastal Maine: **Kennebunk Brewpub**, 65 Portland Rd., Kennebunk 04043; (207) 985-9855; **Portland Brewpub**, 211 Fore St., Portland 04101; (207) 775-2337; and **Scarborough Brewpub**, 201 Southborough Dr., Scarborough 04074; (207) 874-2337; sebagobrewing.com/brewpubs/. The pubs offer different and extensive menus and could include such favorites as baked stuffed haddock and beer-battered fish-and-chips. There is a big selection of year-round beers such as Saddleback Ale and Lake Trout Stout and small-batch and specialty beers that include a lager and a pilsner. Free brewery tours by reservation and tasting room at 616 Main St., Gorham 04038. At least one of the brewpubs is near any coastal trail you might hike in this southern coast and greater Portland section. Open year-round.

Barnacle Billy's, 50-70 Perkins Cove Rd., Ogunquit 03907; (207) 646-5575; barn billy.com. Located near the southern end of Marginal Way, offering "luxury lobster" and "lusty drinks." Claim to fame: The late President George H. W. Bush ate there (the family compound in Kennebunkport is not far), and he would sit at the flagpole table on the deck overlooking Perkins Cove. Indoor and outdoor seating at the full-service restaurant. Open seasonally.

Arundel Wharf Restaurant, 43 Ocean Ave., Kennebunk 04046; (207) 967-3444; arundelwharf.com. Casual waterfront dining and cocktails with a yacht club theme, serving lunch and dinner on the deck or indoors by the fireplace. Lobster and other seafood on the menu, along with other selections. Near Wells Reserve at Laudholm, Vaughn Island, and Timber Point Trail. Family-friendly. Open seasonally.

Franciscan Guest House, 26 Beach Ave., Kennebunk 04043; (207) 967-4865; fran ciscanguesthouse.com. Adjacent to St. Anthony's Franciscan Monastery, this modest nonprofit guest house is within walking distance of Kennebunkport's Dock Square and provides access to tranquil grounds and a continental breakfast. Proceeds benefit the Lithuanian Franciscans' many charities. Close to Wells Reserve at Laudholm, Vaughn Island, and Timber Point Trail. Open seasonally.

Inn by the Sea, 40 Bowery Beach Rd., Cape Elizabeth 04107; (207) 799-3134; inn bythesea.com. Oceanfront luxury resort with suites, rooms, spa, and Sea Glass Restaurant. Pet-friendly. Abuts Crescent Beach State Park; also near Fort Williams Park and Spring Point Shoreway. Open year-round.

Harraseeket Inn, 162 Main St., Freeport 04032; (207) 865-9377; harraseeketinn .com. A family-owned 93-room luxury inn just steps from L.L.Bean and the Amtrak Downeaster train station, featuring two restaurants, the Broad Arrow Tavern and the Maine Harvest Dining Room, a full breakfast buffet, and a lobster Sunday brunch. Near Wolfe's Neck Woods State Park. Open year-round.

The Wiggly Bridge in York, only for walking, is said to be the world's smallest suspension bridge.

CAMPING

Bayley's Camping Resort, 275 Pine Point Rd., Scarborough 04074; (207) 883-6043; bayleysresort.com. Dogs are allowed, maximum of three per campsite. More than 700 sites, including many for RVs and fully equipped trailers up to 35 feet; cabins for rent. This is a family destination with lots of activities, entertainment, beach trolleys, minigolf, three on-site fishing ponds, pools, beach volleyball, kayak rentals and launch, and much more. Near Crescent Beach and Kettle Cove State Parks, Fort Williams Park, and Spring Point Shoreway. Open end of Apr to mid-Oct.

Wolfe's Neck Oceanfront Camping, 134 Burnett Rd., Freeport 04032; (207) 865-9307; freeportcamping.com. Part of the Wolfe's Neck Center for Agriculture and the Environment, offering 130 campsites on 626 acres and 4 miles of oceanfront, the on-site Farm Café, kayak and bike rentals, 3 miles of hiking trails, and livestock education barn. RVs allowed on some sites; dogs allowed at most sites but must be attended to at all times. Near Wolfe's Neck Woods State Park. Open May to Oct, with limited sites in the off-season.

LIGHTHOUSES, MUSEUMS, AND HISTORIC SITES

Two Lights State Park, 7 Tower Dr., Cape Elizabeth 04107; (207) 799-5871; maine .gov/twolights/. Just outside the park, visible at the end of Two Lights Road, are the first twin lighthouses on coastal Maine. Although the lighthouse grounds are closed to the public, you can get a distant view of the 67-foot eastern lighthouse, or Cape Elizabeth Light, at a parking area at the end of Two Lights Road, according to the non-profit American Lighthouse Foundation, which cares for the lighthouse. Edward Hopper painted *Lighthouse at Two Lights* based on the 1874 eastern lighthouse. The eastern light was automated and is active at the south entrance of Portland Harbor. The western light stopped operating in 1924 and is now a private residence. The state park, which charges a fee, offers 41 acres of rocky headlands, picnic tables, and 1.9 miles of shoreline trails. Near Crescent Beach and Kettle Cove State Parks, Fort Williams Park, and Spring Point Shoreway. Park open year-round.

Seguin Light, Seguin Island; contact Friends of Seguin Island Light Station, 72 Front St., Ste. 3, Bath 04530; (207) 443-4808; seguinisland.org. Guided tours available Memorial Day to Labor Day by taking the Seguin Island Ferry, which leaves from **Fort Popham State Historic Site**, 219 Popham Rd., Phippsburg 04562. Seguin Light, the second lighthouse built in Maine, began operating in 1795 after being authorized by President George Washington. The original lighthouse was replaced twice, most recently in 1857. The island is 2.5 miles from shore. Fort Popham, a coastal fort used in the Spanish-American War and World War I, is 2 miles from Popham Beach State Park. Accessible year-round.

Winslow Homer Studio, Portland Museum of Art, 7 Congress Sq., Portland 04101; (207) 775-6148; portlandmuseum.org/homer/visit. Guided 2.5-hour tours to the studio at Prouts Neck in Scarborough leave from the Portland museum twice a day on select days, Apr through Oct. Advance reservation is required, and transportation is by museum-provided luxury van. Near Crescent Beach and Kettle Cove State Parks, Fort Williams Park, Spring Point Shoreway, and Mackworth Island.

COASTAL ATTRACTIONS

Old York, 3 Lindsay Rd., York 03909; (207) 363-1757; oldyork.org. Tour buildings dating back to the 1700s, including The Old Gaol and a warehouse and wharf that John Hancock once had an interest in. Stroll through nearby **Steedman Woods** and cross the **Wiggly Bridge**, said to be the world's smallest suspension bridge and particularly wiggly as the tides change, to join up with **Fisherman's Walk**. Seasonal tours provided by the nonprofit Old York Historical Society (admission charged). Steedman Woods, Wiggly Bridge, and Fisherman's Walk are open year-round. Near Marginal Way and Wells Reserve at Laudholm.

MIDCOAST

The central coast of Maine is a region of peninsulas and deep bays and sounds, with a vast range of hiking, including trips along sandy beaches, high rocky cliffs and ledges, or coves and cobble beaches. This area, called the Midcoast, includes ten coastal hikes from Harpswell to Camden, some of which are on four islands.

Only one island requires a ferry trip—Monhegan, one of the most iconic of Maine's islands, inspiring painters like Jamie Wyeth and Rockwell Kent. Bailey, Orr's, and Georgetown Islands, connected to the mainland by bridges, also provide unforgettable hikes in this part of the state.

The Midcoast has more islands than southern Maine, and they tend to be long and narrow. The area is also one of wild rivers that run for miles and empty into the sea,

The western shore of Wyer Island provides views of Harpswell Sound.

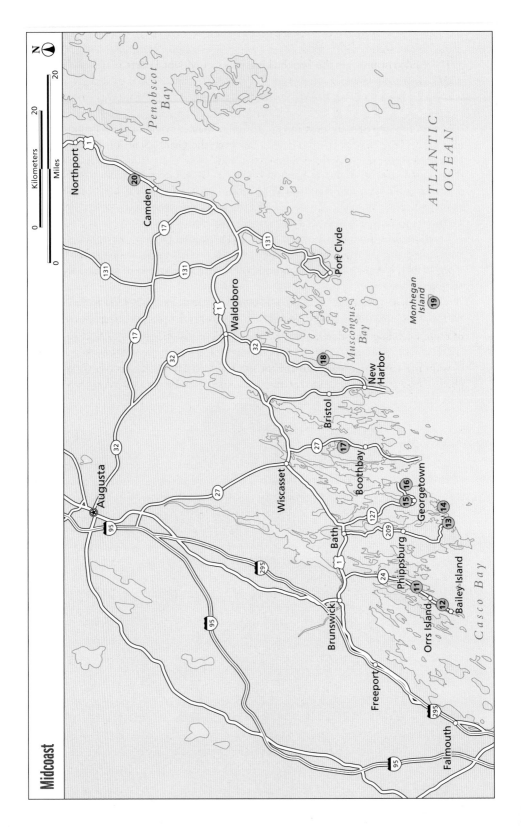

Midcoast

N

0   20
Kilometers

0   20
Miles

Penobscot Bay

Northport

20 Camden

Waldoboro

Port Clyde

Muscongus Bay

New Harbor

18

Bristol

Wiscasset

17 Boothbay

Augusta

Bath

16

15 Georgetown

14

13

Brunswick

Freeport

Phippsburg

11

12 Orrs Island

Bailey Island

Casco Bay

Falmouth

Monhegan Island

19

ATLANTIC OCEAN

including the 170-mile-long Kennebec River, the 66-mile-long Sheepscot River, and the tidal Damariscotta River.

The Midcoast presages the breathtaking peaks of Mount Desert Island to the north with coastal mountains of its own in Camden Hills State Park and Morse Mountain, which rises over the broad sandy beach of the Bates–Morse Mountain Conservation Area.

Many of these hikes are next to major bays in Maine, including West Penobscot Bay off Camden, the northern part of Casco Bay from the Giant's Stairs on Bailey Island in Harpswell, Sheepscot Bay from the lengthy and lovely beaches at Reid State Park in Georgetown, and Muscongus Bay from the LaVerna Preserve in Bristol. Two premier private colleges, Bates College and Bowdoin College, oversee conservation areas with coastal hikes in this region.

The Midcoast boasts several of Maine's most sublime sand beaches, at Popham Beach and Reid State Parks and Bates–Morse Mountain Conservation Area. If you are looking for great blue herons and possibly bald eagles and ospreys among other wild birds, hike the Josephine Newman Audubon Sanctuary or head to Boothbay to visit the Ovens Mouth Preserve.

In Harpswell, the southernmost part of the Midcoast hiking in this book, head to Orr's Island to the Bowdoin College Schiller Coastal Studies Center, which has about 4 miles of trails, including low-tide access to Wyer Island. Just south of Orr's Island, drive over the Cribstone Bridge to Bailey Island for a hike along Casco Bay on the Giant's Stairs.

With the LaVerna Preserve in Bristol and Camden Hills State Park in Camden, the northernmost part of the Midcoast provides some of the best coastal hiking in Maine.

11 BOWDOIN COLLEGE SCHILLER COASTAL STUDIES CENTER

With about 4 miles of well-maintained trails, the Bowdoin College Schiller Coastal Studies Center allows hikers to explore little-known sections of the shoreline on Harpswell Sound and Long Cove and provides many isolated large rocky ledges for quiet time next to the ocean. At low tide you can walk over an exposed bar for a loop hike around wild Wyer Island. You can get great views of ospreys, and you might see harbor seals hauled out near a small island called Dogs Head.

Start: Dipper Cove Path trailhead, off the parking area on the left (west) side of the entrance road
Elevation gain: 217 feet
Distance: 2.9-mile circuit loop
Difficulty: Easy to moderate
Hiking time: 1.5–2.5 hours
Seasons/schedule: Open year-round during daylight hours; best spring through fall and at low tide
Fees and permits: No fees or permits
Trail contact: Bowdoin College Schiller Coastal Studies Center, 6700 College Station, Brunswick 04011; (207) 721-5906; bowdoin.edu/coastal-studies-center/facilities/map-and-directions.html
Dog-friendly: Leashed dogs permitted
Trail surface: Forest floor, rock ledges, log bridges, gravel path, wood chips on forest floor, low-tide sandbar over to Wyer Island
Land status: 118 acres owned and maintained by Bowdoin College
Nearest town: Harpswell
Maps: USGS Orr's Island; Bowdoin College Schiller Coastal Studies Center trail map
Other trail users: Bowdoin College students and faculty, visiting scientists, trail runners, dog walkers, local residents
Special considerations: No facilities. No camping, bicycles, smoking, fires, or hunting allowed. Carry out pet waste. Do not disturb research projects and equipment. For the hike to Wyer Island, accessible only within 1.5 hours on either side of low tide, check the tide chart in local newspapers or at usharbors.com/harbor/maine/south-harpswell-me/tides/.

FINDING THE TRAILHEAD

From US 1 in Brunswick, east of the airport, head south on ME 24 for 10.9 miles onto Orr's Island, part of Harpswell. Turn right (north) onto Bayview Road and travel 1 mile to the parking area for the Bowdoin College Schiller Coastal Studies Center trails. The Dipper Cove Path trailhead is off the parking area on the left (west) side of the entrance road. **GPS:** N43 47.14′ / W69 57.32′

WHAT TO SEE

The dramatic coastline, fields, and forests at Bowdoin College Schiller Coastal Studies Center are in an out-of-the-way spot on Orr's Island and often go unnoticed, even by many students at this historic liberal arts college in central Maine.

Steven Allen, a marine biologist and assistant director at the center, said he is attempting to promote the conservation area and draw more visitors to the college's trails, which

A low-tide walk goes over a short bar to Wyer Island on Bowdoin College conservation land.

are located in Harpswell, some 12 miles from the Bowdoin campus in downtown Brunswick. "It's a hidden gem," Allen said. "And it's open to the public 365 days a year, even though Bowdoin owns the property."

The property is more than a scenic coastal hike to Bowdoin College. Bowdoin uses the center to conduct important research in marine biology and oceanography. For example, field equipment samples water quality, partly to monitor climate change. The Gulf of Maine is warming faster than 95 percent of the world's oceans, said Allen.

"We are on the front-row seat of being able to observe climate change and try to pick it apart and see how it is affecting the biodiversity in the Gulf of Maine," Allen said.

The Schiller Coastal Studies Center is a result of a long history of philanthropy that continues to this day. The property was donated to Bowdoin College in 1981 by Irma and William Thalheimer, an alumnus of the college, with a provision that allowed them to live the rest of their lives in their farmhouse on the land. In 1995 another alumnus, the late L.L.Bean chairman and president Leon Gorman, and his wife, Lisa, provided funds to help develop the property with a marine lab and research facility.

The center was given its current name in 2017 when Philip Schiller, a marketing executive at Apple, and his wife, Kim Gassett-Schiller, donated $10 million to build a state-of-the art dry laboratory linked to the existing marine lab, as well as classrooms, housing, and dining facilities.

The 118-acre property has 2.5 miles of undeveloped oceanfront and about 4 miles of trails including amazing low-tide access to Wyer Island, a small forested island that is linked to Orr's Island with a sandy land bridge exposed when the tide recedes. The property also features views to Dogs Head and other islands, old stone walls, and great access to Harpswell Sound and other oceanfront, especially at low tide.

New England farming families dominated the early years of Orr's Island, which is named for colonist Joseph Orr. The rich history also includes an 1862 book, *The Pearl of Orr's Island*, by abolitionist Harriet Beecher Stowe, famous for writing *Uncle Tom's Cabin*.

We took a 2.9-mile hike that begins at the Dipper Cove Path trailhead at the edge of the parking area on the left (west) side of the entrance road across from the information kiosk.

Walk through a shady forest of red spruce, balsam fir, and white pine, and at just 0.1 mile reach a ridge overlooking Dipper Cove. Turn right (northeast) to walk along the coastline with spectacular views to the northwest of Harpswell Sound, Harpswell Neck across the sound, and Wyer Island. At 0.2 mile on the Dipper Cove Path, reach a junction with a spur trail that goes straight ahead (northeast). Take the spur and reach a rocky point at 0.3 mile. At low tide from this point, you get a beautiful look at the exposed sandbar to Wyer Island, but at high tide, you would never know the bar exists.

If you arrive at low tide as we did, scramble down from the point to the tidal flats and head left (southwest) to the wide and exposed sandbar for the walk to Wyer Island. You can look back at the ridge and see lots of high rocky cliffs, which turn pink and red at sunset. (**Note:** If it is high tide, you won't be able to climb down and do the 0.7-mile out-and-back to Wyer Island. But you can still find some roomy ledges off the ridge for sitting next to the ocean and then continue the hike from the rocky point, as described below.) Check a tide chart, and be aware that low tide occurs about every 12 hours and that it is safe to cross only within 1.5 hours on either side of low tide.

You can get some solitude and a view toward Dogs Head at the Schiller Center on Orr's Island.

The bar to the island, filled with broken sea-shells and also part sandy, is a very easy and pleasant walk. At 0.5 mile in this hike at low tide, after walking 0.2 mile from the rocky point and over the bar, reach the southern point of Wyer Island. Bear left and go clockwise along the western shore with views of Harpswell Sound. Walk along ledge and crushed periwinkle, mussel, and quahog shells on the island, keeping to the shore.

The interior of the island is overgrown and inaccessible. It is rimmed with giant blooming rugosa rose, big bushes of poison ivy, and later a grove of white birch trees and balsam.

At one point we stopped to watch a raft of about fifteen common eiders swimming in the sound at the surface about 100 yards from the island's shore.

It's only a 0.2-mile loop around the shore of the island. Back at the southern tip of the island, head southeast to return across the bar; turn left (northeast) along the coastline and climb back up to the point near the Dipper Cove Path at 1.0 mile. Here, back at the point, you can see an osprey nest built atop a pine tree next to a cliff to the right (east). Keep your distance, and possibly enjoy one of the better views of an osprey nest on coastal Maine.

During late spring and early summer, horseshoe crabs travel from deep ocean waters to the shoreline to breed.

We heard the calls of ospreys and soon spotted two of the birds, one with a fish in its talons, soaring over the exposed nest built of sticks and grass. One later remained in the nest; a couple of others perched on tree tops.

From the rocky point, whether you did the low-tide walk to Wyer Island or not, return southwest via the short spur trail to the junction with the Dipper Cove Path; then turn left (southeast) on the main trail to ascend the ridge to a gravel path by the center's farm-house, which is used for classes, research, and meetings. Turn left (north) onto the gravel path at 1.1 miles into the hike (or 0.4 mile if you didn't do the 0.7-mile low-tide walk to Wyer Island); walk past the farmhouse and barn and head toward a Bowdoin marine lab and sailing center.

At 1.2 miles into the hike, bear right (northeast) to follow Pine Needle Path, indicated by a hiker's sign and green diamond-shaped trail markers as it enters the woods. At 1.4 miles turn right (southeast) onto the Brewer Cove Trail, with blue trail markers. At 1.6 miles, where the trail forks, bear left (east) onto the section of the Brewer Cove Trail that leads to Dogs Head. You get a view of Brewer Cove to the left (north) and an old farm field to the right (south) as you follow along a stone wall and a forest dominated by red oak and white pine. Go up a ridge; at the next intersection, at 1.7 miles, turn left (northeast) to continue on the Brewer Cove Trail toward Dogs Head.

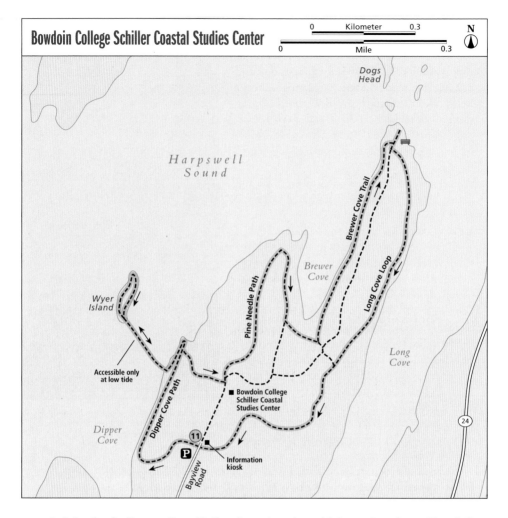

At 2.0 miles the Brewer Cove Trail ends at a junction with Long Cove Loop. Turn left (northeast) onto a spur to a bench at the end of a point overlooking lovely Dogs Head, a tiny island, with views of Uncle Zeke Island, an aquaculture farm, and possibly harbor seals hauled out on open rocks. To the east you can see a bridge that connects Orr's Island to Sebascodegan Island.

Note: Please respect the private property beyond the point.

Retrace your steps, passing the Brewer Cove Trail that comes in on the right (west). Bear left (southeast) at the next intersection, at 2.1 miles, to follow the scenic coastal section of the Long Cove Loop instead of climbing up a wooded ridgetop. From the Long Cove Loop, you can look back at Dogs Head and soon Long Cove itself, which is nestled at the base of two stretches of land along Orr's Island.

At 2.5 miles, where the upland section of the Long Cove Loop comes in on the right, go straight ahead (southwest) on the Stone Wall Walk. Skirt an old field at 2.9 miles and arrive back at the parking area.

MILES AND DIRECTIONS

0.0 Start at the Dipper Cove Path trailhead, at the edge of the parking area on the left (west) side of the entrance road.

0.1 Reach a ridge overlooking Dipper Cove; turn right (northeast) to continue on the Dipper Cove Path along the coastline.

0.2 Reach a junction. The main trail heads to the right (southeast), but first head straight (northeast) to explore a rocky point.

0.3 Reach the rocky point. If you arrive at low tide, scramble left (west) down to the tidal flats and head southwest to the sandbar that connects to Wyer Island. Be mindful of the tide—it's safe to cross only within 1.5 hours on either side of low tide.

0.5 Reach the southern point of Wyer Island and bear left to go clockwise along the western shore.

0.6 Reach the northern point of Wyer Island and circle back along the eastern shore.

0.7 Back on the southern tip of the island, head southeast back across the sandbar, turning left (northeast) along the coastline back to the rocky point.

1.0 Climb back up the point, then head southwest on the spur to return to the junction with the main Dipper Cove Path.

1.1 Turn left (southeast) on the main trail and ascend the ridge to a gravel path by the center's farmhouse and barn. Turn left (northeast) past the farmhouse and barn and head toward the marine lab and sailing center.

1.2 Bear right to follow the Pine Needle Path, indicated by a hiker's sign and green diamond-shaped trail markers, as it enters the woods.

1.4 At the junction with the Brewer Cove Trail, marked by blue diamond-shaped trail markers, turn right (southeast).

1.6 At the next intersection turn left (east) to follow the section of the Brewer Cove Trail toward Dogs Head.

1.7 Go up a ridge; at the next intersection turn left (northeast) to continue on the Brewer Cove Trail.

2.0 As the Brewer Cove Trail ends at the junction with the Long Cove Loop, turn left (northeast) onto a short spur toward a bench overlooking Dogs Head. Please respect private property beyond here.

2.1 Retrace your steps, passing where the Brewer Cove Trail comes in on the right (west). Bear left (southeast) at the next junction to follow the scenic coastal section of the Long Cove Loop rather than climb up the wooded ridgetop.

2.5 Reach an intersection where the upland section of the Long Cove Loop comes in on the right (west). Go straight ahead (southwest) on the Stone Wall Walk to circle back to the parking area.

2.9 Skirt an old field and arrive back at the parking area.

12 GIANT'S STAIRS

So fantastic are the cliffs that make up the Giant's Stairs that they're featured in *The Life of Captain Marvel*, a comic-book series that filled in the superhero's backstory, just before she starred in the 2019 blockbuster movies *Captain Marvel* and *The Avengers: Endgame*. In real life, this Bailey Island preserve draws families, hikers, and Bowdoin College faculty and students to enjoy the marvelous views of Casco Bay and explore the science, from geology to marine biology.

Start: The seasonal All Saints by the Sea Episcopal Chapel
Elevation gain: 14 feet
Distance: 0.8 mile out and back
Difficulty: Easy
Hiking time: 30 minutes–1 hour
Seasons/schedule: Open year-round; best spring through fall, either early or late in the day during summer peak
Fees and permits: No fees or permits
Trail contact: Town of Harpswell, PO Box 39, Harpswell 04079; (207) 833-5771; harpswell.maine.gov
   Harpswell Heritage Land Trust, PO Box 359, Harpswell 04079; (207) 721-1121; hhltmaine.org
Dog-friendly: Dogs under owner control permitted, preferably leashed
Trail surface: Graded gravel, rock ledges, paved road
Land status: 2.5 acres along the coast owned and managed by the Town of Harpswell, with an adjoining 1-acre McIntosh Lot Preserve owned and managed by the nonprofit Harpswell Heritage Land Trust
Nearest town: Harpswell
Maps: USGS Bailey Island; Harpswell Heritage Land Trust trail map

Other trail users: Trail runners, birders, local residents, dog walkers
Special considerations: Park only where allowed, either at the small lot for the seasonal All Saints by the Sea Episcopal Chapel (except in July and August during Sunday morning services) or at limited town-provided parking areas located at the south end of Washington Avenue, marked by signs. The better parking option during busy times is a 15-minute walk away at the Harpswell Heritage Land Trust's Johnson Field Preserve, off Abner Point Road on the west side of ME 24, 0.4 mile north of the junction with Washington Avenue. The hike description starts from the chapel parking lot near the northern end of the Giant's Stairs Trail, although there is also access near the southern terminus of the trail via the McIntosh Lot, off the south end of Washington Avenue. No facilities. Trail partly accessible for visitors with wheelchairs or strollers. Watch out for poison ivy, wet rocks, and surf. Please respect private property owners' rights. If visiting with dogs, pick up after them.

FINDING THE TRAILHEAD

From Cooks Corner in Brunswick, take ME 24 south for 14.5 miles, crossing the Cribstone Bridge onto Bailey Island; turn left (east) onto Washington Avenue. Park in front of the seasonal All Saints by the Sea Episcopal Chapel, just before Washington turns sharp right (south). Walk east on Ocean Street to pick up the northern end of the Giant's Stairs Trail. If you park at the town-provided parking areas at the south end of Washington Avenue, walk back to the chapel to head east on Ocean Street. **GPS:** N43 43.35' / W69 59.40'

WHAT TO SEE

Hundreds of millions of years of geologic forces—from tectonic collisions to volcanic activity—are written in the rugged rocks of Giant's Stairs and the surrounding coastline.

Formed by a wide swath of black volcanic rock that intruded between jagged pink and gray metamorphic rock and eroded over eons into a steplike cliff, Giant's Stairs looks otherworldly enough for a colossus to climb out of Casco Bay—or to be featured in a superhero comic book, *The Life of Captain Marvel*.

A gift to Harpswell in 1910 from Captain William Henry Sinnett, a lifelong resident of Bailey Island, and his wife, Joanna, the Giant's Stairs Trail, though short, is jam-packed with sights and sounds. Look out on Casco Bay and you may see a lobster boat plying the waters. Off to the east are Pond and Ragged Islands. At the southern tip of the trail, beyond the well-graded path and skirting private property, you can get views of a cleft in the cliffs known as Thunder Hole, Pinnacle Rock jutting up into the sky, and Jaquish Island just off shore.

The Giant's Stairs Trail offers so much that one Audubon field trip in December 2017 documented twenty-nine species, including a peregrine falcon consuming prey on a rock ledge east of Thunder Hole. Faculty and students from nearby Bowdoin College come to study the geology and marine biology.

The hike described here is out and back, allowing twice the opportunity to take in the coastal views. But if you prefer loop hikes, you can head inland on the McIntosh Lot Trail near the southern tip of the Giant's Stairs Trail and turn right (north) on Washington Avenue back to the car.

From the All Saints by the Sea Episcopal Chapel parking lot, head east on Ocean Street, reaching the northern end of the Giant's Stairs Trail at 0.1 mile. Turn right (south) onto the graded gravel path, being mindful of poison ivy, wet rocks, and surf if you decide to go off the path to explore the vast rocky ledges.

Hundreds of millions of years of geologic forces are evident along the Giant's Stairs Trail.

A plaque marks the top of the Giant's Stairs, formed by a wide swath of volcanic rock, known as a black dike, that steps down to the sea.

It was surprising right at the start of the trail to see a large grove of jack pines, which generally do not grow south of Mount Desert Island in Maine. Jill E. Weber, Acadia National Park consulting botanist, said the jack pines at Giant's Stairs might be outliers that are pushing the geographic limits, or a single tree might have been planted and spread progeny.

Another thrilling sight, a half dozen laughing gulls skimmed over the ocean just beyond the rocks onshore. Laughing gulls, a state listed species of special concern, are less common than herring or black-backed gulls in Maine and stand out for their black heads and red beaks in summer.

The late spring air was filled at times with the melody of song sparrows, which moved in the thickets along the shore. The trail was also lined with blooming white flowers on trees that turned out to be apple, a member of the rose family that persists for years on a landscape after being planted by people or dispersed to the site by animals.

At 0.3 mile reach the top of the Giant's Stairs, marked by a plaque commemorating the gift of this land by the Sinnetts. Look down on the black dike (as the wide band of volcanic rock is known) as it steps down to the ocean, and marvel at the jagged pink and gray cliffs towering above it on either side.

Just after the junction with the McIntosh Lot Trail on the right (west), reach the end of the graded gravel path, where most people turn around. But for additional views, head onto the rugged rock ledge, being respectful of the private homes that abut the southern end of the Giant's Stairs Trail.

Follow the faint red blazes painted on the rock ledge, passing near Pinnacle Rock, with Jaquish Island in the background, and going around the corner to Thunder Hole at 0.4 mile, where you might hear a gurgle in calm seas, as we did, or possibly a loud clap at times of rough surf.

As with all coastal trails, be wary of high surf, slippery rocks, and cliff edges.

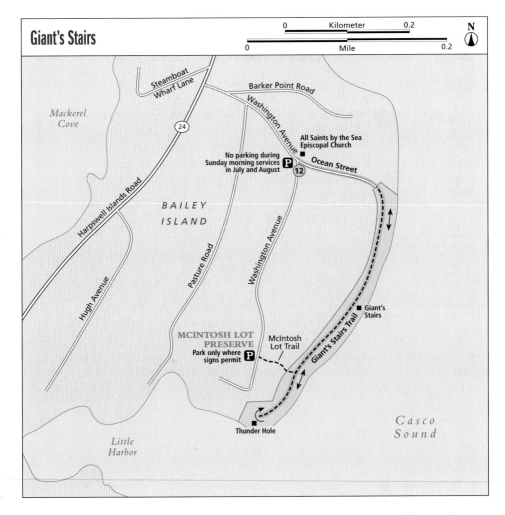

Giant's Stairs

Mackerel Cove

Steamboat Wharf Lane

Barker Point Road

Washington Avenue

24

All Saints by the Sea Episcopal Church

No parking during Sunday morning services in July and August

Ocean Street

12

BAILEY ISLAND

Harpswell Islands Road

Pasture Road

Washington Avenue

Hugh Avenue

MCINTOSH LOT PRESERVE

Park only where signs permit

McIntosh Lot Trail

Giant's Stairs Trail

Giant's Stairs

Thunder Hole

Little Harbor

Casco Sound

Return the way you came, or, if you like loops, turn left on the McIntosh Lot Trail and then right on Washington Avenue.

MILES AND DIRECTIONS

0.0 Start at the All Saints by the Sea Episcopal Chapel parking lot and head east on Ocean Street.

0.1 Reach the northern end of the Giant's Stairs Trail; turn right (south).

0.3 Reach the top of the Giant's Stairs.

0.4 Pass the McIntosh Lot Trail on the right (west). Go beyond the end of the graded gravel path and onto the rock ledge, following faint red blazes on the ledge, and round the point to Thunder Hole. Return the way you came.

0.8 Arrive back at the chapel parking lot.

13 BATES–MORSE MOUNTAIN CONSERVATION AREA

The Bates–Morse Mountain Conservation Area allows you to hike over a mountain with spectacular views and then walk along a large sand beach and sand flats situated between two tidal rivers. It's an important research area for Bates College, allowing study of a coastal environment free of such development as seawalls or jetties. Owners strive for exemplary stewardship and limit access with some rules that are stricter than at state and other public beaches.

Start: Southeast on Morse Mountain Road, past the gate outside the parking lot

Elevation gain: 499 feet

Distance: 4.6 miles out and back

Difficulty: Easy to moderate

Hiking time: 2.5–3.5 hours

Seasons/schedule: Open year-round during daylight hours; best spring through fall, either early or late in the day during summer peak, and at low tide

Fees and permits: No fees or permits

Trail contact: Bates–Morse Mountain Conservation Area, Bates College, Hedge Hall, Rm. 213, Lewiston 04240; (207) 786-6078; bates.edu/bates-morse-mountain-shortridge/

Dog-friendly: No dogs allowed

Trail surface: Partly paved road, forest floor, rock ledges, sandy beach, tidal flats

Land status: 600 acres of salt marsh and coastal uplands owned by the private nonprofit Bates–Morse Mountain Conservation Area Corporation; much of Seawall Beach owned by the private nonprofit Small Point Association

Nearest town: Phippsburg

Maps: USGS Small Point; Bates–Morse Mountain Conservation Area map

Other trail users: Local residents, seasonal renters of private houses within the conservation area, trail runners, birders, beachgoers

Special considerations: No facilities. No beach umbrellas, cabanas, radios, balls, kites, drones, Frisbees, or bicycles. No lifeguard on duty. No camping or fires. No collecting of plants without permission. Carry out what you carry in. Stay on road, trail, or beach; do not climb on dunes. Do not disturb research equipment, signs and markers, or nesting piping plovers and least terns. Bring insect repellent. Be prepared for a 2-mile walk before reaching the beach. Watch for authorized vehicles along the road. Once the parking lot is full, which can be as early as 10 a.m. during peak season, access is suspended; no other parking is available nearby.

FINDING THE TRAILHEAD

From US 1 in Bath, take ME 209 south onto the Phippsburg peninsula. At 11.6 miles, when ME 209 turns sharply left (east) to Popham Beach State Park, head straight (south) on ME 216 for 0.4 mile. Turn left (southeast) onto Morse Mountain Road; park in the lot on your left. Start at the gate outside the parking lot and head southeast on Morse Mountain Road. **GPS:** N43 44.42' / W69 50.15'

WHAT TO SEE

The Bates–Morse Mountain Conservation Area and Seawall Beach in Phippsburg is a one-of-a-kind coastal hike, but it is also a living lab that requires an elevated appreciation of a unique natural environment. For visitors it's a rare area that allows you to hike to a mountaintop and then spend hours next to the ocean on a spectacular sandy barrier beach—all in one day and devoid of the crowds that can spoil the peace on other nearby beaches. For researchers it is an opportunity to observe a natural coastal system—unaltered by development such as seawalls or jetties—undergoing significant environmental change.

Faculty and students at Bates College, based in Lewiston, conduct research in the area and monitor a variety of conditions in the salt marshes, on the beach, and in the forests—all in the context of exceptionally rapid warming in the Gulf of Maine.

Laura Sewall, recently retired director of the Bates–Morse Mountain Conservation Area, said that the enhanced conservation behavior required by the rules ensures that the area is relatively undisturbed by human use. "Morse Mountain provides a unique opportunity to observe rapid change in a large natural system," Sewall said. "We document changes on the beach and in the marsh in order to learn how coastal systems naturally respond to increases in the frequency and intensity of storm events, warming waters, and sea level rise."

At Seawall Beach you can get this view toward the Morse River and Popham Beach State Park.

One focus of the monitoring is to determine if the salt marsh is "accreting" or growing in elevation at a pace that will keep up with sea level rise. "Some of the salt marsh appears to be handling sea level rise quite well," said Sewall, director of the conservation area for eleven years and now succeeded by marine scientist Caitlin Cleaver. "Other areas of the marsh are losing ground and becoming waterlogged, or what we refer to as lumpy marsh. Overall, the marsh is transitioning."

Another long-term monitoring project profiles the beach and records the movement of sand or sediment in the area over time. This has revealed a significant loss of dune front—approximately 15 meters in the last twenty-five years—in the central portion of the beach.

The 600-acre Morse Mountain area covers land from the Sprague River to the Morse River and to the upland edge of Seawall Beach. This special coastal hike takes you along a mostly unpaved road through a spruce and balsam forest and a salt marsh to the peak of 180-foot Morse Mountain and then to a huge sand beach. Sometimes called "the biggest little mountain in Maine," Morse Mountain offers views southwest over Casco Bay and northwest all the way to Mount Washington in New Hampshire on a clear, crisp day.

A clamshell sits on Seawall Beach at low tide.

The hike, recommended at low tide, culminates with a breathtaking walk along sandy and expansive Seawall Beach, bordered by U-shaped dune woodlands and offering views of an assortment of islands, including Seguin Island with its light station.

The conservation area is managed by Bates College and the Bates–Morse Mountain Conservation Area Corporation, a nonprofit that includes members of the St. John family, Bates College, and the general public. Bates College uses the property for environmental research and educational purposes. The nonprofit Small Point Association owns the beach and shares management with the college and the Bates–Morse Mountain Conservation Area Corporation. In addition, The Nature Conservancy holds three conservation easements to the property and ensures that management is consistent with the stipulations and provisions of those easements.

Public access to the beach and area is limited in number and by rules designed to preserve it for nature's sake, for research and education, and also for nature lovers. Attendants oversee a dirt parking lot for about forty cars, but during the gatekeeping season, from April to the end of November, depending on the weather, the parking area is often full by 10 a.m. each day. Access is suspended when the lot is full, and walk-ins are not allowed. This keeps the

The peak of Morse Mountain, the "biggest little mountain in Maine," towers over the Sprague River and the sea.

area free of the crowds that can often mar state beaches in the vicinity on a sunny day. A newer "turnaround" loop allows cars to easily depart when the lot is full. If you see a "Parking Lot Full" sign near the entrance, use the turnaround, return to ME 216, and try again later.

The 4.6-mile hike begins at the gate off the parking lot and heads southeast on Morse Mountain Road. Sewall said the road "is a good thing" because it goes directly to the beach and can handle many visitors without impacting the rest of the conservation area. It is important for people to remain on the road.

During late spring and early summer, be sure to pack repellent to ward off marsh mosquitoes and deerflies. On a morning hike on July 1, we encountered some relentless bug attacks and soon needed to double back for repellent. The road is first nicely shaded by spruce and balsam and then white pine and deciduous trees such as oaks, birches, and maples.

At 0.4 mile the Sprague River Salt Marsh stretches to a wooded horizon on either side of the road. The salt marsh, called the Great Marsh by local residents, is nourished by the Gulf of Maine through the Sprague River inlet and is protected by dense shrubs, the barrier beach, and dunes. Cordgrass is abundant and provides habitat for wildlife such as the glossy ibis, which is often seen foraging for food with its curved bill and is the topic of one of the most frequently asked questions at the conservation area over the past decade.

At 0.9 mile you will reach a junction with Summit Circle, a private road marked by a sign that says "View Point to Right." To go to the top of Morse Mountain, bear right (south) onto the road, being cautious to avoid trespassing on private property. You quickly reach a granite outcrop framed by pitch pine and then the Morse Mountain summit, which provides views to the southwest over the ocean and the Sprague River as it winds and flows through the marsh and empties into the sea. A rock bench, located atop a rounded granite outcropping, provides a nice resting place if your repellent is strong enough to keep biting bugs at bay.

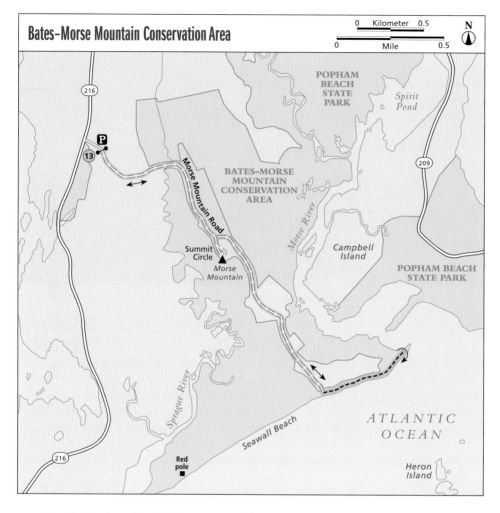

Bates–Morse Mountain Conservation Area

Turn back after taking in the views and then turn right (east) to continue on Morse Mountain Road. At about 1.7 miles into the hike, or 0.6 mile past the intersection with Summit Circle, you can hear the sound of the surf.

At 2.0 miles you will reach Seawall Beach, which is bounded by two tidal rivers—the Morse River to the east and the Sprague River to the west. Turn left (northeast) toward the mouth of the 1.7-mile-long Morse River, stopping to read an exhibit on the "Shorebirds of Seawall Beach." The beach supports some of the largest numbers of migrating shorebirds in Maine, such as plovers, sandpipers, dowitchers, and whimbrels. Enjoy the sight of the steep rocks and upland dunes and woods that border a section of the beach, but please do not climb on the dunes or ledges.

(**Option:** Turn right [southwest] on Seawall Beach toward the 2.5-mile-long Sprague River. If you go this way, you must turn around at a prominent red pole before you reach the mouth of the Sprague.)

At low tide, heading left toward the Morse River, the beach is mammoth with lots of room to walk on packed sand and along the waves as they lap the shore. You get incredible views out to the Gulf of Maine and to small islands and Seguin Island Light. We did not see many rocks or shells on the beach toward the Morse River, just expansive and pleasant sand for walking. The beach narrows considerably at high tide, so aim to visit at low tide.

Reach the mouth of the Morse River at 2.4 miles; you can see Popham Beach State Park on the other side and maybe some terns diving into the river. Stop for a swim or a wade in the ocean, then return the way you came, bypassing the private road up to Morse Mountain, to arrive back at the parking lot.

MILES AND DIRECTIONS

0.0 Start at the gate outside the parking lot, and head southeast on Morse Mountain Road.

0.4 Cross Sprague Marsh.

0.9 Reach a junction with Summit Circle, a private road; bear right (south) up it, being mindful not to trespass on private property.

A glossy ibis, with its trademark curved bill, is a frequent sight at the Bates–Morse Mountain Conservation Area.

1.0 Reach the summit of Morse Mountain and take in views from the open ledge. Return down the private road to the junction with Morse Mountain Road.

1.1 Turn right (east) to continue on Morse Mountain Road.

2.0 Reach Seawall Beach; turn left (northeast) to head toward the mouth of the Morse River.

2.4 Reach the mouth of the Morse River and a view across to Popham Beach State Park. Return the way you came, bypassing the private road up to Morse Mountain.

4.6 Arrive back at the parking lot.

14 POPHAM BEACH STATE PARK

Popham Beach State Park can be a hiker's paradise. When the tide is at its lowest level, it uncovers a giant sandy beach with more space to hike east or west than any other coastal area in the state, plus a heavenly low-tide walk to Fox Island.

Start: "Center Beach" sign at the southern edge of the parking lot
Elevation gain: 69 feet
Distance: 1.2 miles out and back
Difficulty: Easy
Hiking time: 1–2 hours
Seasons/schedule: Open year-round 9 a.m. to sunset; best spring through fall, either early or late in the day during summer peak, and at low tide
Fees and permits: Day-use fee
Trail contact: Popham Beach State Park, 10 Perkins Farm Ln., Phippsburg 04562; (207) 389-1335; maine.gov/pophambeach
Dog-friendly: Leashed dogs permitted Oct 1 through Mar 31; prohibited other times of year
Trail surface: Sandy beach, tidal flats, rock ledges

Land status: 605-acre park owned and maintained by the State of Maine
Nearest town: Phippsburg
Maps: USGS Small Point
Other trail users: Beachgoers, surfers, trail runners, local residents; Oct 1 through Mar 31, horseback riders and dog walkers
Special considerations: Facilities include bathhouses, freshwater solar rinse-off showers, and picnic areas with charcoal grills. Lifeguards on duty mid-June to mid-August. Beach and tidal flats are accessible with assistance (beach wheelchair available). Off-season visitors can park in the turn lane on ME 209 outside the gate.

FINDING THE TRAILHEAD

From US 1 in Bath, take ME 209 south onto the Phippsburg peninsula; follow it 15 miles to Popham Beach State Park. Turn right (south); pass the entrance station and proceed to the "Center Beach" sign in the middle of the southern edge of the parking lot. **GPS:** N43 44.12' / W69 47.48'

WHAT TO SEE

With its outstanding ocean and island views, the low-tide walk to Fox Island at Popham Beach State Park can be an unforgettable and spellbinding experience. The hike goes along the Fox Island tombolo, a large sandbar, exposed and accessible only about 1.5 hours on either side of low tide. The tombolo, which is all sand and no rocks, connects isolated Fox Island to the mainland state park in Phippsburg.

Popham is one of Maine's most popular beaches and can be crammed with up to 2,500 people on a sunny day. In order to savor the spirit of this special hike, try to go in the early morning or late afternoon and at dead low tide, when the sandy beach seems boundless.

The state park offers much more than the Fox Island tombolo. It is home to some substantial dunes; views of a series of islands, including two with lighthouses; a variety of shorebirds such as sandpipers and plovers; a pitch pine forest; and the Morse River, an outstanding tidal waterway. Instead of the walk to Fox Island, you can also hike next to dunes or the ocean about 0.5 mile southwest to the Morse River, with its spectacular upland marsh and soft sandy shore, or 0.5 mile to the northeast to the boundary with the

private Hunnewell Beach and, at low tide, possibly farther to municipal Popham Beach and Fort Popham State Historic Site near the mouth of the Kennebec River.

Sean M. Vaillancourt, park manager who grew up in the region, said Popham Beach is his favorite place on Earth. "This is a very happy place," he said one summer evening while looking out over the beach. "This is sacred to me."

Popham and its open spaces were also sacred to those responsible for saving it some fifty years ago. The creation of Popham Beach State Park as Maine's ninth state park in 1968 was mainly the result of some far-sighted work behind the scenes by two active environmentalists, lawyer Lawrence M. C. Smith and his wife, Eleanor Houston Smith, who lived on a farm in Freeport and in Philadelphia.

In order to prevent developers or speculators from buying the beach, the Smiths quietly began purchasing parcels in Popham in 1960, acquiring most of the shoreline over a three-year period. The Smiths held the land with the goal of eventually selling it to the state for the same amount they spent acquiring it. That occurred in 1967 when, after years of refusing to finance efforts to purchase the beach, the state legislature finally appropriated money for Popham. The Smiths sold their 353 acres at cost ($112,000) to allow dedication of Popham as a state park in 1968. An additional 170-acre parcel in the park, located inland of the beach next to Spirit Pond, the source of the Morse River, was also acquired from the Smiths.

Lawrence Smith, who died in 1975, and Eleanor Smith, who died in 1987, attended a dedication of Popham Beach State Park in 1968, along with then-governor Kenneth Curtis. A year later, the Smiths also donated land that became Wolfe's Neck Woods State

You can hike to the top of mostly barren Fox Island at Popham Beach State Park.

Park in Freeport. The *Maine Sunday Telegram* in Portland, the state's largest newspaper, wrote in an August 1968 editorial that Maine should be "everlastingly grateful" to the Smiths for their work in saving Popham.

These days, some powerful natural forces are putting the beach at peril. Over the years, the shoreline and dune profile of Popham has changed dramatically, a "give and take" that "is very unusual for a Maine beach," resulting from nearby rocky islands, the Kennebec and Morse Rivers, as well as storms, according to a series of Maine Geological Survey reports.

The most problematic dynamic is the Morse River's direction, seemingly as unpredictable as the weather and as unstoppable as the tide. Between 2005 and 2007, 525 feet of beach and dunes were lost, and a new bathhouse at the corner of the parking lot was being threatened in 2009, leading the geological survey to call it the "worst erosion cycle Popham Beach State Park has ever experienced."

Officials seemed hopeful in 2010 when the Morse River channel appeared to be switching course, heading more directly to sea (south) rather than continuing its damage by meandering to the east and at times breaching the sandbar connecting Popham to Fox Island. But by 2011 a new phase of erosion prompted emergency measures: stacking of cement blocks and fallen trees, and "beach scraping," where 10,000 cubic yards of sand were moved with heavy equipment to redirect the river. Officials kept piping plover habitat and natural coastal processes in mind when completing the federally and state-permitted beach scraping project. A 2013 University of Maine study of the project called it "an example of engineering activity that saved beach property without harming the beach."

Indeed, during our visit at low tide, the Morse River appeared to be going safely out to sea, away from the sandbar attaching Popham to Fox Island, and the bathhouse appeared to be at no risk of toppling.

Perhaps there is no better way to appreciate the preservation of Popham than to complete the 1.2-mile round-trip hike to Fox Island at low tide. The walk, which we completed three times in 2018 and 2019, starts at a flagpole and the sign for Center Beach in the middle of the southern edge of the massive parking lot. Although the 382 spots in the lot provide a lot of access, some 30 percent of the dunes at the beach were destroyed during the state's construction of the lot.

From the parking lot, amid the sounds of surf, head down a sandy path lined with pink rugosa rose when in bloom and pitch pine. Walk toward the sandy tombolo, with Fox Island looming over the horizon. At high tide the sandbar to the island is submerged, but at low tide the bar is open and vast.

From Center Beach, before stepping onto the tombolo, you can see Fox Island and Seguin Island, to the southeast behind Fox. To the left (east) you can see Wood Island, then Stage Island and the small Sugarloaf Islands in the distance. From this vantage, Pond Island, with an automated light atop an 1855 brick tower, is in the background between Wood and Stage Islands. Pond can be seen more clearly from Fox Island or more toward the east or west ends of the beach. We were amazed to see a bald eagle fly over the ocean and land on the wooded west end of Pond, which is part of the Maine Coastal Islands National Wildlife Refuge. From Center Beach the tombolo was mesmerizing during a couple of leisurely walks to the northern shore of Fox Island on sunny June days.

At the foot of the island at 0.4 mile, a stack of rocks may mark the beginning of an informal trail. Bear right at the base and then left (northeast) up a moderate rocky ridge to reach the high point at 0.5 mile. It's amazing to stand on the top of Fox Island and look back at the tombolo connecting the island to the mainland or look out at the powerful ocean waves crashing on the island's steep ledges and creating swirling tide pools in crevices.

To the northwest, looking beyond Popham Beach, you can see Morse Mountain sloping on the mainland and, closer by, Morse River emptying out to sea between Popham and Seawall Beaches. Little Fox Island and two smaller ledges are just to the west and southwest. You can also see larger Heron Island to the southwest in the distance.

Looking to the northeast you can see Pond Island Lighthouse, which is near the mouth of the Kennebec River. To the horizon on the southeast is a close-up view of Seguin Island and its automated and historic light station, owned and preserved by the Friends of Seguin Island Light Station.

While Fox Island is mostly a barren top with volcanic rock and ledges, it is also alive with bright stretches of strand plants such as cordgrass, seaside goldenrod, quack grass, and bent grass, as well as thick rugosa rose. On the peak, a memorial plaque serves as a reminder of the potential danger of the ocean currents by noting the death of a Bates College student who drowned in 1963. More recently, in early March 2011, a pediatrician and her daughter became stranded on Fox Island for about 8 hours during high tide and were rescued by Phippsburg and state emergency personnel, with the mother near death from hypothermia.

Fox Island provides a view of Morse River to the west.

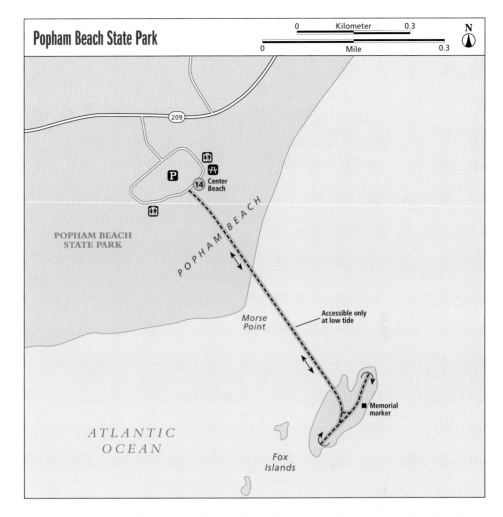

Popham Beach State Park

Kilometer 0 0.3

Mile 0 0.3

N

209

P

14 Center Beach

POPHAM BEACH
STATE PARK

POPHAM BEACH

Morse
Point

Accessible only
at low tide

Memorial
marker

ATLANTIC
OCEAN

Fox
Islands

Continue along the ridge to the northeast tip of Fox, which is not quite 0.2 mile from one end to the other, for a different perspective. Retrace your steps and head to the southwest tip of the island at 0.7 mile. Head back across the tombolo and arrive at the Center Beach parking lot at 1.2 miles to complete the hike. **Option:** Hiking east toward the Kennebec River or west toward the Morse River, or both directions, if it remains low tide and the gigantic beach remains exposed.

On our first visit to Popham, the weather pivoted rapidly and a thunderstorm rumbled and drenched the beach after we were back in our car. In what may be a sign of heaven on earth, the storm passed quickly and left a giant rainbow of salmon pink, yellow, and green in the enormous sky over the sea.

MILES AND DIRECTIONS

0.0   Start at the "Center Beach" sign in the middle of the southern edge of the parking lot, and walk southeast toward the sandbar, which is safe to cross only within 1.5 hours on either side of low tide.

0.4   Reach the northern shore of Fox Island.

0.5   Bear left (northeast) up rocky ridge to reach the summit and memorial marker.

0.6   Continue on the ridge to reach the northeastern end of the island.

0.7   Retrace your steps and head to the southwestern end of the island.

0.8   Retrace your steps; turn left (northwest) to head back across the sandbar.

1.2   Arrive back at the parking lot.

CLIMATE CHANGE THREATENS THE MAINE COAST

With more coastline than just about any other state, and the most forested state in the United States, Maine is dealing with some dramatic changes because of climate change and rising temperatures.

- The center of activity for the nation's No. 1 lobster industry has moved farther north in Maine waters, and the dunes at one of the state's leading beaches have lost tremendous ground because of climate change.
- If sea levels keep rising, salt marshes may eventually vanish and migratory birds could decrease due to a possible loss of their food supplies and the flooding of islands and other stopover spots.
- An invasive bug is eating away at majestic groves of coastal hemlock trees, and rates of Lyme disease have increased in recent years as winters have become warmer.
- Atop Cadillac Mountain in Acadia National Park, subalpine species at the southern edge of their range, like alpine azalea, may not be around much longer.

"There is a lot of concern about how the climate along the Maine coast will warm in the future," said Sean Birkel, Maine state climatologist and research assistant professor at the Climate Change Institute and School of Earth and Climate Sciences at the University of Maine. He said the precise trajectory of climate change is uncertain and hinges on worldwide efforts to reduce carbon dioxide emissions from coal plants and other sources of fossil fuels. Carbon dioxide and methane trap the sun's heat and warm the Earth.

The Gulf of Maine is warming faster than 99 percent of the world's oceans, helping to dramatically increase lobster stocks since the late 1980s but also slowly luring new species from the south, such as red hake, blue crab, butter-fish, and such creatures as seahorses and ocean sunfish, according to *Maine's Climate Future: 2015 Update* (MCF 2015), produced by the Climate Change Institute and Maine Sea Grant at the University of Maine, Orono.

A 2019 report by the National Audubon Society said that Maine has warmed 3°F in the last century, twice as much as the rest of the nation, increasing the risk of floods and droughts and threatening vulnerable populations. Sea levels have risen up to 8 inches since 1950, depending on location, and could increase another 6 inches in the next 16 years. By the end of the century, nearly two-thirds of North American birds could go extinct, including some of Maine's best-known species.

Birds also face an immediate threat from plastics. Birds get tangled in plastics or die after ingesting plastics such as bags or bottle caps. Plastics are related to global warming, since petroleum, a fossil fuel, is used as a raw material to manufacture plastics.

The effects of climate change could intensify over the next ten to fifty years, but research shows that the effects of rising temperatures in Maine are already hitting the coast. Local sea level, as measured at Portland, has risen by 7 inches since 1912, and global sea level is expected to rise at an accelerated rate in the next century. That's much faster than at any time in the past 5,000 years, noted MCF 2015. "Future sea-level rise could have major implications for coastal beaches," said Birkel.

For example, Popham Beach State Park in Phippsburg, one of the more popular and spectacular beach complexes in the state, saw its dunes significantly decline, partly because of intense storms. The West Beach at Popham declined an average of 1.1 feet between 2017 and 2018, while the East Beach lost 4.6 feet and the Center Beach grew an average of 3.5 feet.

Because of increasing water temperatures, the center of Maine's lobster industry, the largest in the United States, has shifted farther north and Downeast, beyond Penobscot Bay, from Casco Bay in the Midcoast, as demonstrated by landings and the populations of juveniles on the ocean floor. Populations of Atlantic cod, once a valuable part of the Maine fishing industry, have disintegrated because of overfishing. Recovery efforts have fallen short, partly because cod are unable to spawn in the warmer waters. Cod also feed on juvenile lobsters, and the collapse of cod stocks has helped boost lobster numbers.

Warming temperatures could also be making trees on the coast more vulnerable to invasive species of insects. A small aphid, which has trouble tolerating cold winters, is feeding on eastern hemlocks, including a grove at Wolfe's Neck Woods State Park in Freeport, and a beetle from Asia, first found in Maine in 2018, is destroying ash trees in certain parts of the state, although cold is considered a "speed bump" to the ash-boring beetle, according to the Maine Department of Agriculture, Conservation and Forestry.

Lyme disease has increased sharply because of global warming and other factors, with total cases in Maine jumping by 87 percent, from 752 in 2010 to 1,405 in 2018. Ticks that spread the disease, and the deer that host the ticks, may find it easier to survive during warmer winters, and the ticks' range has moved farther north in Maine.

Salt marshes, which are vital for protecting the coast, may eventually disappear if annual sea levels continue to rise as they have during the past sixty years, according to MCF 2015.

Climate change is having a mixed effect on coastal agriculture, including blueberries, apples, and cranberries. The growing season has increased by about two weeks, but benefits could be offset by more pests moving north and increased rain that can damage seeds and cause more erosion, according to the Climate Change Institute's 2018 report, *Coastal Maine Climate Futures*.

Another problem is the growing acidity of the oceans, an increase tied to higher levels of carbon dioxide. Shellfish managers in Maine have experimented with adding crushed shells to clam flats to buffer against acidity, which can weaken the shells of clams, mussels, and oysters.

In 2019 Maine passed a law to significantly reduce the state's greenhouse gas emissions by 45 percent below 1990 levels by 2030 and at least 80 percent by 2050. "Maine is at the forefront of making serious efforts to reduce greenhouse-gas emissions," Birkel said.

Acadia consulting botanist Jill E. Weber, atop Cadillac Mountain, checks on research plots marked by sandbags and rope as part of an effort to better understand how to bring back the summit's fragile vegetation. Climate change threatens Cadillac's subalpine species, like alpine azalea.

15 JOSEPHINE NEWMAN AUDUBON SANCTUARY

The attractive shoreline of Robinhood Cove, a classic coastal cove that juts into Georgetown Island, is the centerpiece of a hike at the Josephine Newman Audubon Sanctuary. As a habitat for birds such as ospreys, herons, and egrets, the sanctuary epitomizes the goals of the Audubon Society to protect birds and the places they need.

Start: Gate at the south end of the parking area
Elevation gain: 287 feet
Distance: 2.3-mile loop
Difficulty: Easy to moderate
Hiking time: 1.5–2.5 hours
Seasons/schedule: Open year-round during daylight hours; best spring through fall, low tide for shorebird viewing
Fees and permits: No fees or permits
Trail contact: Maine Audubon, 30 Gilsland Farm Rd., Falmouth 04105; (207) 781-2330; maineaudubon.org/visit/josephine-newman/
Dog-friendly: No dogs allowed
Trail surface: Forest floor, footbridge, bogwalks, rock ledges

Land status: 119-acre preserve owned and maintained by the nonprofit Maine Audubon
Nearest town: Georgetown
Maps: USGS Boothbay Harbor; Josephine Newman Audubon Sanctuary trail guide
Other trail users: Trail runners, birders, local residents
Special considerations: No facilities. Benches at viewpoints. No bicycles and no firearms. Download the Self-Guiding Trail brochure from maineaudubon.org/visit/josephine-newman/ and bring it along on the hike to learn what the numbered posts along the trail are about.

FINDING THE TRAILHEAD

From the junction of US 1 and ME 127 in Woolwich, head south on ME 127 for 9.1 miles to Georgetown. Turn right (south) at the sanctuary sign, and follow the entrance road to the parking area. Start the hike at the gate at the south end of the parking area. **GPS:** N43 48.02' / W69 45.03'

WHAT TO SEE

The Josephine Newman Audubon Sanctuary brings you to the shoreline of a massive tidal cove in Georgetown with some outstanding opportunities for watching shorebirds and ospreys and the chance to see a phenomenon known as a reversing falls. The little-used 119-acre sanctuary also includes some challenging up-and-down hiking on a ridge above Robinhood Cove and through dense mixed forests.

The land was donated in 1968 to Maine Audubon in the will of Josephine Oliver Newman, a noted naturalist whose father bought the land for a family farm. Before her death at age 90, Newman loved to walk the land with friends and other visitors and share her expertise on botany and the landscape. In bequeathing the land to Maine Audubon, she ensured that the property would be kept as open space and that generations of people could continue to enjoy the refuge in much the same condition as she left it.

There are nine species of woodpeckers in Maine, including the hairy, with one seen at the Audubon's Joseph Newman Sanctuary.

One modest change since her death is that about 0.5 mile of the 2.5 miles of trails include numbered posts placed at special geological, historical, and other features along the way. Each stop is detailed in a comprehensive self-guided trail brochure that can be obtained from the sanctuary's website at maineaudubon.org/visit/josephine-newman/.

A 2.3-mile loop hike starts on the self-guided trail at the gate at the south end of a small parking area. At an information kiosk, turn left (northeast) on the blue-blazed Geology Trail, through a gap in a stone wall near a quiet meadow with goldenrod in late summer. Head downhill and, on the right, pass a reedy cattail marsh; at 0.2 mile bear left (northeast) to continue on the Geology Trail toward the east branch of Robinhood Cove.

According to Maine Audubon, seven species of cone-bearing trees grow in the refuge, including eastern white pine (Maine's state tree), spruce, and balsam. Look also for the red pines, which have red-scaled bark.

At 0.3 mile, on a late blue-sky August day, we heard the sharp, distinctive chirps of flying ospreys and began to see the waters of Robinhood Cove. The cove cuts into the center of Georgetown and is created by the Sasanoa River to the north. Reach a bench at the cove where it begins to narrow to a channel, and later ascend along a pine needle path.

If you hit the tide right, as we did, when it just starts to ebb, you can see the waters of the channel begin to pick up speed and create a relatively rare phenomenon called a reversing falls—a rush of whitewater generally formed by the outgoing tide and under-water bedrock or ledges. These reversing falls are unique to Maine along the US East Coast, a result of the state's geology and narrow passages where rivers and bays meet the ocean, according to the University of Maine Sea Grant Program, which highlights eight such reversing falls on its website, although Robinhood Cove isn't among them.

At 0.5 mile come to a rare section of exposed outcropping of bedrock and then ascend steeply along a narrow, wooded spine with open views south to where the cove widens again. At 0.6 mile descend wooden steps to explore the cove and what we found to be a hot spot for watching ospreys and later, at low tide, a heron, an egret, and other foraging birds. There's lots of room to explore the cove from this spot.

We watched for more than an hour as three or four ospreys glided high over the water, sometimes flapping and spreading their wings, which were white underneath. The

ospreys flew up and down across the sky and one dived and splashed into the cove. Later, at low tide, the ospreys were nowhere in sight, possibly an indication that the higher waters in the cove are better for the birds to catch fish. A bald eagle flew in the empty sky, stretching its wide wings and distinctive for its white tail.

The mudflats across the cove attracted some large wading birds, including two great blue herons, a snowy egret, and four yellowlegs, aptly named for their long bright-yellow legs. The herons stabbed their beaks into the water and caught fish, swallowing their prey after straightening their sinuous necks.

Climb back up the steps to the main trail. Go up a ridge and cross a wooden footbridge with asphalt shingles for a good grip and enter a dense canopy of spruce. The blue-blazed Geology Trail passes a conspicuous giant boulder, or glacial erratic, which was transported by glacial ice from an area several miles to the north and east. The Geology Trail ends at 0.8 mile at the red-blazed Rocky End Trail, where you turn left (south). At 1.0 mile descend over the exposed roots of old giant white pine and spruce to a bench and a view of the cove.

At 1.1 miles reach another bench and a junction with a spur to a viewpoint at the end of a rocky finger of land. Go straight (southwest) on the spur to enjoy some of the best close-up views of the cove. Take in the scenery and return to the junction at 1.3 miles; turn left (west) on the main Rocky End Trail. Follow the trail steeply up a rocky knob to the highest elevation in the preserve and then descend.

Turn right (northwest) at 1.6 miles before an old stone wall and follow the trail as it hugs and then diverges from the wall. Reach a junction at 1.7 miles and turn right (north) to continue following the Rocky End Trail. The trail to the left heads to The

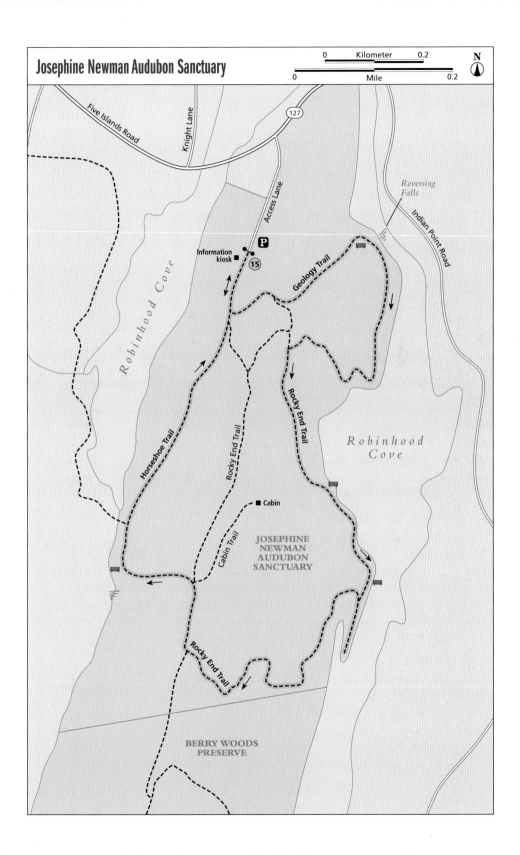

Josephine Newman Audubon Sanctuary

Kilometer
0   0.2

Mile
0   0.2

N

Five Islands Road

Knight Lane

127

Access Lane

Reversing
Falls

Indian Point Road

P

Information
kiosk

15

Geology Trail

Robinhood Cove

Horseshoe Trail

Rocky End Trail

Rocky End Trail

Robinhood
Cove

Cabin

Cabin Trail

JOSEPHINE
NEWMAN
AUDUBON
SANCTUARY

Rocky End Trail

BERRY WOODS
PRESERVE

Nature Conservancy's adjoining 377-acre Berry Woods Preserve, which protects another 3,500 feet of shoreline on Robinhood Cove.

At 1.8 miles reach a four-way intersection and turn left on the orange-blazed Horseshoe Trail, where we watched a hairy woodpecker pecking for insects on a conifer. Step over the remnants of a stone wall and reach a junction at 1.9 miles with a spur to another bench overlooking a creek and falls below the west branch of Robinhood Cove. Turn right (north) along the creek banks to loop back to the parking lot on the Horseshoe Trail.

At 2.2 miles come to the edge of a meadow, where a couple of white-tailed deer looked at us and then leaped away. Walk past the kiosk and the start of the Geology Trail, arriving back at the parking area at 2.3 miles.

MILES AND DIRECTIONS

0.0   Start at the gate at the south end of the parking area.

0.1   Turn left (northeast) at an information kiosk to follow the blue-blazed Geology Trail.

0.2   Reach a junction with the north end of the red-blazed Rocky End Trail; bear left (northeast) to continue on the Geology Trail.

0.3   Reach a bench overlooking Robinhood Cove, where you may see the reversing falls created by the ebbing tide.

0.5   Reach exposed bedrock, then climb a ridge and descend a narrow wooded spine.

0.6   Go down wooden steps to explore Robinhood Cove. Climb back up the steps to continue on the Geology Trail, climbing to the top of a ridge and crossing a wooden footbridge.

0.8   The Geology Trail ends; turn left (south) onto the red-blazed Rocky End Trail.

1.0   Wind down to a bench and view of the cove.

1.1   Reach another bench and a junction with a spur to a viewpoint at the end of a rocky finger of land. Go straight (southwest) on the spur.

1.3   Take in the views, then return to the junction and turn left (west) on the main Rocky End Trail.

1.6   Turn right (northwest) before a stone wall and follow the trail as it hugs then diverges from the wall.

1.7   Reach a junction and turn right (north) to continue on the Rocky End Trail. The trail to the left heads to The Nature Conservancy's neighboring Berry Woods Preserve.

1.8   Reach a four-way intersection; turn left (west) on the orange-blazed Horseshoe Trail.

1.9   Reach a junction with a spur to another bench overlooking a creek and falls below the west branch of Robinhood Cove. Bear right (north) to continue on the Horseshoe Trail.

2.2   Reach the edge of a meadow; walk past the information kiosk and start of the Geology Trail.

2.3   Arrive back at the parking area.

16 REID STATE PARK

Reid State Park is unusual along the rockbound Maine coast because it offers a more than 1-mile-long hike along two adjoining sandy beaches. The park also includes a spectacular tidal river with a wide salt marsh and seasonal blooming flowers like blue flag and beach pea, the northernmost large undeveloped dune system in Maine, and the opportunity to see bald eagles, snowy egrets, and piping plovers.

Start: Southwest corner of Griffith Head parking lot, to the right of the restrooms
Elevation gain: 45 feet
Distance: 2.8 miles out and back
Difficulty: Easy
Hiking time: 1.5–2 hours
Seasons/schedule: Open year-round 9 a.m. to sunset; best spring through fall, either early or late in the day during summer peak, and at low tide for shorebird viewing
Fees and permits: Day-use fee
Trail contact: Reid State Park, 375 Seguinland Rd., Georgetown 04548; (207) 371-2303; maine.gov/reid
Dog-friendly: Leashed dogs permitted Oct 1 through Mar 31; prohibited other times of year

Trail surface: Sandy beach, tidal flats, rock ledges, boardwalk, paved and dirt paths
Land status: 770-acre park owned and maintained by the State of Maine
Nearest town: Georgetown
Maps: USGS Boothbay Harbor; Reid State Park map
Other trail users: Beachgoers, birders, local residents
Special considerations: Facilities include picnic area (group picnic shelter by reservation only), benches along boardwalk, and restrooms. Bring insect repellent—mosquitoes and ticks can be a problem at times. Beach and tidal flats are accessible with assistance (beach wheelchair available).

FINDING THE TRAILHEAD

From the junction of US 1 and ME 127 in Woolwich, head south on ME 127 for 12 miles to Georgetown. Turn right on Seguinland Road and follow it for 1.5 miles to the park. Pass the entrance station and proceed to the Griffith Head parking lot, where the hike starts from the southwest corner, to the right of the restrooms. **GPS:** N43 46.58' / W69 43.21'

WHAT TO SEE

Reid State Park in Georgetown includes a beautiful hike along two different sandy beaches backed by large grass-covered dunes and flanked on one end by a powerful tidal river. Mile Beach, the longest beach, is bookended by rocky headlands called Griffith Head to the northeast and the Little River Ledges to the southwest. Mile Beach is linked by a short path around the Little River Ledges to Half Mile Beach, a barrier spit; they combine for a scenic coastal hike along the Gulf of Maine.

Samantha Wilkinson, manager of Reid State Park, said the park is unique in Maine because it boasts more than a mile of nearly uninterrupted sandy beach in a state otherwise dominated by rocky coastline. "During the summer, we generally tell people that our beaches make our best trails," said Wilkinson, who grew up less than a mile from the

park. "You can walk in the woods anywhere, but our beaches are unique and unusual on the coast of Maine."

Reid State Park is also noted for large dunes that line the beaches and constitute the most northern large dune area in Maine, bigger than the more moderately sized dunes to the north at Acadia National Park's Sand Beach. Reid stands out in Maine for its large undisturbed dune field, with front ridges and extensive back dunes.

Begin the hike at the southwest corner of the parking lot for Griffith Head. Turn right (west) onto the boardwalk; go straight past benches and down to the start of Mile Beach, a barrier beach known for its brown, coarse sand that slopes down from dunes. Look at the ocean to the northeast and you can see what appears to be a wooded peninsula but is actually the big island of Southport, which is connected to Boothbay Harbor by a swing bridge. Rachel Carson worked on her iconic book *Silent Spring* in her summer cottage on Southport.

Off the tip of Southport, you can see Damariscove Island. Out on the horizon to the southwest is Seguin Island and its famed light station.

The walk along the undeveloped beach is made possible by the man who gave the oceanfront land to the state. Reid State Park is the first saltwater beach to be owned by the State of Maine. Georgetown native and wealthy businessman Walter E. Reid donated the beach to the state in 1946, and it became the centerpiece for what is now a 770-acre state preserve. Reid was known as "the mystery man of Wall Street" because he avoided publicity, but the eponymous park is no mystery. Up to 2,500 people a day visit on a sunny summer weekend day, and about 150,000 people visit the park each year.

Another interesting part of the history of the beach is that before it became a state park, World War II fighter pilots from a nearby US Navy base trained by flying over the ocean and shooting rockets at a barge as they zoomed toward the beach.

Although the park is popular, the beaches were practically empty during a hike on a gorgeous weekend late morning in mid-June, an ideal time of year to visit. The air was filled with constant sounds of herring gulls and the ocean hitting the shore.

At about 0.4 mile along Mile Beach, just in front of the dunes, a fenced-in area shielded a nest for piping plovers, a tiny shorebird listed as endangered in Maine. Each year, Reid State Park hosts successful nests for the plovers, with four chicks fledging at two nests in 2018. The state protects the plovers at Reid and other parks with rules, including one that asks people to avoid approaching the nests. Yet sometimes you can watch plovers as they scamper and feed on worms and insects at low tide. The plovers also benefit from state protection of the fragile dunes at Reid State Park. No one is allowed to walk on the dunes because they are easily damaged. In any event, only the foolhardy would invade the dunes, which are rife with ticks, other biting bugs, and poison ivy.

On the edge of the dunes, we spotted bright pink beach-pea in bloom and later purple blue flag, a type of iris, blooming amid American dune grass. The park is also home to the state's northernmost coastal stands of beach heather, a 3- to 8-inch-tall shrub with bright yellow flowers that grows in the dunes.

At 0.7 mile reach the end of Mile Beach and go up a dirt path on the right (west) just before rocky, volcanic bedrock that separates the two beaches. Head toward the Todds Point parking lot; turn left before the lot to follow a paved path past restrooms and a picnic area on the way to Half Mile Beach. Reach an overlook on the left, where you can

A snowy egret lands in the Little River marsh at Reid State Park.

Little River Ledges can be viewed off the picnic area near the Todds Point parking lot.

view and explore the Little River Ledges, located right off the parking lot. Standing here, you can see Mile Beach to the northeast and Half Mile Beach to the southwest. Continue straight on a sandy path with blooming thickets of white and red rugosa rose on either side, past a spur path that comes in on the right from the parking lot and a side trail on the left, and down to Half Mile Beach at 1.0 mile.

Beach pea flourishes in the sand at Reid State Park.

As soon as we reached the beach, we watched in awe as several sandpipers foraged at the ocean's edge and then rapidly burst into flight and glided over the water in front of us. About twenty species of sandpipers can be seen in Maine, but these appeared to be semipalmated sandpipers, considering their short wings, short bill, and slightly rusty tones to feathers and crown.

Once on Half Mile Beach, turn right (southwest) along fine sand that slopes more gradually, and dunes that are lower, than those on Mile Beach. A large area near the dunes is fenced off for nesting piping plovers, and then the Little River comes into view. At 1.2 miles, near the end of Half Mile Beach, you stand on a sandy spit called Todds Point, shaped by the 4-mile-long Little River, which meets the Atlantic here and marks the western end of Reid State Park. During a rising tide, the ocean can be turbulent at the river's mouth, with huge whitecaps striking the shore. A colony of least terns used to nest near the Little River, but they no longer do so, perhaps because of development on the private side of the river and heavy park visitation.

Round Todds Point and follow the eastern bank of the Little River behind the dunes of Half Mile Beach. Near the river, your feet sink deep into soft sand; beach peas fill the base of grassy dunes to the east. Reach a vast salt marsh, where we spotted a large willet and then saw a snowy egret soar from the west and land in the marsh in front of us with its trademark white feathers and big yellow feet. Bright green cordgrass grew in the brackish water of the saltmarsh at this spot.

According to the park manager, Reid also has a huge array of various sea ducks, an occasional gannet, a large white bird with a long bill, all sorts of hawks, bald eagles, golden eagles, and ospreys.

As the Little River meanders inland, turn around at 1.4 miles and retrace your steps to the Griffith Head parking lot to complete this spectacular coastal hike.

MILES AND DIRECTIONS

0.0 Start at the southwest corner of the Griffith Head parking lot, to the right of the restrooms; turn right (west) onto the boardwalk and out onto the beach.

0.1 Turn right (southwest) onto Mile Beach.

0.7 Reach the end of Mile Beach and go up a dirt path on the right (west) before the rocky ledges, toward the Todds Point parking lot. Turn left (southwest) before the parking lot; follow the paved path past the restrooms and picnic area to head toward Half Mile Beach.

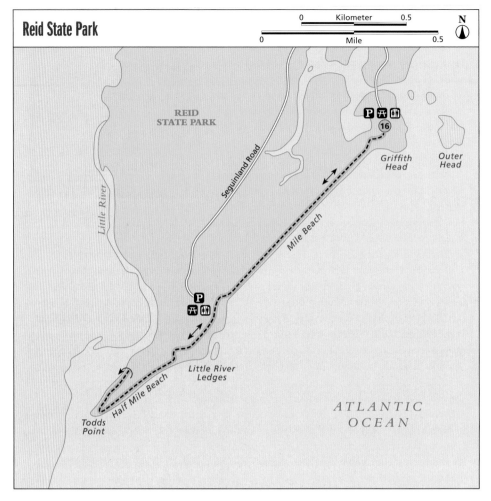

Reid State Park

REID
STATE PARK

Seguinland Road

Little River

Mile Beach

Griffith
Head

Outer
Head

Little River
Ledges

Half Mile Beach

Todds
Point

ATLANTIC
OCEAN

0   Kilometer   0.5

0   Mile   0.5

N

0.8   Pass an overlook, a spur coming in on the right from the parking lot, and a side trail on the left; continue on the main path down to Half Mile Beach.

1.0   Reach Half Mile Beach and turn right (southwest).

1.2   Reach the end of Half Mile Beach at Todds Point.

1.4   Round the point and follow the eastern bank of the Little River behind the dunes of Half Mile Beach to the edge of a salt marsh. Retrace your steps.

2.8   Arrive back at the Griffith Head parking lot.

17 OVENS MOUTH PRESERVE

Benches to watch the tide rush in, remnants of an 1880s dam and ice pond, great blue herons high-stepping across mudflats, and lobster boats plying the waters: These are among the discoveries to be made at this Boothbay Region Land Trust preserve, hidden along a narrow deepwater channel carved into rock walls. A distinctive footbridge connects the property's two peninsulas, Ovens Mouth East and Ovens Mouth West.

Start: White-blazed trail next to the information kiosk, on the north side of the Ovens Mouth East parking lot
Elevation gain: 288 feet
Distance: 2.2-mile figure-eight loop
Difficulty: Easy to moderate
Hiking time: 1.5-2 hours
Seasons/schedule: Open year-round; best spring through fall
Fees and permits: No fees or permits
Trail contact: Boothbay Region Land Trust, PO Box 183, Boothbay Harbor 04538; (207) 633-4818; bbrlt.org
Dog-friendly: Leashed dogs permitted
Trail surface: Forest floor, rock ledges, footbridges

Land status: 175 acres owned by the nonprofit Boothbay Region Land Trust
Nearest town: Boothbay
Maps: USGS Westport; Boothbay Region Land Trust Ovens Mouth Preserve trail map
Other trail users: Local residents, dog walkers
Special considerations: No facilities. Bring insect repellent during blackfly and mosquito season. The western loop involves some steep sections. Be careful to return to the Ovens Mouth East parking lot and not the Ovens Mouth West lot, which is miles away.

FINDING THE TRAILHEAD

From US 1 east of Wiscasset, take ME 27 south for 8 miles to Adams Pond Road. Turn right (southwest) onto Adams Pond Road and then right (north) in another 0.2 mile onto Dover Road. Follow Dover Road for 2 miles to a junction with Dover Cross Road that curves to the left; make a sharp right (north) to stay on Dover Road. Reach the Ovens Mouth East parking lot in another 0.4 mile. Take the white-blazed trail next to the information kiosk to head north from the lot. **GPS:** N43 55.46' / W69 38.24'

WHAT TO SEE

Sit on one of the benches along a rockbound deepwater passage and you can imagine how early English explorers navigating through here may have thought they were entering a narrow oven's opening, reportedly calling this place Ovens Mouth. Crossing a wooden footbridge linking the preserve's two rocky fingers of land, you can envision the 1880s dam that spanned this same stretch to form a freshwater pond for making blocks of ice to meet the refrigeration needs of Boston and New York. As you walk along the shore of the Cross River basin, you can see great blue herons, snowy egrets, and other shorebirds feeding at low tide, or recreational boaters going by.

These are among the aspects of Ovens Mouth Preserve that make it a standout coastal hike in the Boothbay region. Among the features highlighted by Nicholas J. Ullo,

A footbridge connects Ovens Mouth East to Ovens Mouth West, with remnants of an old ice pond dam visible at low tide to the north of the bridge.

executive director of the nonprofit Boothbay Region Land Trust, which bought this property in 1994: "First of all, there is the iconic bridge which connects Ovens Mouth East to Ovens Mouth West. Having these two preserves connect allows visitors to easily choose the length and difficulty of their hike," with the eastern loop easier than the western one of this figure eight–shaped hike. "The other thing that makes Ovens Mouth so unique is the vast, undeveloped shoreline of the Cross River basin," he said.

For Winston Wood, a longtime visitor to the Boothbay area, the history and the way the wooded peninsula opens up to water views draw him back to the preserve time and again to hike with grandchildren and other family members, or any of his legion of friends. "I've walked the Ovens Mouth trail in winter and summer, and it never gets old," Wood said; "one of the highlights of the Boothbay region."

He especially likes the "payoff of an interesting cove where ice was once harvested in winter for transport to Boston and New York. With hardly any houses in sight, it's easy to imagine ships at anchor in the river waiting to load the huge blocks." When Wood has hiked the trail at dawn, he's seen lobstermen hauling their traps. "Makes the place all the more picturesque," he said.

According to the land trust's Ovens Mouth Preserve trail guide, available online at bbrlt.org, during the Revolutionary War, both American and British ships hid in the coves near here. The peninsulas, now largely wooded, were once cleared for sheep pasture or cut for lumber during both World Wars. The nonprofit manages the forest for recreational use, aesthetics, timber production, and wildlife habitat.

From the Ovens Mouth East parking lot, take the white-blazed trail next to the information kiosk and head north through the woods. Cross a yellow-blazed trail at 0.1 mile and continue on the white-blazed trail to a junction at 0.2 mile with a short spur to the first vista. Bear right (east) onto the spur and immediately come to a view of the vast Cross River basin, where you may spot a couple of great blue herons craning their necks and stalking across the flats, or see one take flight over an exposed lobster trap, as we did one day at low tide. From this vista we counted at least ten terns diving into the receding waters, saw a snowy egret swoop onto the mudflats near the great blue herons, heard the sounds of gulls, and marveled at an osprey soaring overhead. We also saw an eastern phoebe—distinctive for its brown back and long tail—hopping from one tree limb to another elsewhere on the trail.

Head back on the spur and bear right (northeast) to continue on the white-blazed trail as it parallels the shoreline. Step over the remnants of a stone wall, perhaps built by the Tibbetts-Welsh family, who owned this property for more than one hundred years, beginning soon after the Civil War.

At 0.5 mile reach a second vista at the eastern end of the narrow rockbound channel known as Ovens Mouth, where there is a bench to sit and enjoy what can be the fast-moving currents of the Cross River. A sign identifies a red oak here, a fun way to introduce children to nature along this easy eastern shoreline loop. The white-blazed trail now circles the tip of the Ovens Mouth East peninsula, heading west along the channel that gets so constricted, you could almost reach out and touch a passing boat.

At 0.7 mile arrive at the northwestern tip of the eastern peninsula, where there is a memorial bench and a yellow-blazed trail that comes in from the south. You can see

Look across to Ovens Mouth West from this bench at the northwestern tip of Ovens Mouth East.

across to Ovens Mouth West from here to a matching bench. Continue on the white-blazed trail as it now rounds south toward the old ice pond.

Reach the footbridge that connects Ovens Mouth East and Ovens Mouth West at 0.8 mile. At low tide, paralleling the bridge, remnants of the nineteenth-century dam reveal themselves. Locals call the former pond "Ice House Cove" for the structure that once stood here to store ice, awaiting schooners bound for the big city. Now "a magnificent salt marsh has replaced the ice pond," notes the preserve's trail guide.

Turn right across the bridge to head to the steeper Ovens Mouth West loop, where there are nice views from high on the bluffs. (**Option:** If you are pressed for time, or looking for an easier walk, skip crossing over to the hillier peninsula and continue south on the white-blazed trail. This would bring you back to the Ovens Mouth East parking lot in a simple 1.1-mile loop.)

Once over the bridge, turn right (north) to follow the white-blazed trail around the northeastern tip of Ovens Mouth West, reaching the bench that allows you to look back toward the matching one on Ovens Mouth East at 0.9 mile. As you sit here near the west end of Ovens Mouth, you could watch boats roll in or wave back at slower-paced members of your hiking party still enjoying the bench across the cove on the eastern peninsula.

Continue on the white-blazed trail, turning right (north) at a double blaze (indicating a change of direction) to head downhill to the shoreline and around the peninsula tip, passing a couple more benches along the way.

At 1.2 miles reach a junction marked with a double white blaze; bear left (southeast), up the hill and away from the water, to start looping back toward the footbridge. Be sure to watch for this junction—if you miss it and keep following the shoreline south, you may find yourself heading to the Ovens Mouth West parking lot, miles from the start.

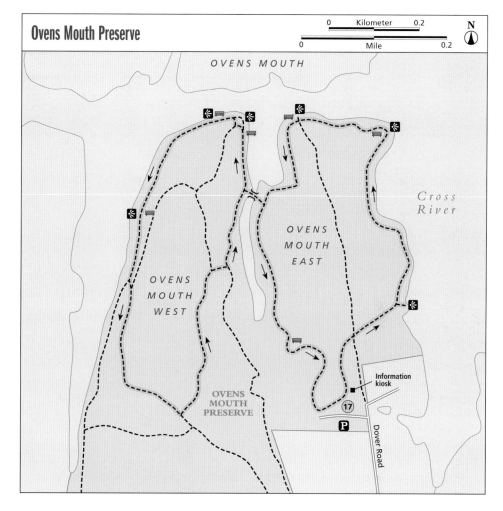

OVENS MOUTH

Cross
River

OVENS
MOUTH
EAST

OVENS
MOUTH
WEST

OVENS
MOUTH
PRESERVE

Information
kiosk

17

P

Dover Road

At 1.5 miles reach a junction with a blue-and-yellow-blazed trail and turn left (north), away from an information kiosk to follow what is now a two-colored trail for a short stretch as you continue circling the western peninsula.

At 1.7 miles turn right (east) to follow what is now only a yellow-blazed trail as you head downhill to the old ice pond, which is transitioning to marshland, then turn left (north) onto a white-blazed trail, following signs pointing toward "Vista" and "Kiosk." At 1.8 miles the white-blazed trail forms a switchback down to the west shore of the old pond as it heads north to the footbridge back to Ovens Mouth East to complete the western loop.

Cross east over the bridge at 1.9 miles and turn right (south) on the white-blazed trail to start closing the eastern loop along the east shore of the former pond. Reach the end of the marsh on the white-blazed trail at 2.1 miles, arriving back at the Ovens Mouth East parking lot at 2.2 miles.

A rowboat navigates the Cross River at slack tide.

MILES AND DIRECTIONS

0.0 Start at the Ovens Mouth East parking lot, taking the white-blazed trail near the information kiosk to head north.

0.1 Cross a yellow-blazed trail and follow the sign pointing toward a vista.

0.2 Bear right (east) at a short spur to the vista overlooking the Cross River basin.

0.3 Back at the junction with the main white-blazed trail, bear right (northeast) to continue along the shoreline.

0.5 Reach a viewpoint with a bench by the east end of Ovens Mouth.

0.7 Reach a viewpoint with a bench at the northwestern tip of the Ovens Mouth East peninsula, where you can look across a cove to a twin bench on the tip of Ovens Mouth West.

0.8 Turn right (west) across the wooden footbridge, with remnants of the nineteenth-century dam visible at low tide. Turn right (north) again to head toward the northeastern tip of Ovens Mouth West. (**Option:** For a shorter loop hike, instead of crossing the bridge, continue straight [south] on the white-blazed trail to circle back to the Ovens Mouth East parking lot in another 0.3 mile.)

0.9 Reach a bench offering views back across the cove to the twin bench on Ovens Mouth East. Continue on the white-blazed trail, turning right (north) at a double blaze to head down to the shoreline and circle the western peninsula, passing a couple more benches along the way.

1.2 Reach a junction at a double white blaze; bear left (southeast), up the hill and away from the water, to loop back around the west peninsula. Be sure to watch for this junction, or else you may find yourself at the Ovens Mouth West parking lot, miles away from the start.

1.5 At a junction with a blue-and-yellow-blazed trail, turn left (north), away from a kiosk, and follow the two-colored trail for a short stretch to start circling back to the footbridge.

1.7 Turn right (east) to follow what Is now only a yellow-blazed trail, then turn left (north) onto a white-blazed trail, following signs pointing toward "Vista" and "Kiosk."

1.8 Switchback down the ridge and along the west shore of the former ice pond to return on the white-blazed trail to the bridge, completing the western loop of the figure-eight hike. Turn right (east) to cross back to Ovens Mouth East; immediately turn right again (south) on the white-blazed trail to head along the east shore of the old ice pond as you start closing the eastern loop of the hike.

2.2 Arrive back at the Ovens Mouth East parking lot.

18 LAVERNA PRESERVE

LaVerna Preserve, named for the Italian monastery where St. Francis of Assisi went to pray, seems a sacred place with its 3,600 feet of magnificent shoreline and splendid views of the sea and islands. The steward of the preserve says he thanks God every time he visits; if you hike this trail, you might feel blessed too.

Start: Hoyt trailhead on the east side of ME 32, across from the parking area
Elevation gain: 377 feet
Distance: 3.5-mile lollipop
Difficulty: Moderate
Hiking time: 2-3 hours
Seasons/schedule: Open year-round during daylight hours; best spring through fall
Fees and permits: No fees or permits
Trail contact: Coastal Rivers Conservation Trust, PO Box 333, Damariscotta 04543; (207) 563-1393; coastalrivers.org
Dog-friendly: Leashed dogs permitted
Trail surface: Forest floor, rock ledges, footbridges, cobble beach
Land status: 120-acre preserve owned and maintained by the nonprofit Coastal Rivers Conservation Trust with the sponsorship of Masters Machine Company

Nearest town: Bristol
Maps: USGS Louds Island; LaVerna Preserve trail guide
Other trail users: Local residents, dog walkers, trail runners
Special considerations: No facilities. Hunting is allowed in season; be aware of the hunting seasons and wear blaze orange for safety. No camping or fires. Respect private property owners' rights; part of the hike is a right-of-way over private land. Bring insect repellent, as mosquitoes can be a problem. Beware of poison ivy, especially on Leighton Head. Coastal Rivers Conservation Trust, formed in 2019 with the union of the Pemaquid Watershed Association and Damariscotta River Association, provides information about the LaVerna Preserve at these pages: coastalrivers.org/trail/la-verna-preserve/ and coastalrivers.org/wp-content/uploads/2019/10/La-Verna-Preserve-trail-guide-2019.pdf.

FINDING THE TRAILHEAD

 From the junction of US 1 and ME 32 in Waldoboro, head south on ME 32 for 16.8 miles to the LaVerna Preserve parking area, on the right (west) side of the road. Cross to the east side of ME 32 (watch out for traffic) for the Hoyt Trail.
GPS: N43 54.09' / W69 28.47'

WHAT TO SEE

LaVerna Preserve in Bristol takes you through a thick evergreen and hardwood forest to a long oceanfront of cliffs, ledges, and coves with spectacular views of islands in Muscongus Bay. The preserve, located on the Pemaquid Peninsula northeast of Boothbay Harbor, is owned by Coastal Rivers Conservation Trust of Damariscotta and is named for the Italian monastery that was given as a gift to St. Francis of Assisi, patron saint of ecology, during the thirteenth century.

Billy Claflin, steward of the preserve, says LaVerna is a sacred place. With 3,600 feet of shoreline and glorious views of the sea, you get to fully explore and experience the

The layered ledges at LaVerna Preserve are right next to the bay.

Maine coast. "Every time you go there, you look up and thank the Lord," Claflin said. "It is a beautiful spot."

The preserve was begun more than fifty years ago by Elizabeth Ellis Hoyt, a philosopher, social scientist, and internationally known economist. A smaller version of the current preserve was owned by her family's charitable and educational foundation; she called it the LaVerna Nature Preserve.

Hoyt was a professor for fifty-five years at Iowa State University, but during summers she returned to her childhood home in Bristol, on the Pemaquid Peninsula. In 1965 she and her sister, Anna Mavor, donated 30 acres. Their family charitable and educational foundation, the LaVerna Foundation, gave 55 acres to The Nature Conservancy to manage and own LaVerna Preserve in Bristol. The Nature Conservancy also bought 34 acres to expand the preserve.

A trailblazer in consumer economics with a doctorate from Radcliffe Graduate School at Harvard, Hoyt completed early research that helped create the widely-known Consumer Price Index and was also recognized for improving libraries in Africa. Coming from a family that goes back generations in Bristol, including great-great grandparents who lived in a log cabin, she also loved nature and viewed herself as part of a broader effort to save open space in the town.

In a twenty-four-page booklet titled *Man and Nature in Bristol*, self-published in 1965 to celebrate the bicentenary of her hometown, she wrote in detail about the plants, animals, and wild birds in the preserve. She also expressed her fears of environmental damage in the region, including the spraying of herbicides along state roads, which she said destroyed beautiful stands of plants, and the indiscriminate picking of orchids and other wildflowers. Writing before a ban on DDT, she said she had seen no eastern bluebirds for five years in Lincoln County and attributed it to wide use of insecticides on apple trees, a favorite of the birds. She wrote that the LaVerna preserve "is away from human dwellings and dedicated to the conservation of nature and the study of nature. Thus, it is a part of the services to posterity of the Town of Bristol . . . the beauty remains, entrusted to us."

Ownership of LaVerna Preserve changed in 2009 when The Nature Conservancy transferred the preserve to the former Pemaquid Watershed Association. The association merged with another nonprofit into the Coastal Rivers Conservation Trust in 2019.

The LaVerna Preserve is replete with colorful rock that contrasts with blue sea.

The 3.5-mile hike starts across the preserve parking lot on ME 32 in Bristol and follows the blue-blazed Hoyt Trail southeast along a right-of-way across private property. Owners of the preserve ask that people please respect the private property.

Soon pass a LaVerna sign and follow the trail along a moss-covered stone wall and thick green ferns on either side of footbridges. Stay on the Hoyt Trail as it jogs left (north) and eventually becomes the LaVerna Trail and crosses the boundary into the preserve. As you near Meadow Brook at 0.5 mile, you start to walk on a series of long footbridges, which during our hike in mid-August were lined with blooming orange touch-me-not, also known as jewelweed.

Reach a junction at 0.9 mile and turn left (northeast) to follow the yellow-blazed Ellis Trail. Stay on the Ellis Trail, climbing gradually up a ridge and veering to the right (south-southeast) before descending toward the shore, sometimes steeply amid the smell of sea salt in the air.

Switchback down to Browns Head Cove and at 1.6 miles reach the first ledges, which are among the oldest rocks in Maine. Reach a cobble beach at 1.7 miles and bear right up a knob. In this area you get views of some major islands in Muscongus Bay. Louds Island is the first big island, located to the northeast, with smaller islands—sandy Bar Island, Ross Island, and forested Haddock Island—to the right (south) of Louds. Another big island, hilly Allen Island, owned by painter Jamie Wyeth, is located far on the horizon of the bay to the east. Monhegan Island is unmistakable on the horizon to the right (southeast).

Claflin, the preserve's steward, said islands are "stars on earth." He said people can also peer on the horizon to the east for Franklin Island, identified by a 45-foot automated light on a brick tower that looks like a pencil from the shore of LaVerna. "If you walk LaVerna and walk the 3,600 feet of oceanfront, the islands will appear and disappear, depending on your perspective," Claflin said. "Sometimes you can see Franklin, and sometimes you can't."

A freshwater pool is a special sight at the end of the Contemplative Trail at the LaVerna Preserve.

For the next 0.2 mile you hike along some giant, gray-colored bedrock, with many layers in different directions. According to the Maine Geological Survey, the layered bedrock along the shore at LaVerna started as sediment more than 400 million years ago. The most abundant type of rock was transformed by heat and pressure and comes in many varieties of color and texture, with some steeply tilted and folded.

At 1.9 miles the Ellis Trail rejoins the blue-blazed LaVerna Trail as you near Leighton Head. Turn left (east) on the LaVerna Trail to continue paralleling the shore, and when it ends at Leighton Head, continue on the green-blazed Tibbitts Trail, named for a family that also transferred land for the preserve. During our visit, four eiders were climbing on the rocks below and several cormorants flew along the surface of the ocean.

Follow the rocky shore on the Tibbitts Trail and reach the junction with the short, orange-blazed Lookout Trail on the left (east), where the Lookout Trail dead-ends, providing great views of Monhegan Island. Continue on the Tibbitts Trail and at 2.2 miles walk over footbridges to the base of an osprey nest, where the raptors return year after year and often can be heard as you approach. You can also see huge rocks dragged and left onshore by the glaciers. We watched herring gulls and at least one great black-backed gull feeding on shellfish among sea moss on the rocks.

At 2.3 miles come to the junction with the Contemplative Trail on the left (south). This short side trail dead-ends at the small Freshwater Pool, rimmed by rusty, weathered rocks, just about 100 feet from the crashing ocean surf. Continue on the Tibbitts Trail as it heads inland (north-northwest), often crossing or skirting stone walls and heading over footbridges.

The Tibbitts Trail ends at a junction with the LaVerna Trail at 2.6 miles. Turn left (northwest) to follow the blue-blazed LaVerna Trail. Pass the yellow-blazed Ellis Trail on the right and stay straight on the blue-blazed LaVerna Trail as it becomes the Hoyt Trail and takes you back along the right-of-way through private property. Arrive back at the parking area at 3.5 miles.

LaVerna Preserve

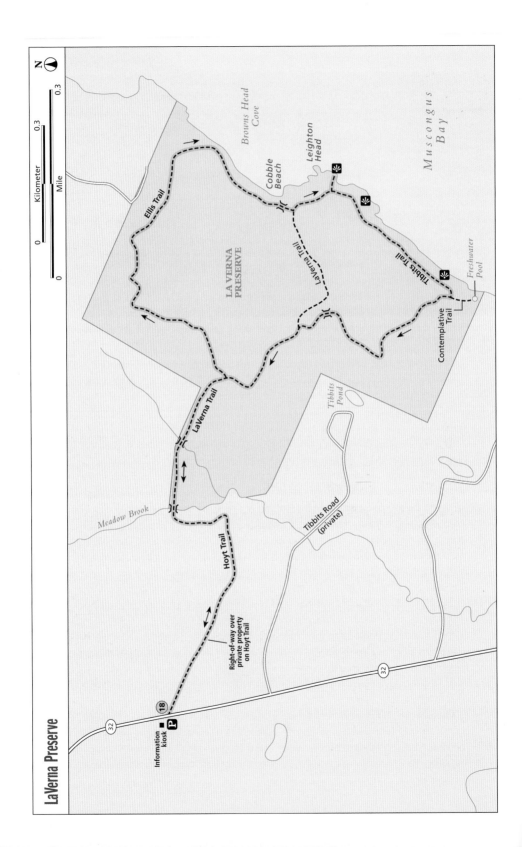

N

Kilometer
0   0.3

Mile
0   0.3

Ellis Trail

Browns Head
Cove

LA VERNA
PRESERVE

LaVerna Trail

Cobble
Beach

Leighton
Head

Tibbits Trail

Muscongus
Bay

Freshwater
Pool

Contemplative
Trail

LaVerna Trail

Meadow Brook

Hoyt Trail

Tibbits Pond

Tibbits Road
(private)

Right-of-way over
private property
on Hoyt Trail

Information
kiosk

P

18

32

32

MILES AND DIRECTIONS

0.0 Start across ME 32 from the preserve parking area, following the blue-blazed Hoyt Trail southeast along a right-of-way across private property.

0.4 Follow the Hoyt Trail as it jogs to the left (north) and eventually becomes the LaVerna Trail, crossing the boundary into the preserve.

0.9 At a junction turn left (northeast) to follow the yellow-blazed Ellis Trail rather than continuing straight on the blue-blazed LaVerna Trail.

1.6 Switchback down to Browns Head Cove and reach the first ledges.

1.7 Reach a cobble beach. Bear right, up the knob.

1.9 Reach the end of the Ellis Trail as it rejoins the blue-blazed LaVerna Trail. Turn left (east) to continue following the shore on the LaVerna Trail until it ends at Leighton Head. Continue on the green-blazed Tibbits Trail, paralleling the shore. Take a short spur onto the orange-blazed Lookout Trail on the left (east) for views of Monhegan Island to the southeast.

2.3 Reach a junction with the short orange-blazed Contemplative Trail on the left (south), which you can take to explore the small Freshwater Pool along the rocky shoreline. Continue following the Tibbits Trail as it circles inland.

2.6 Tibbits Trail ends at a junction with the LaVerna Trail. Turn left (northwest) to follow the blue-blazed trail back, passing the yellow-blazed Ellis Trail that goes to the right and staying straight on the LaVerna Trail as it becomes the Hoyt Trail and takes you back along the right-of-way across private property.

3.5 Arrive back at the parking area.

A bald eagle glides over the LaVerna Preserve.

19 MONHEGAN ISLAND

Catch the early boat to Monhegan or stay overnight on the island so that you can hike this rugged loop along dramatic ocean cliffs. See just why artists like Edward Hopper, Rockwell Kent, and Jamie Wyeth, and even actor Zero Mostel of *Fiddler on the Roof* fame, an artist in his own right, have been drawn here. If you are into birding, microbrews, lighthouses, or museums—even more reason to make the trip to this small island.

Start: Wharf on Wharf Hill Street
Elevation gain: 514 feet
Distance: 4.6-mile lollipop
Difficulty: Moderate to strenuous
Hiking time: 3–5 hours
Seasons/schedule: Open year-round; best late May through early to mid-Oct, when boat service is most frequent
Fees and permits: No fees or permits
Trail contact: Monhegan Associates, Inc., PO Box 97, Monhegan 04852; monheganassociates.org; e-mail: info@monheganassociates.org
Dog-friendly: Leashed dogs permitted
Trail surface: Forest floor, rock ledges, footbridges, unpaved roads
Land status: More than 350 acres privately owned and maintained by the Monhegan Associates, Inc., a private nonprofit land trust
Nearest town: Monhegan, technically a "plantation," as it is not large enough to be a town
Maps: USGS Monhegan; Monhegan Associates trail map
Other trail users: Birders, local residents, artists, tourists
Special considerations: Advance reservations for boat passage

and lodging recommended. Visit monheganwelcome.com for information about boat, lodging, dining, and other services. No car ferry, no public telephones, no public trash cans, and no medical services. Limited cell coverage and toilet facilities. For businesses that do not accept credit cards or personal checks as payment, there are ATMs available. Bring insect repellent. Beware of poison ivy, cliff edges, wet rocks, and surf. Monhegan Associates, Inc., requests that there be no technical climbing, smoking, fires, camping, or drones. Visitors enter the privately owned wildlands at their own risk. Carry out what you carry in. Do not miss the day's last boat, and be sure to take the right one back, as there are three boat lines. The Monhegan Boat Line out of Port Clyde provides the earliest departure during the high season, 7 a.m., and the latest return trip, 4:30 p.m., allowing as many as 8 hours on the island. The *Balmy Days II* boat out of Boothbay Harbor, the farthest port from Monhegan, allows about 3.75 hours on the island; the Hardy Boat out of New Harbor, a maximum of about 5 hours.

FINDING THE TRAILHEAD

Head uphill from the wharf on Wharf Hill Street to Main Street. Turn right (southwest) to start circling the island counterclockwise via unpaved road and the rugged Cliff Trail (Trail #1). **GPS:** N43 45.55' / W69 19.16'

WHAT TO SEE

Theodore Edison, son of inventor Thomas Edison, so loved the island he began summering on as a boy in the early 1900s that he acquired land to save it from development and founded the private nonprofit that has done so much to preserve the "simple, friendly way of life" and wildlands of Monhegan. As a result, the same special island culture and rugged sea cliffs—including the highest on the Maine coast—that have attracted artists, writers, summer residents, nature lovers, and tourists for more than a century continue to exert their magnetic pull.

About 350 acres, or about two-thirds of the not-quite 1-square-mile island, are now owned and managed by the private nonprofit Monhegan Associates, Inc., the land trust founded by Ted Edison in 1954, providing public access to the wooded interior, open cliffs, and hidden coves over a network of about 9 miles of trails and helping preserve the island's rich bird and plant life.

Monhegan is such a hot spot for birds, it's included in the Maine Birding Trail and well-known as a "migrant trap," with heavy concentrations of birds stopping to rest and feed along their transoceanic journey. The last three weeks of May and from late August through early October are peak times for birding, according to the birding trail brochure, available from the Maine Office of Tourism. Among the species that can be spotted from the cliffs are northern gannets, common eiders, black guillemots, and sharp-shinned hawks. The songs of as many as twenty different species of warblers can be heard in just one morning just walking around the village.

Monhegan is also a hotbed of botanical study, and is listed as a National Natural Landmark by the National Park Service for its near-virgin stands of red spruce and other flora. One early plant list of 165 species was published in the journal *Rhodora* in 1901. Another list of about eighty species of trees, herbs, wildflowers, shrubs, and ferns, compiled in 2006 by a University of Maine researcher, is available on the Monhegan Associates' website. In 2014 Monhegan Associates published the *Monhegan Nature Guide*, which includes a list of island wildflowers, among other highlights. During our visit to the island in late September, we saw plenty of New York aster and rough-stemmed goldenrod in bloom and horizontal juniper lining the trails.

Whitehead allows you to look back toward Gull Rock on Monhegan Island.

The hike on Monhegan Island brings you quickly to the *D.T. Sheridan* shipwreck.

But nature, in all its diversity and magnificence, is not the only draw to Monhegan. There's the Monhegan Museum of Art & History at the lighthouse, the Rockwell Kent–James Fitzgerald House & Studio, the Monhegan Brewing Company (whose beer is not available off-island), gift shops, dining, lodging, and even a shipwreck.

Being able to visit the museum on the same trip as your hike around the island adds immeasurably to the experience, allowing you to learn about the geology and see the island through artists' eyes. But it takes some logistics, as the museum is open only from 11:30 a.m. to 3:30 p.m. in July and August and 1:30 to 3:30 p.m. in late June and September. You either need to have overnight lodging or take the 7 a.m. boat from Port Clyde, as we did, for up to 8 hours on the island.

The 4.6-mile lollipop hike described here takes you around the length and breadth of the 1.7-mile long, 0.7-mile-wide island. The Cliff Trail, the longest and most spectacular, constitutes the bulk of the hike. Marked "#1" on small wooden signs nailed to trees and on the Monhegan Associates trail map, the Cliff Trail is the one that trails committee cochair Rick Cameron said he and his family make "a beeline for," as it "meanders high and low along the edge of Monhegan Island" and moves "from one majestic view to another."

Be sure to print out a trail map in advance or buy one for $1 on the boat or from the box nailed to a tree along the road that heads uphill from the wharf. With the spotty cell coverage, you can't depend on downloading a map on your phone. The map highlights the difficult parts of the trail network, primarily located along the rocky headlands that this loop traverses, and shows interior trails if you need to cut the hike short to catch the day's last boat back.

To reach the Cliff Trail, head uphill from the wharf on Wharf Hill Road and turn right (southwest) onto Main Street. Yield to work trucks and golf carts on the island's narrow unpaved roads. At 0.2 mile, by the church, a side road goes left (east) uphill to the only public restrooms—pay toilets behind the Monhegan House—available near the hike.

At 0.4 mile bear left (south) at a fork in the road, passing Monhegan Brewing Company on your right. At 0.5 mile follow the sign left toward Lobster Cove, then bear right (south) down a footpath, reaching the cove near the southern tip of the island at 0.6 mile. There's nothing but Atlantic Ocean to the south of you.

Walk across a black sand beach past a life preserver ring, a reminder of how dangerous the surf can be here, and at 0.7 mile reach the rusted wreck of the *D. T. Sheridan*, a tugboat that ran aground in 1948. The shipwreck, immortalized in paintings by Rockwell Kent and Jamie Wyeth, is a popular subject for artists and photographers and an easy destination for those who want only a short hike.

Head east from the shipwreck, paralleling the rocky shore, and pick up the Cliff Trail, marked "#1" on small wooden signs nailed to trees. It's a trail less traveled, as it is the longest and not among those described on the Monhegan Associates map as being "best for short visits." It's strenuous in spots too, taking you down to coves and back up to the highest cliffs on the Maine coast, 160 feet above sea level. But without a doubt, the Cliff Trail is the most scenic, and it is what you will now be following to traverse most of the perimeter of Monhegan, keeping the sea to your right.

Pass Christmas Cove with its scent of balsams at 0.8 mile, and reach a junction with a tree marked "#1" at 0.9 mile. Bear right to continue on the Cliff Trail (#1) at this and the next junction at 1.0 mile. (The trail to the left at both junctions is #1A, a parallel route that veers a little inland, useful during stormy weather and high surf. The junctions may be a little confusing here, but if you end up on #1A by mistake, it will eventually bring you back to #1.) There are rock faces to clamber up and steep drop-offs in this stretch as the trail nears Gull Rock, so be careful. The Cliff Trail now starts heading north-northeast along the back side of the island with its high, rocky headlands.

At 1.3 miles the Underhill Trail, marked by a "#3" on a log, comes in on the left. Stay straight on the Cliff Trail (#1). At 1.4 miles bear right to continue on the Cliff Trail (#1) as it traverses the rocky headland known as Burnt Head, elevation 140 feet. (The trail to the left is another #1A stormy-weather bypass, which provides access to the Burnt Head Trail [#4] back to Main Street and the only public toilets.)

At 1.5 miles you get the first views of Whitehead, which, along with Black Head, farther up Monhegan's coast, has the highest ocean cliffs in Maine, both at 160 feet above sea level.

The restored keeper's house at the Monhegan Island Lighthouse also serves as a museum.

Descend to Gull Cove at 1.6 miles, where the Gull Cove Trail (#5) comes in on the left. Stay straight on the Cliff Trail, being mindful of the poison ivy here, and start climbing up Whitehead, bearing right at the tree marked "#1" to continue paralleling the cliff. As you reach the top of Whitehead at 1.8 miles, look back to the south to see Gull Rock and Burnt Head. To the west from this high point, you can see the village. The Whitehead Trail (#7) comes in from the west here, and because it is the most direct route between the wharf and the spectacular views of Whitehead, you may find you have company here.

Continue north-northeast on the Cliff Trail, down to the base of Little Whitehead then up and over it. Continue bearing right to stay along the cliff tops on #1 as other trails marked "#12" and "#1A" go off to the left and inland.

Reach Squeaker Cove at 2.2 miles and continue on Trail #1, passing Trails #11, #10, and #1A that go left and inland.

Climb to the top of Black Head, the twin of Whitehead at 160 feet elevation, at 2.5 miles. As you round the headland to the northwest, you start getting glimpses of the mainland to the north and Burnt and Allen Islands in between. At 2.6 miles cross a mini-chasm and see Pulpit Rock come into view. Pass Trails #1A and #18 coming in on the left at 2.7 miles, and continue along the Cliff Trail as it skirts a grassy field close to Pulpit Rock.

At 3.0 miles the Cliff Trail heads away from the ocean's edge as it rounds Green Point at the northernmost part of the island and starts curving west. As it heads inland, the Cliff Trail passes #17, the Fern Glen Trail, and #15, the Evergreen Trail, coming in on the left (south).

At 3.4 miles the Cliff Trail skirts the shore at Pebble Beach and #14, the Pebble Beach Trail, comes in on the left (south). A big white erratic—a glacially deposited rock, seemingly so out of place on the coast here—hints at the powerful glacial forces that shaped this island. Seal Ledges and Duck Rocks come into view, where you may see harbor seals hauled out.

At 3.7 miles, as the Cliff Trail rounds the northwestern edge of the island, Manana Island across from the Monhegan wharf becomes visible, as does the rocky knob known as Smutty Nose. Manana Island represents the tail of Monhegan's distinctive whale-shaped profile, visible as you approach by boat.

The Cliff Trail heads away from the shore again, passing #14 on the left (north) and ending at a junction with the Black Head Trail, #10, at 4.0 miles. Turn right (southwest) onto the Black Head Trail and follow that as it merges onto Main Street at 4.1 miles. Follow Main Street back to the village; turn right (southwest) onto Wharf Hill Road, and return to the wharf at 4.6 miles.

If you find you have plenty of time before your return boat trip, you can grab a bite to eat or stop in for a brew, or perhaps even climb Lighthouse Hill to visit the Monhegan Art & History Museum before it closes at 3:30 p.m.

Every year the museum features a special art exhibit, such as the one in 2018 when we visited, marking the museum's fiftieth anniversary, highlighting Monhegan as an artist colony and featuring works by Andrew Wyeth, Rockwell Kent, Edward Hopper, and others. Through the end of 2020, the museum is working to match a $1 million challenge grant from the Wyeth Foundation for American Art.

You can also see works by Zero Mostel, who came to Monhegan in the 1950s after being blacklisted for refusing to cooperate with the House Un-American Activities Committee, and other artists who've lived and worked on the island.

That's Burnt Head in the distance from behind Gull Rock on Monhegan Island.

You can learn about the island's natural and Native American history, with a timeline starting in 1500; visits by Samuel de Champlain and John Smith in the 1600s; the fishing and tourist industries; the life cycle of the lobster (including a giant lobster claw "found in the attic of an old Monhegan home"); and how Ted Edison and others came to preserve so much of the island through Monhegan Associates.

If the lighthouse happens to be open, you can take a tour. Or you can simply sit on one of the benches at the top of Lighthouse Hill, appreciating the grand view of the village below and how Ted Edison's deep love for the island helped save the wildlands of Monhegan.

MILES AND DIRECTIONS

0.0 Start from the wharf on Wharf Hill Road; head uphill and turn right (southwest) onto Main Street.

0.2 Pass the church and the side road that leads left (east) to the only public restroom; stay straight (southeast) on Main Street as it becomes Lobster Cove Road.

0.4 Bear left (south) at a fork in the road and pass Monhegan Brewing Company on your right.

0.5 Follow the sign pointing to Lobster Cove and bear right (south) down a footpath.

0.6 Reach Lobster Cove, near the southern tip of the island, and walk across a black sand beach.

0.7 Reach the wreck of the *D.T. Sheridan*, a tugboat that ran aground in 1948.

0.8 Heading east from the shipwreck, pick up the Cliff Trail, marked "#1" on small wooden signs nailed to trees. Pass Christmas Cove and continue following #1 around the edge of the island.

0.9 Reach a junction with a stormy weather bypass trail marked "#1A"; bear right (east) to continue on the Cliff Trail.

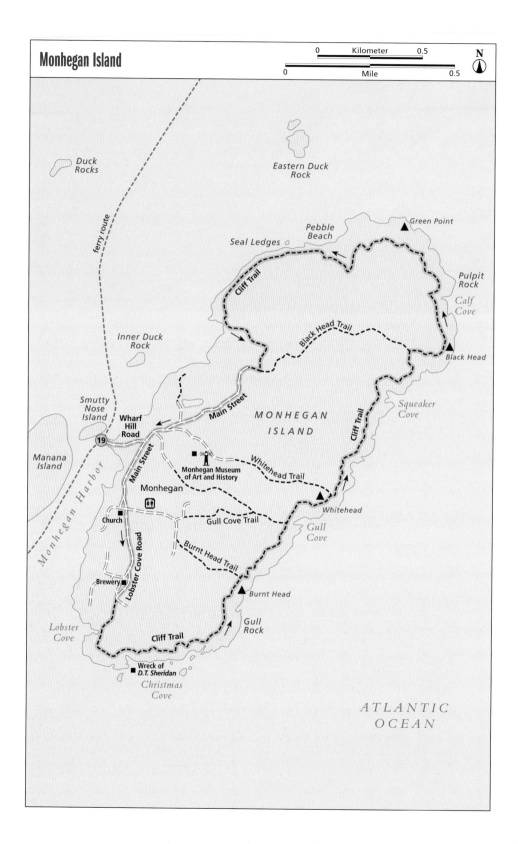

Monhegan Island

0   Kilometer   0.5

0   Mile   0.5

N

Duck Rocks

Eastern Duck Rock

ferry route

Pebble Beach

Green Point

Seal Ledges

Cliff Trail

Pulpit Rock

Calf Cove

Inner Duck Rock

Black Head Trail

Black Head

Smutty Nose Island

Wharf Hill Road

Main Street

MONHEGAN ISLAND

Squeaker Cove

19

Main Street

Cliff Trail

Manana Island

Monhegan Museum of Art and History

Whitehead Trail

Monhegan Harbor

Monhegan

Whitehead

Church

Gull Cove Trail

Gull Cove

Lobster Cove Road

Burnt Head Trail

Brewery

Burnt Head

Lobster Cove

Cliff Trail

Gull Rock

Wreck of D.T. Sheridan

Christmas Cove

ATLANTIC OCEAN

1.0 Bear right (southeast) at a junction with another #1A bypass; continue on the Cliff Trail.

1.3 Reach a junction with the Underhill Trail, marked "#3" on a log; stay straight (northeast) on the Cliff Trail.

1.4 Bear right (east) to continue on the Cliff Trail, away from the #1A bypass that leads to the Burnt Head Trail (#4), and ascend Burnt Head, elevation 140 feet.

1.6 Reach Gull Cove, where the Gull Cove Trail (#5) comes in on the left. Stay straight and then bear right (northeast) at the next junction, away from bypass #1A, to stay on the Cliff Trail.

1.8 Reach the top of Whitehead, at 160 feet elevation, the highest ocean cliff in Maine. The Whitehead Trail (#7), comes in on the left. Continue following the Cliff Trail, bearing right at several junctions to keep paralleling the shore as you head up and over Little Whitehead.

2.2 Reach Squeaker Cove and stay on the Cliff Trail to parallel the shore as trails marked "#12" and "#1A" go off to the left and inland.

2.5 Reach the top of Black Head, at 160 feet elevation, tied with Whitehead as the highest ocean cliff in Maine.

2.7 Stay straight on the Cliff Trail as Trails #1A and #18 come in on the left; pass a grassy field close to Pulpit Rock.

3.0 Follow the Cliff Trail as it heads in a westerly direction and rounds Green Point, away from the ocean's edge. Pass junctions with Trails #17 and #15 coming in on the left (south).

3.4 Follow the Cliff Trail as it skirts the shore again at Pebble Beach and Trail #14 comes in on the left (south).

3.7 Manana Island and the Monhegan wharf come into view as the Cliff Trail rounds the northwestern edge of the island.

4.0 The Cliff Trail ends at the Black Head Trail. Turn right (southwest) and take the Black Head Trail to Main Street.

4.1 Follow Main Street southwest back to the village. Turn right (southwest) onto Wharf Hill Road.

4.6 Arrive back at the wharf.

Whitehead on Monhegan Island is a good place to take a break and enjoy the considerable ocean views.

Hike up to Ocean Lookout on the shoulder of wooded Mount Megunticook, the highest mainland peak on the US Atlantic coast, then down to Mount Battie with its stone tower. Be inspired by the same views of Camden Harbor and Penobscot Bay that moved Edna St. Vincent Millay to write "Renascence," one of her best-known poems.

Start: Tablelands trailhead at the second parking lot on the right, 0.9 mile up Mount Battie Road
Elevation gain: 1,257 feet
Distance: 3.5-mile circuit loop
Difficulty: Moderate to strenuous
Hiking time: 2–2.5 hours
Seasons/schedule: Trails open year-round 9 a.m. to sunset; day-use areas open May 1 through Oct 15; best spring through fall
Fees and permits: Day-use fee
Trail contact: Camden Hills State Park, 280 Belfast Rd., Camden 04843; (207) 236-3109 (May 1 through Oct 15), (207) 236-0849 (Oct 16 through Apr 30); maine.gov/camdenhills
Dog-friendly: Leashed dogs permitted
Trail surface: Forest floor, rock ledges, pavement, stone tower steps, footbridges

Land status: 5,700-acre park owned and maintained by the State of Maine
Nearest town: Camden
Maps: USGS Camden; Camden Hills State Park trail map
Other trail users: Motorists who drive up Mount Battie Road, bus tour passengers, dog walkers, local residents; and snowshoers, snowmobilers, and cross-country skiers in winter
Special considerations: Facilities include picnic areas, campground, and restrooms. Check the state park's calendar of events at maine .gov/dacf/parks/discover_history_ explore_nature/activities/index .shtml. Parts of Mount Battie along the summit parking lot are accessible to visitors using wheelchairs or strollers. Parking for 15 cars at the Tablelands trailhead lot. Hunting allowed in season (except Sunday).

FINDING THE TRAILHEAD

From US 1 in Camden, head north 2 miles and turn left (west) to enter Camden Hills State Park. After the entrance station, turn left (southwest) onto Mount Battie Road and drive 0.9 mile up to the second parking lot on the right (north). Pick up the Tablelands Trail at the northwestern corner of the parking lot. **GPS:** N43 13.43' / W69 03.60'

WHAT TO SEE

Atop Mount Battie, with its close-up views of Penobscot Bay below and forested Mount Megunticook behind, it seems little has changed since Edna St. Vincent Millay wrote these words:

> *All I could see from where I stood*
> *Was three long mountains and a wood;*
> *I turned and looked another way,*
> *And saw three islands in a bay . . .*

Ocean Lookout, situated on a shoulder of Mount Megunticook, offers a panorama of Camden Harbor.

These opening lines of "Renascence," published in 1912 when St. Vincent Millay was just a teenager, are set in a plaque on the summit of her favorite of the Camden Hills.

And while there is now an auto road to the summit, built in 1963; the Mount Battie Tower, a 26-foot stone tower completed in 1921 to honor those who served in World War I; and a series of displays naming the islands in the distance, the surrounding view dwarfs everything, as it did for St. Vincent Millay:

> And all at once things seemed so small
> My breath came short, and scarce at all . . .

Camden Hills State Park, whose main attractions include Mount Battie and Mount Megunticook, had its beginnings during the Great Depression, when the federal government bought up languishing farmland, turned it into a park, and then transferred it to the State of Maine. Now considered one of the state's most popular day use areas, with more than 25 miles of trails, picnic areas, and the summit road that is open May through October, the park is particularly a magnet during the fall, when the hills are ablaze with color. The state park is also a top destination to watch for migrating hawks and includes two of the state's Natural Heritage Hikes, one of which goes up to Ocean Lookout on Mount Megunticook, the first destination of this hike.

By starting at the Tablelands trailhead partway up Mount Battie Road, this hike provides a more gradual and relatively less busy approach than if you begin at "Hiker's Parking" for the Megunticook Trail near the base of the road or at the parking lot at the Mount Battie summit. The other advantages of the hike as described: By looking out upon the more-distant ocean vistas near the top of Megunticook first and then descending to the more intimate views of Battie, you save the best for last. And any islands you can't identify from Ocean Lookout, you'll most likely learn the name of on the series of displays near Battie's stone tower.

From the Tablelands trailhead parking lot, head north away from Mount Battie Road toward Megunticook, staying straight on the blue-blazed trail and passing the Nature Trail that comes in on the right at 0.1 mile and the Carriage Trail that comes in on

For first-rate views, climb the spiral stairs in this stone tower memorial atop Mount Battie at Camden Hills State Park.

the left at 0.3 mile. The Tablelands Trail now starts getting rougher and steeper, going up stone steps in spots. Pass the Jack Williams Trail that comes in on the left at 0.7 mile, and follow the blue blazes straight ahead and up toward Ocean Lookout.

At 0.8 mile reach a junction with the Adam's Lookout Trail coming in on the right, which you will be returning on. Turn left (northwest) to head steeply up to Ocean Lookout. You'll be teased by views of Camden at a couple of outcroppings, as you skirt cliffs up to the lookout. These cliffs are among the features mentioned in the state's Natural Heritage Hikes description, in a section entitled "Peregrines and Poetry," for being both good nesting habitat for peregrine falcons and part of the view that inspired St. Vincent Millay.

At 1.0 mile reach Ocean Lookout, an open rock ledge with expansive views east and southeast of Maine's largest bay and picturesque Camden Harbor. Fall colors were just starting to tinge the landscape below during our late-September visit.

Ocean Lookout offers the best views from Megunticook, the highest mainland mountain on the US Atlantic coast at 1,385 feet (a little shorter than Acadia National Park's Cadillac, which is technically the highest mountain on all of the US Atlantic coast but is on an island and not the mainland). From here you can see Deer Isle to the east and Vinalhaven with its windmills; below rises the road up Mount Battie.

If there's a landmark you're uncertain of, take a photo to match it up with the wayside exhibits atop Battie, the next destination of this hike. There was one high island we couldn't identify from Ocean Lookout, and we were surprised to discover from the Mount Battie displays that it was Isle au Haut, the most remote part of Acadia.

To continue on the hike, look for the junction with the Megunticook Trail in the woods just beyond Ocean Lookout. Instead of taking the white-blazed trail northwest 0.4 mile up to the wooded summit, follow it northeast and steeply down in the direction of the campground to head to the Adam's Lookout Trail for the return.

At 1.5 miles as the trail levels off at a junction, turn right (southwest) onto the Adam's Lookout Trail to loop back to the Tablelands Trail. The lookout trail is relatively level for a stretch and then goes steeply up to the Tablelands junction at 1.8 miles, where you turn

left (southwest) to start descending back to the parking lot. Retrace your steps down the blue-blazed trail, returning to the Tablelands parking lot partway up the road at 2.5 miles.

Now for the best views of the hike, cross the road (watch for traffic in both directions), bear to the right (southwest), and look for the blue blaze in the woods to continue on the Tablelands Trail to Mount Battie. The trail parallels the road and reaches the parking lot atop Mount Battie at 2.9 miles. Follow the blue blazes, marked on rocks along the parking lot and gravel paths, and reach the stone tower and summit displays at 3.0 miles.

At 800 feet elevation, Mount Battie is the closest of the Camden Hills to town, and you can imagine a young St. Vincent Millay walking from her home to this very same place more than a century ago. Read her opening lines of "Renascence" on the plaque to the right (west) of the stone tower, and learn the names of some of the hundreds of islands in Penobscot Bay on the two wayside exhibits to the left (east). Among the landmarks visible from Mount Battie are, from left (east) to right (south): Mount Desert Island, Deer Isle, Isle au Haut, Vinalhaven, Curtis Island at the mouth of Camden Harbor, Camden, and Rockport.

Climb the spiral staircase of the World War I memorial stone tower, which underwent a $100,000 repair in 2016 and has been home to a giant Mount Battie Star, lighting up the Camden night sky for the holidays for more than fifty years. Look back above at Mount Megunticook and once more at Penobscot Bay below; you too will have your breath taken away like Edna St. Vincent Millay.

Return the way you came, arriving back at the Tablelands trailhead parking at 3.5 miles.

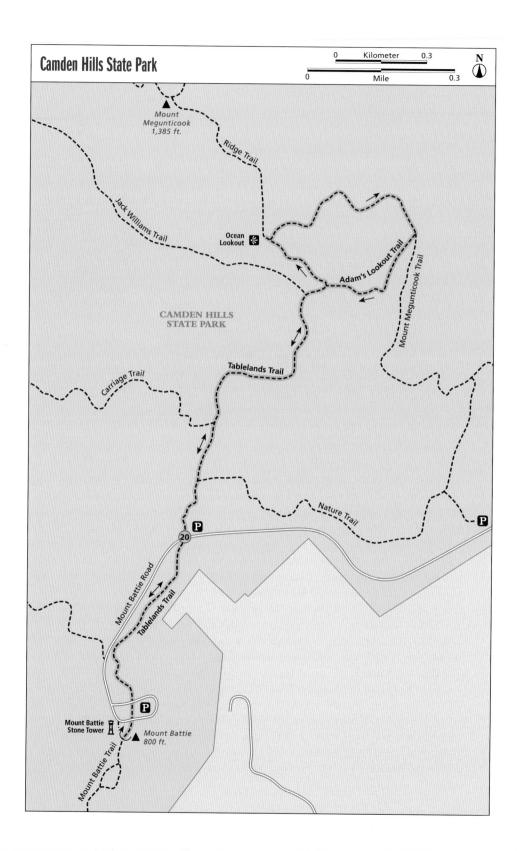

0   Kilometer   0.3

0   Mile   0.3

N

Mount
Megunticook
1,385 ft.

Ridge Trail

Jack Williams Trail

Ocean
Lookout

Adam's Lookout Trail

Mount Megunticook Trail

CAMDEN HILLS
STATE PARK

Carriage Trail

Tablelands Trail

Nature Trail

P

P

20

Mount Battie Road

Tablelands Trail

Mount Battie
Stone Tower

P

Mount Battie
800 ft.

Mount Battie Trail

MILES AND DIRECTIONS

0.0 Start at the Tablelands trailhead at the second parking lot on the right, 0.9 mile up Mount Battie Road; follow the blue-blazed trail north.

0.1 Pass the Nature Trail on the right.

0.3 Pass the Carriage Trail on the left.

0.7 Pass the Jack Williams Trail on the left.

0.8 Reach a junction with the Adam's Lookout Trail on the right, which will be your return. Turn left (northwest) to head steeply up to Ocean Lookout.

1.0 Reach the open rock ledge of Ocean Lookout. Descend on the white-blazed Mount Megunticook Trail as if heading to the campground rather than climbing another 0.4 mile on the Ridge Trail to the wooded summit.

1.5 Turn right (southwest) onto the Adam's Lookout Trail.

1.8 Turn left (southwest) onto the Tablelands Trail; retrace your steps to the trailhead parking lot.

2.5 From the parking lot, cross Mount Battie Road and bear right (southwest) to pick up the blue-blazed Tablelands Trail section that heads to Mount Battie.

2.9 Reach the Mount Battie parking lot; follow the blue blazes along the lot and gravel paths.

3.0 Reach the summit with its stone tower and wayside exhibits. Retrace your steps to the Tablelands trailhead.

3.5 Arrive back at the Tablelands trailhead parking lot.

MORE IN MIDCOAST

BREWERIES, EATS, AND SLEEPS

Bath Brewing Co., 141 Front St., Bath 04530; (207) 560-3389; bathbrewing.com. This neighborhood brewpub is located on the banks of the Kennebec River in downtown Bath. The small brewery is on-site, and the tap lists rotate but could include Long Reach Lager, Bath Pale Ale, and Milk Stout. The restaurant serves such items as lobster roll, grilled eggplant sandwich, and crispy haddock cake, and starters such as grilled shrimp skewers and lobster fritters. Near Bowdoin College Schiller Coastal Studies Center, Giant's Stairs, Bates–Morse Mountain Conservation Area, Popham Beach State Park, Josephine Newman Audubon Sanctuary, and Reid State Park. Open year-round.

Monhegan Brewing Company, 1 Boody Ln., Monhegan 04852; (207) 596-0011; monheganbrewing.com. "Craft beer, 10 miles out to sea" is the motto for this family-owned business, which brews eight months a year, Apr through Nov, with the last batches aging over the winter months. Draft and bottled beers only sold on Monhegan Island. Accessible only by boat. Open seasonally.

Rock Harbor Pub and Brewery, 416 Main St., Rockland 04841; (207) 593-7488; rockharborbrewing.com. Try the Haddock Rockefeller and the Twin Screw Pale Ale at the pub. Offers sixteen beers on tap, with five to nine brewed in-house at any given time. You can also see how the beer is made and packaged in a tour of the taproom and then try out the product at 5 Payne Ave., Rockland; (207) 466-9245. Near Camden Hills State Park. Open year-round.

One way to beat the crowds at Red's Eats is to get your lobster roll at night, just before closing.

Kennebec Tavern, 119 Commercial St., Bath 04530; (207) 442-9636; kennebectavern .com. Casual outside and inside dining along the banks of the Kennebec River, featuring steaks and seafood. Near Bowdoin College Schiller Coastal Studies Center, Giant's Stairs, Bates–Morse Mountain Conservation Area, Popham Beach State Park, Josephine Newman Audubon Sanctuary, and Reid State Park. Open year-round.

Red's Eats, 41 Water St., Wiscasset 04578; (207) 882-6128; redseatsmaine.com. With the motto "World's Best Lobster Shack" and a whole lobster's worth of meat on a roll, no wonder there are often long lines here. Dine on outside picnic tables or take out. Near Ovens Mouth Preserve and LaVerna Preserve. Open seasonally.

Fish House Fish Market, 7 Horns Hill Rd., Monhegan 04539; (207) 594-9342; facebook.com/pg/fishhousemonhegan/. Fish market and lunch and dinner menu, featuring such items as fish tacos, lobster BLT, and other specialties. On Fish Beach, Monhegan Island; accessible only by boat. BYOB. Open seasonally.

McLoons Lobster Shack, 315 Island Rd., Spruce Head Island 04858; (207) 593-1382; mcloonslobster.com. Known for its lobster roll, which has been featured by national and regional media. Other menu items include crab cakes, lobster stew, and roasted little-neck clams. Can hand-select your own lobster if ordering a steamed lobster dinner, as the lobsters are right from McLoons Wharf. Near Camden Hills State Park. Open seasonally.

Residence Inn by Marriott, 139 Richardson St., Bath 04530; (207) 593-1382; marri ott.com/hotels/travel/pwmba-residence-inn-bath-brunswick-area/. All-suite extended-stay lodging; includes breakfast. Near Bowdoin College Schiller Coastal Studies Center, Giant's Stairs, Bates–Morse Mountain Conservation Area, Popham Beach State Park, Josephine Newman Audubon Sanctuary, and Reid State Park. Open year-round.

The East Wind Inn, 21 Mechanic St., Tenants Harbor 04860; (207) 372-6366; east windinn.com. Historic seaside inn that's close enough to comfortably catch the first mailboat out of Port Clyde to Monhegan Island. Offers full breakfast with reservation, and a total of 19 rooms, suites, and an apartment. Small pets allowed for a fee in the Meeting House Annex only. On-site Wan-E-Set Restaurant and Quarry Tavern. Near Port Clyde mailboat to Monhegan Island and Camden Hills State Park. Open seasonally.

CAMPING

Sagadahoc Bay Campground, 9 Molly Point Ln., Georgetown 04548; (207) 371-2014; sagbaycamping.com. A total of 58 sites, including tent and RV sites, and 4 rental units. Some RV and tent sites on the ocean at the tip of Georgetown Island. All sites have running water; most have electricity. Al Roker and Craig Melvin of NBC's *Today* show did a recent "Great Outdoors" segment at the campground with their RV and hammocks. Septic at some RV sites; others have access to dump station. Dogs allowed; please keep pets on leash when walking them. Near Josephine Newman Audubon Sanctuary and Reid State Park. Open May 1 to Oct 31.

Lake Pemaquid Campground, PO Box 967, 100 Twin Cove Ln., Damariscotta 04543; (207) 536-5202; lakepemaquid.com. More than 200 sites, including some for RVs, plus cabin and cottage rentals. Sand beach on lake with swimming, boating, and fishing. Dogs are allowed on leash. Near Ovens Mouth Preserve and LaVerna Preserve. Open Memorial Day to Sept 30.

Camden Hills State Park, 280 Belfast Rd., Camden 04843; (207) 236-3109, (207) 236-0849 after Labor Day; maine.gov/camdenhills. More than 100 sites, some for RVs and campers. Dogs allowed on-leash. Starting in early February, reservations at Maine State Park campgrounds may be made online at maine.gov/dacf/parks/camping/reservations/ or by calling (207) 624-9950. Open May 15 to Oct 15.

LIGHTHOUSES, MUSEUMS, AND HISTORIC SITES

Marshall Point Lighthouse, 178A Marshall Point Rd., Port Clyde 04855; (207) 372-6450; marshallpoint.org. *Forrest Gump*, which won the Academy Award for best picture in 1994, thrust the Marshall Point Lighthouse into Hollywood history of sorts. Forrest, played by Tom Hanks, slowly jogs up the lighthouse's 100-foot walkway, the Gulf of Maine glittering in the background, as he appears to cap his epic run across the USA—until he decides to turn around and run back. Although the lighthouse is closed to the public, its automated light still directs boaters in and out of the fishing village of Port Clyde. Visitors may roam the grounds and stand right next to the 1858 lighthouse. The restored 1880 keeper's house is also a museum, open Memorial Day to the second Monday in October, with exhibits on the history of the lighthouse and the St. George Peninsula. Near Camden Hills State Park and the Port Clyde mailboat to Monhegan Island.

In the movie, Forrest Gump reaches the apex of an epic cross-country run at the wooden walkway of Marshall Point Lighthouse.

Owls Head Light, 186 Lighthouse Rd., Owls Head 04854; (207) 594-4174; lighthousefoundation.org/what-we-do/programs/lighthouse-tours/tour-owls-head-light/. The 1852 Owls Head Light is located on a promontory in Owls Head State Park overlooking Penobscot Bay. The 26-foot-tall lighthouse, with an automated light, is licensed to the nonprofit American Lighthouse Foundation. Volunteers lead tours from Memorial Day through the second Monday in October. A keeper's house, interpretive center, and gift shop are open year-round, weather permitting. Near LaVerna Preserve and Camden Hills State Park.

Maine Maritime Museum, 234 Washington St., Bath 04530; (207) 443-1316; maine maritimemuseum.org. Located in the "City of Ships" on the grounds of a former ship-yard along the Kennebec River, the Maine Maritime Museum offers indoor and outdoor exhibits, seasonal lighthouse and nature cruises, and the chance to board the schooner *Mary E*, placed on the National Register of Historic Places in September 2019 by the National Park Service. Near Bowdoin College Schiller Coastal Studies Center, Giant's Stairs, Bates–Morse Mountain Conservation Area, Popham Beach State Park, Josephine Newman Audubon Sanctuary, and Reid State Park. Open year-round.

Farnsworth Art Museum, 16 Museum St., Rockland 04841; (207) 596-6457; farns worthmuseum.org. Celebrating Maine's role in American art and featuring works of Andrew, N. C., and Jamie Wyeth among others, the Farnsworth has 15,000 works in its nationally recognized collection. Near LaVerna Preserve and Camden Hills State Park. Open year-round.

COASTAL ATTRACTIONS

Project Puffin Visitor Center, 311 Main St., Rockland 04841; (207) 596-5566; pro jectpuffin.audubon.org. The next best thing to going on a puffin cruise is to see live video of puffins and other seabirds at this Audubon visitor center, which celebrates the success of Project Puffin in bringing the colorful birds back to their historic nesting islands. You can also find schedules for puffin cruises, see exhibits, buy puffin-themed gifts, and learn about Audubon's conservation work in Maine. Near LaVerna Preserve and Camden Hills State Park. Open seasonally.

Maine Lobster Festival, Harbor Park, 1 Pleasant St., Rockland 04841; (800) 576-7512; mainelobsterfestival.com. Celebrating all things lobster for more than seventy years, the Maine Lobster Festival is held annually the first weekend in August. Near LaVerna Preserve and Camden Hills State Park.

ACADIA NATIONAL PARK AND BAR HARBOR

The Acadia National Park and Bar Harbor region is unlike any other in Maine because of its mountains with spectacular ocean views, wide-ranging coastal access, and long history of activism and philanthropy that helped win federal protection. Acadia National Park is also special for its ancient geology, primarily the beautiful pink granite that can be found on Cadillac Mountain, the highest peak on the East Coast of the United States, and along the eastern and western shores of Mount Desert Island. The park is also noted for its glacially carved features such as giant Somes Sound, rounded and barren mountain tops, and U-shaped valleys.

Eleven of the thirteen hikes in this section are on Mount Desert Island, the largest island off the coast of New England. The 108-square-mile island, connected to the mainland by a bridge, is the sixth-largest island in the contiguous United States. Most of the trails are in Acadia National Park, consisting of some 50,000 acres, including 13,000 acres of conservation easement.

Acadia is also ranked as the country's eighth most visited national park and set an attendance record in 2017 with more than 3.509 million visits, up 40 percent from 2.5 million in 2010.

Like many major parks, heavy traffic, overflowing lots, and illegal roadside parking can be a problem during the busy season. To better manage traffic, the park service is starting

The surf is up at Sand Beach after an October rainstorm.

Acadia National Park and Bar Harbor

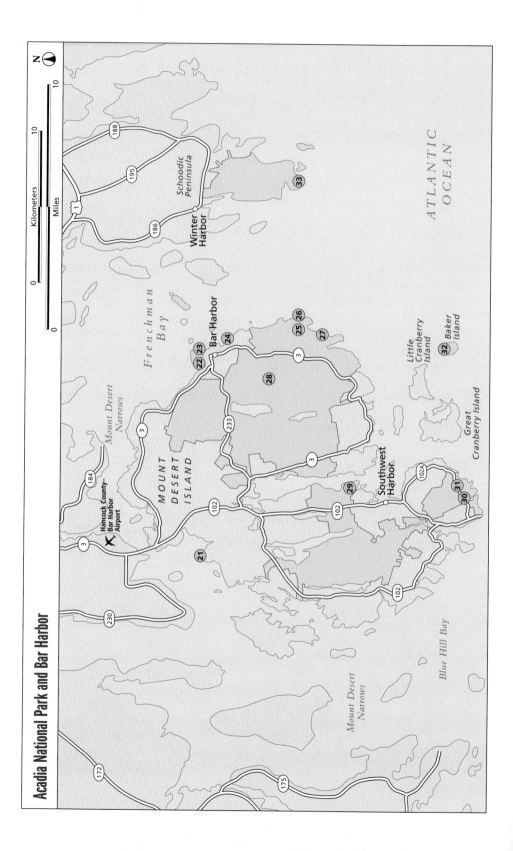

a reservation system for motor vehicles at Cadillac Mountain, planned to operate for its first full season, mid-June to mid-October, in 2021, after a pilot in 2020. Go to recreation. gov to reserve a time to drive up Cadillac (small fee applies). Length of stay is unlimited.

No earlier than 2022, the system is planned to include Sand Beach Entrance Station (access to Sand Beach, Thunder Hole, Ocean Path, and Gorham Mountain) and the Jordan Pond area.

Unlike most national parks, Acadia is composed of mostly private donations of land and was set aside largely through the work of wealthy summer residents who were alarmed by the development that threatened the island at the turn of the twentieth century and believed it needed to be saved for future generations.

John D. Rockefeller Jr., the only son of a wealthy oil magnate, donated about 10,000 acres of land to the park and paid to build 45 miles of carriage roads and sixteen stone bridges on those roads. Harvard President Charles W. Eliot led the creation of an organization in 1901 to conserve land and build paths that became the foundation for the park. George B. Dorr, the park's first superintendent, spent all of his family's fortune to help create the park and worked to persuade political leaders in Washington and Maine to back his vision for the park.

The epic struggle of Dorr, Eliot, Rockefeller, and many others resulted in President Woodrow Wilson approving a national monument in 1916 and Congress passing a law for a national park in 1919. Their legacy of idealism and volunteerism is carried on today by the Friends of Acadia, a nonprofit group in Bar Harbor founded in 1986 that works closely with the National Park Service to help protect and promote Acadia for public use in myriad ways. In 2000 the Friends and NPS blazed a new path when they established a first-in-the-nation endowment to maintain trails, funded with $9 million in private donations and $4 million in park user fees.

Acadia National Park is unusual for a national park because it is so tightly connected to the communities on Mount Desert Island, notably Bar Harbor. The historic seaport is the gateway to the park and a drawing card for tourists and cruise ships.

Two of the more beautiful coastal trails—the Bar Island Trail and the 125-year-old Shore Path—are right in busy downtown Bar Harbor; a third, the Compass Harbor Trail, includes the remains of Dorr's former estate and is just outside the downtown.

Some of the coastal trails are among the oldest and most historic in the park, including the Bar Island Trail, Ocean Path, Sand Beach and Great Head Trail, Gorham Mountain and Cadillac Cliffs Trails, and the loop trail atop 1,530-foot Cadillac Mountain. Another loop hike includes 284-foot Flying Mountain, the smallest of the park's twenty-six peaks, and the lone trail in this book along Somes Sound—a 5-mile-long fjord-like inlet that separates the east and west sides of Mount Desert Island. At the tip of the western side of Mount Desert Island are Wonderland and the Ship Harbor Trail.

While a lot of the island is dominated by evergreens such as spruce, balsam, and pine, the diversity of the forest was increased in 1947 when a huge fire burned a large part of the eastern side of Mount Desert Island and formed the conditions for new eastern deciduous trees such as maple, birch, beech, and oak.

Three of the coastal trails are in more remote and quieter areas: Baker Island, located about 3 miles off the coast of Mount Desert Island and accessible only by boat; the Sundew Trail, the lone hike in this book on the Schoodic Peninsula, the only part of the national park on the mainland; and Indian Point Blagden Preserve, owned by The Nature Conservancy.

21 INDIAN POINT BLAGDEN PRESERVE (BAR HARBOR)

Located in a less-visited part of Mount Desert Island, the Indian Point Blagden Preserve includes frontage on a vast bay and a quiet pebble beach. The preserve, with trails noted for solitude, includes a mature forest that was not hit by the great fire of 1947 on Mount Desert Island, a field, and an old apple orchard, and offers a decent chance of seeing harbor seals.

Start: Big Wood trailhead, next to the information booth at the parking lot
Elevation gain: 199 feet
Distance: 2.3-mile circuit loop
Difficulty: Easy to moderate
Hiking time: 1.5–2 hours
Seasons/schedule: Open year-round sunrise to 6 p.m.
Fees and permits: Donations suggested; groups of 12 or more should make prior arrangements.
Trail contact: The Nature Conservancy, 14 Maine St., Ste. 401, Brunswick 04011; (207) 729-5181; e-mail: naturemaine@tnc.org
Dog-friendly: No dogs allowed
Trail surface: Forest floor, wooden footbridges, paved road, rock ledges, pebble beach

Land status: 110 acres owned and maintained by The Nature Conservancy, a global environmental nonprofit
Nearest town: Bar Harbor
Maps: USGS Acadia National Park and Vicinity; Nat Geo Trails Illustrated Topographic Map: Acadia National Park; Indian Point Blagden Preserve trail map, available at https://www.nature.org/content/dam/tnc/nature/en/documents/me-indian-point-trail-map.pdf
Other trail users: Trail runners, local residents
Special considerations: Insect repellent may be needed, especially if a wet spring or summer; no facilities; no camping, fires, bicycling, or commercial tours allowed; respect abutting private property.

FINDING THE TRAILHEAD

After crossing the Trenton Bridge onto Mount Desert Island on ME 3, bear right at the first fork in the road and head south on ME 102 toward Somesville. Turn right (southwest) at 1.8 miles onto Indian Point Road; in another 1.7 miles bear right at the junction with Oak Hill Road to stay on Indian Point Road. In another 200 yards turn right (northwest) onto Higgins Farm Road at the Indian Point Blagden Preserve sign. The parking lot is immediately on the left. The Big Wood Trail begins at the information booth and heads into the woods at the northwest corner of the parking lot. **GPS:** N44 22.58' / W68 21.54'

WHAT TO SEE

The Indian Point Blagden Preserve is a nearly hidden jewel that offers the chance to see harbor seals and to walk some stunning coastline with beach and granite. Located on a peninsula in the northwest corner of Mount Desert Island, the preserve often is overshadowed by the trails of nearby Acadia National Park and therefore offers hikers a chance to enjoy a less-visited part of Maine's largest island. Bring some binoculars for viewing harbor seals on rocky ledges in the distance.

Doug Radziewicz, preserve steward for The Nature Conservancy, which owns the 110-acre preserve, said the place is special because of the privacy it offers. A relatively small number of people visit the preserve each year, and most come during the summer months. "When people hike on the Indian Point Blagden Preserve, it seems as though they have a special place of their own," he said. "That is what attracts a lot of people to this preserve—the solitude that it offers."

The preserve has roughly 1.5 miles of hiking trails, and as an alternative you can walk a paved road that is open to authorized private vehicles. The trails are easy to moderate and go through a mature forest to a quiet and beautiful bay largely devoid of motorboats.

From the northwest corner of the parking lot, the hike ascends slightly at the start on the yellow-blazed 0.9-mile-long Big Wood Trail, a path covered by pine needles that cuts through tall red spruce, cedar, and balsam trees. The dark spruce and other evergreens on this part of the preserve are similar to a boreal forest found in Downeast Maine, largely because the area escaped a fire that burned much of the eastern side of Mount Desert Island in 1947.

At 0.8 mile on the Big Wood Trail, after crossing a gravel road, look for the start of a stand of tall tamarack, an unmistakable conifer with long, wispy branches and soft green needles that become yellow in the fall. Tamarack, seen again after you cross three bridges, is the only native deciduous conifer tree, losing its needles every fall.

Before reaching the shore you emerge from the forest into a field and old apple orchard, where the Big Wood Trail ends at 0.9 mile.

Turn left (west) onto a paved road and follow a blue wooden arrow to the Shore Trail, turning right (northwest) before a private drive at 1.0 mile. Come out to a grassy area with a nice wooden bench with a bronze memorial plaque. Bear left to continue following the Shore Trail to the west; pass a second bench. Reach a fork, where you

You might find some solitude on a chair by the shore at the Indian Point Blagden Preserve.

bear right to the shore and see two more benches and then a rocky ridge with two red Adirondack-style chairs at 1.2 miles. You might hear the barking of seals in the distance and possibly see ospreys and bald eagles over Western Bay.

A big attraction of the preserve is its 1,000 feet of shoreline on Western Bay. To the left (west) on the shoreline, you will find gray-and-white granite called the Ellsworth schist, some of the oldest rock on Mount Desert Island. A pebble beach and tree-covered uplands are to the right (east). A sign on a wooden post marks the start of private property to the west and cautions people against walking to a tiny island at low tide. Please make sure you stay on the preserve and respect private property.

From this spot on the coast near the west end of the preserve, you get sweeping open ocean views, with great vistas to the west of Western Bay, north to the Mount Desert Narrows, and northwest to Alley Island. Looking southwest, spot Blue Hill Mountain with its communications tower. Goose Cove and Haynes Point are to the north.

From the rocks at the western end of the preserve, point your binoculars at several ledges in the distance to spot harbor seals hauled out, some with their heads raised. We spotted at least a half dozen and heard an occasional honk or bark from the seals.

"People can see harbor seals primarily in spring and summer after pups are born and seals rest on ledges," said Radziewicz. "The seals are best viewed at low tide, when ledges and small islands are exposed."

Retrace your steps on the Shore Trail back to the grassy area with the first bench. But instead of turning sharply right into the woods back to the paved road, go diagonally across the grassy area and turn left (north) to the shore, reaching a pebble beach at 1.4 mile. About 0.1-mile long, the beach provides some comfortable spots for sitting and enjoying the massive bay waters and leads to the Fern Trail, which represents the eastern end of the preserve and the start of private property.

Turn right to walk northeast along the beach to the first big granite ledge, and look right into the woods for a red wooden arrow for the Fern Trail at 1.5 miles. Follow the Fern Trail to the end at 1.6 miles and turn left (west) onto Higgins Farm Road.

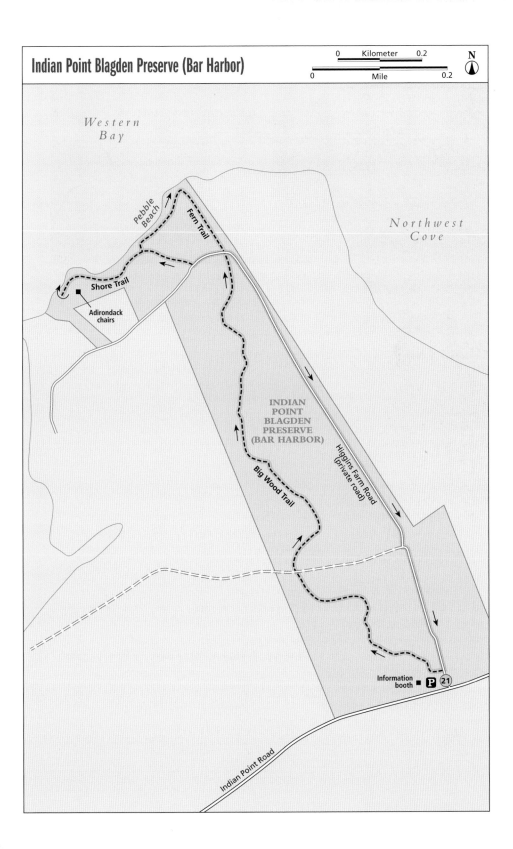

Indian Point Blagden Preserve (Bar Harbor)

0   Kilometer   0.2

0   Mile   0.2

N

Western Bay

Northwest Cove

Pebble Beach

Fern Trail

Shore Trail

Adirondack chairs

INDIAN
POINT
BLAGDEN
PRESERVE
(BAR HARBOR)

Big Wood Trail

Higgins Farm Road (private road)

Information booth   P   21

Indian Point Road

At the end of this pebble beach is the Fern Trail at the Indian Point Blagden Preserve.

Follow the road as it bears right, and take it back to the parking lot at 2.3 miles. Watch out for occasional motor vehicles that could be on this private road.

MILES AND DIRECTIONS

0.0   Start at the Big Wood trailhead next to the information booth; turn right at the northwest corner of the parking lot, following a yellow wooden arrow into the woods.

0.3   Turn left (west) on a gravel road, following a yellow wooden arrow, then immediately right (north) back into the woods at another yellow wooden arrow just before the preserve boundary sign.

0.9   Reach the end of the Big Wood Trail at an old orchard; turn left (west) on the paved road and follow a blue wooden arrow to the Shore Trail.

1.0   Turn right (northwest) onto the Shore Trail before a private drive, coming out to a grassy area with a wooden bench and bearing left (west), paralleling the shore.

1.2   Reach two red Adirondack-style chairs on a rocky outcropping, where you get expansive views across Western Bay and possible sightings of seals, ospreys, and bald eagles.

1.3   Retrace your steps on the Shore Trail back to the grassy area with the first wooden bench. Instead of turning sharply right through the woods and back to the paved road, go diagonally across the grassy area and turn left (north) down to the shore.

1.4   Turn right (northeast) along the short stretch of pebble beach.

1.5   At the first big granite ledge at the far end of the beach, look into the woods for a red wooden arrow; turn right (south) to pick up the Fern Trail.

1.6   Reach the end of the Fern Trail at Higgins Farm Road; turn left (east) and follow the road as it bears right to loop back to the parking lot.

2.3   Arrive back at the trailhead.

22 THE SHORE PATH (BAR HARBOR)

Although not part of Acadia National Park, the Shore Path is as scenic and historic as almost any coastal trail in the more celebrated federal property. On the Shore Path, hikers get extensive views of the Porcupine Islands and giant cruise ships while walking along Frenchman Bay and a rocky shoreline with geological oddities like Balance Rock and elegant signs about the path's rich history.

Start: Shore Path trailhead at the top of the municipal boat ramp across from Agamont Park, at the foot of West and Main Streets
Elevation gain: 13 feet
Distance: 1.2 miles out and back
Difficulty: Easy
Hiking time: 45 minutes–1 hour
Seasons/schedule: Open year-round; best spring through fall, particularly early morning or late afternoon in summer and fall to avoid crowds and cruise ship passengers who've come ashore
Fees and permits: No fees or permits
Trail contact: Bar Harbor Village Improvement Association, PO Box 52, Bar Harbor 04609; https://barharborvia.org/contact-us/
Dog-friendly: Leashed dogs permitted
Trail surface: Graded gravel path, paved road

Land status: Private but open to the public; maintained by the nonprofit Bar Harbor Village Improvement Association
Nearest town: Bar Harbor
Maps: USGS Acadia National Park and Vicinity; Nat Geo Trails Illustrated Topographic Map: Acadia National Park
Other trail users: Cruise ship passengers who've come ashore, trail runners, dog walkers
Special considerations: There are public restrooms at Agamont Park near the trailhead, a picnic area at Grant Park about halfway along the Shore Path, and limited parking that is metered until 8 p.m. from May 15 to Oct 31 along West and Main Streets and in lots throughout town. While the path is accessible for visitors with wheelchairs or strollers, busy times can make it difficult to navigate through the crowds.

FINDING THE TRAILHEAD

From the Acadia National Park Hulls Cove Visitor Center, head south on ME 3 for about 2.5 miles toward downtown Bar Harbor. Turn left (east) onto West Street at the first intersection after the College of the Atlantic, and head toward Main Street and the town pier. The closest Island Explorer stop is Bar Harbor Village Green, which is available on the Campgrounds, Eden Street, Sand Beach/Blackwoods, Jordan Pond, Brown Mountain, and Southwest Harbor lines. **GPS:** N44 23.28' / W68 12.14'

WHAT TO SEE

With its unbeatable views of islands and cruise ships, strong ties to the Gilded Age, and easy access to the coast, the Shore Path in Bar Harbor may be unlike any other coastal trail in Maine. Located directly along the rockbound coast of Frenchman Bay in downtown Bar Harbor, the path is also unusual because it is on private property and kept open

The schooner *Margaret Todd* sails among the Porcupine Islands, as seen from the Shore Path in Bar Harbor.

to the public through the generosity of property owners for more than 125 years; the path and the seawall are maintained by the Bar Harbor Village Improvement Association.

The path is a nice complement to the downtown and especially the Bar Harbor Inn, a historic resort next to the path. Winston Wood, who stayed at the Bar Harbor Inn with his family, said he hiked the Shore Path every morning to work up an appetite for breakfast. "All in all, the path is one of the real attractions in Bar Harbor," Wood said. "Having been in a number of coastal Maine communities—Boothbay Harbor, Camden, Rockland, Rockport, Searsport, Lincolnville, and York Harbor—I can't think of anything like it."

Generally heading north to south, the path begins across from Agamont Park, at the top of the boat ramp at the municipal pier at the foot of West and Main Streets. The 0.6-mile-long path ends at Wayman Lane.

Right from the start are dazzling views of the Porcupine Islands, from west to east: Bar Island and then the four Porcupines—Sheep, Burnt, Long, and later Bald, which has steep cliffs—and Ironbound farther east.

In the distance to the southeast, look for the historic Bar Harbor breakwater, a trapezoidal stone mound structure built by the US Army Corps of Engineers in 1917 with federal dollars. The breakwater extends 2,510 feet southwesterly from Bald Porcupine Island toward Cromwell Cove near the shore of Mount Desert Island. While the structure's length was finished as planned, a superstructure is 88 percent complete, left unfinished because of World War I, according to the Corps. The breakwater, though in need of repair, still provides significant protection to Bar Harbor and the outer anchorage areas from southerly swells and waves.

You can also see the *Margaret Todd*, a four-masted touring schooner, sailing among the Porcupines, as well as any of the estimated 150 cruise ships that anchor in the bay and tender passengers to the downtown during the spring-to-fall season.

There are lots of places to stop along the path, including to read about history on the detailed "The Museum in the Streets" signs placed along the pathway.

The path soon crosses in front of the Bar Harbor Inn, with its expansive lawn and historic "Reading Room," a club visited by President William Howard Taft in 1910 and with members like George B. Dorr, the father of Acadia National Park, and Charles Eliot, a Harvard president who worked with Dorr to create Acadia in the early twentieth century. It was high culture, but the club was also begun as a nonprofit and therefore was free from Maine's oldest-in-the-nation prohibition laws.

The path is also noted for its geologic peculiarities, including Pulpit Rock and Balance Rock, a giant boulder left by melting glaciers more than 10,000 years ago, similar to Bubble Rock on the peak of South Bubble in Acadia.

The path has many spots to step down to the cobblestone beach or bedrock granite that lines the shore. It is rough in some spots, but don't miss five convenient granite steps in front of the southern end of the Bar Harbor Inn.

The path is meticulously maintained and includes the open space of Grant Park, located right behind Balance Rock at 0.3 mile. Named for a New York lawyer who built an estate that helped launch the booming Gilded Age in Bar Harbor, the park was purchased by the town about one hundred years ago. The Shore Path includes fine benches for sitting next to the ocean, perhaps none better than two picnic tables on a brick patio and another six benches lined outside a separate patio near Grant Park. You will also find another seven granite steps down to the water in front of Grant Park. Often during the hike, you will see the wide green lawns of grand estates, such as the gable-roofed "cottage" originally built by John Innes Kane and on the National Register of Historic Places.

A nice long stone bench sits at a point under a big birch tree and affords fantastic looks at the four Porcupine Islands and Egg Rock with its lighthouse.

At low tide, which can be 8 to 12 feet less than high tide, the Shore Path is enhanced by tide pools where kids might enjoy looking for shells, snails, periwinkles, and other creatures exposed by the receding waters. Be careful on the seaweed and rocks, which can be very slippery.

At about 0.5 mile, at Reef Point, is the location of the family home of Beatrix Farrand, a noted landscape architect who designed more than fifty estate gardens in Bar Harbor and chaired the planning committee of the Bar Harbor Village Improvement Association. The Farrand home was torn down, and another home now stands there.

Reach the end of the path along the shore and some open space that was the location of the Briars Cottage, which boasts a long history that includes the Hope Diamond and served as the birthplace of the late Vice President Nelson Rockefeller.

Return the way you came for a different perspective on the spectacular views, or turn right on Wayman Lane to make a loop through town on Main Street.

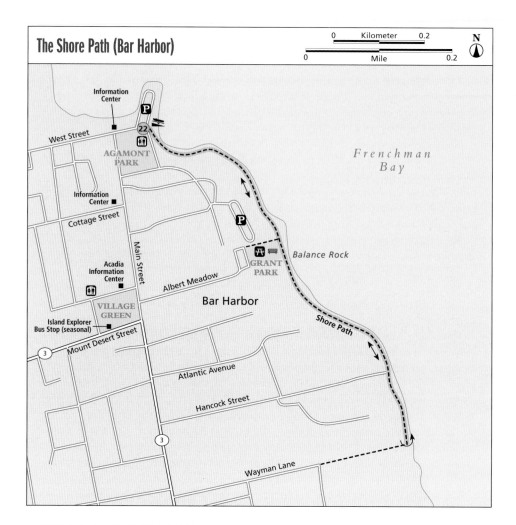

The Shore Path (Bar Harbor)

0 Kilometer 0.2
0 Mile 0.2
N

Information Center

West Street

AGAMONT PARK

Information Center

Cottage Street

Main Street

Acadia Information Center

VILLAGE GREEN

Island Explorer Bus Stop (seasonal)

3

Mount Desert Street

Albert Meadow

Bar Harbor

Atlantic Avenue

Hancock Street

3

Wayman Lane

GRANT PARK

Balance Rock

Shore Path

Frenchman Bay

MILES AND DIRECTIONS

0.0 Start at the Shore Path trailhead at the top of the municipal boat ramp across from Agamont Park, at the foot of West and Main Streets; follow the paved walkway southeast along the waterfront.

0.1 Pass the dock for the schooner *Margaret Todd*, and follow what has now become a graded gravel path taking you by the Bar Harbor Inn and Pulpit Rock at Birch Point.

0.3 Reach picnic tables and benches next to Grant Park, with a view of Balance Rock.

0.6 Cross a wooden footbridge and reach the end of the path at Wayman Lane. Retrace your steps. (**Option:** Turn right on Wayman Lane to loop back through town on Main Street.)

1.2 Arrive back at the trailhead.

23 BAR ISLAND TRAIL

A low-tide walk leads to a rocky island off Bar Harbor, providing a unique perspective back toward town and its mountain backdrop. The trail can also offer a close-up view of gulls feeding or starfish exposed by the tide.

Start: Bar Island trailhead at the foot of Bridge Street, the first left (north) off West Street on the edge of downtown Bar Harbor
Elevation gain: 130 feet
Distance: 2.0 miles out and back
Difficulty: Easy
Hiking time: 1–1.5 hours
Seasons/schedule: Open year-round, low tide only; best spring through fall, particularly early morning or late afternoon in summer to avoid the crowds
Fees and permits: Acadia National Park pass required May through Oct
Trail contact: Acadia National Park, PO Box 177, Bar Harbor 04609; (207) 288-2338; nps.gov/acad
Dog-friendly: Leashed dogs permitted

Trail surface: Low-tide gravel bar, gravel road, forest floor, rock ledges
Land status: Acadia National Park
Nearest town: Bar Harbor
Maps: USGS Acadia National Park and Vicinity; Nat Geo Trails Illustrated Topographic Map: Acadia National Park
Other trail users: Trail runners, dog walkers, motorists on gravel bar
Special considerations: Accessible only within 1.5 hours on either side of low tide. Check tide chart on Bar Island, in local newspapers, or at usharbors.com/harbor/maine/bar-harbor-me/tides/. There is a public restroom at the intersection of West and Main Streets.

FINDING THE TRAILHEAD

From the park's visitor center at Hulls Cove, head south on ME 3 for about 2.5 miles toward downtown Bar Harbor. Turn left (east) onto West Street at the first intersection after the College of the Atlantic. The trail, visible only at low tide, leaves from Bridge Street, the first left (north) off West Street on the edge of downtown. There is limited on-street parking (metered until 8 p.m. from May 15 to Oct 31) on West Street. The closest Island Explorer stop is Bar Harbor Village Green, which is available on the Campgrounds, Eden Street, Sand Beach/Blackwoods, Jordan Pond, Brown Mountain, and Southwest Harbor lines. **GPS:** N44 23.30' / W68 12.35'

WHAT TO SEE

The Bar Island Trail is a short, easy jaunt within shouting distance of Bar Harbor, but you feel transported to another world. That is the beauty of being on an island, even a small one, so close to a busy summer resort town. It's easy enough for the least-seasoned hiker, with Dolores's mother, April, a first-time visitor to Acadia at 71, effortlessly strolling across. But the Bar Island Trail also provides a bit of risk to satisfy the thrill-seeking adventurer—it can only be traveled at low tide, when a gravel bar connecting Bar Harbor and the island is exposed. The incoming tide can quickly cover the bar and prevent people from hiking off the island.

"Time your hike carefully" a sign warns hikers once they reach the island's rocky shores. "The tide changes quickly. Plan to be off the bar no later than 1.5 hours after

Fall colors frame the view back to Bar Harbor from the summit of Bar Island in Acadia National Park.

low tide," lest you become stuck. For your convenience, a tide chart is posted, as well as phone numbers for a water taxi and Acadia dispatch if a water taxi is unavailable. Don't become one of the visitors who periodically get stranded on the island, or whose cars get swamped while parked on the gravel bar.

The trail was used by the rusticators, the popular name for visitors who came to Maine for extended summer vacations during the mid- to late nineteenth century, and was first described in 1867 according to *Pathmakers: Cultural Landscape Report for the Historic Hiking Trail System of Mount Desert Island*, published by the National Park Service's Olmsted Center for Landscape Preservation. It was closed for a period then reopened by the National Park Service in 1990 when the island was still partly privately owned. The NPS completed ownership of the island in 2003 when it purchased 12 acres from former *NBC News* correspondent Jack Perkins and his wife, Mary Jo, who lived on the island for thirteen years in a small home they built there. Perkins, who died in 2019, called the island his "garden of Eden" and detailed his time there in his 2013 book, *Finding Moosewood, Finding God*.

Maybe you can also discover God, or at least a sign of God, during a hike to the 0.5-mile-long island, as we perhaps did on a cloudless early evening in September 2017 when a bald eagle hovered for a while just above our heads near the start of the wooded island.

The hike begins at the foot of Bridge Street in Bar Harbor. Be forewarned: On a sunny summer weekend day or holiday, the walk can almost become circus-like, with big crowds and passing vehicles—and maybe one or two becoming stuck in the sand.

For a more tranquil coastal trek, try early morning or late afternoon on a weekday for the low-tide hike.

Walk northwest across the gravel bar, catch a view of nearby Sheep Porcupine Island and reach Bar Island at about 0.4 mile. Some of the resort town's historic summer "cottages"—really mansions—are visible along Bar Harbor's shoreline to the left (southwest) as you cross the gravel bar. At the end of the bar, a newer sign warns people "Do not remove or stack cobbles." A violation of Leave No Trace principles, rock stacking is an annoying form of vandalism that is increasingly marring open spaces across the country and which the NPS is attempting to prevent.

Once you reach Bar Island, head northeast up the gravel road behind the gate. The trail soon levels off at a grassy field. At about 0.6 mile bear left (northeast) at a trail sign pointing into the woods toward Bar Island summit. At a fork at about 0.8 mile, marked by a cairn (a pile of rocks to mark a change in trail direction), bear right (southeast) up a rocky knob.

At about 1.0 mile you reach the summit, with its views toward Bar Harbor as well as several Acadia peaks: from left to right, Champlain Mountain, Huguenot

Driftwood on the shore of Bar Island provides a convenient resting place.

Head, and Dorr and Cadillac Mountains. From here you can hear the town's church bells, see the fishing and recreational boats along the harbor, and take in the smells of the sea and the views of the mountains.

Return the way you came.

MILES AND DIRECTIONS

- 0.0 Start at the Bar Island trailhead, at the foot of Bridge Street.
- 0.4 Reach the shore of Bar Island. Check the posted tide chart to time your return; otherwise you'll have to wait more than 12 hours for the next low tide. Head northeast up the gravel road behind the gate.
- 0.6 Cross a grassy field and come to a junction; bear left (northeast) into the woods at the trail sign.
- 0.8 Reach another junction marked by a cairn; bear right (southeast) up to the island's summit.

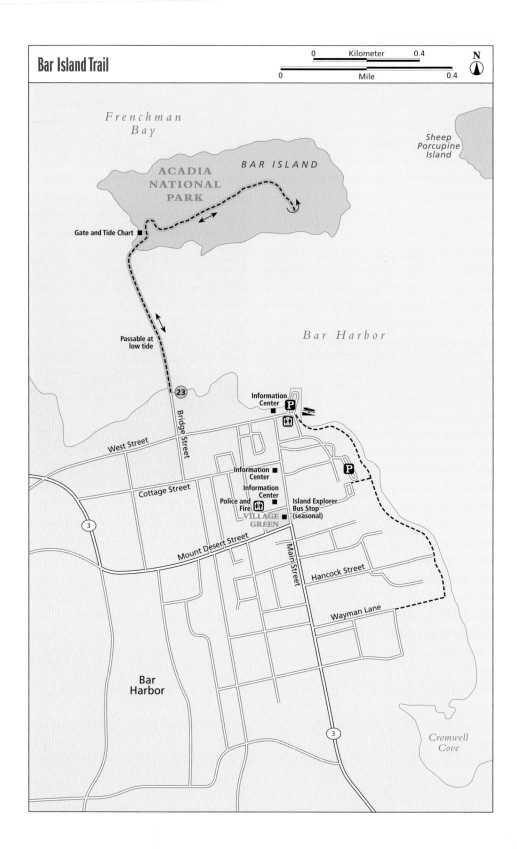

0   Kilometer   0.4

0   Mile   0.4

N

Frenchman Bay

Sheep Porcupine Island

ACADIA NATIONAL PARK

BAR ISLAND

Gate and Tide Chart ■

Bar Harbor

Passable at low tide

23

Information Center ℙ

West Street

Bridge Street

Information Center ■

Cottage Street

Information Center ■

Police and Fire ■

VILLAGE GREEN

Island Explorer Bus Stop (seasonal) ■

ℙ

Mount Desert Street

Main Street

Hancock Street

3

Wayman Lane

Bar Harbor

3

Cromwell Cove

1.0 Reach the island's summit, with views back toward Bar Harbor and the mountains. Retrace your steps.

2.0 Arrive back at the trailhead.

Coauthor Dolores Kong, on right, walks with her mother, April, across the bar at low tide to Bar Island. MICHELLE KONG

24 COMPASS HARBOR TRAIL

Situated just outside downtown Bar Harbor, this easy trail offers both important history—it's the former site of park pioneer George B. Dorr's Oldfarm estate—and, with its point right on Frenchman Bay, sweeping ocean and island views. The trail features some remnants of Dorr's family home, older growth trees, Dorr Point, and sights along the bay.

Start: Compass Harbor trailhead, off parking lot on east side of ME 3, just south of Nannau Wood, a private road
Elevation gain: 44 feet
Distance: 0.8 mile out and back
Difficulty: Easy
Hiking time: About 30 minutes
Seasons/schedule: Open year-round; best spring through fall, particularly off-peak times
Fees and permits: Acadia National Park pass required May through Oct
Trail contact: Acadia National Park, PO Box 177, Bar Harbor 04609, (207) 288-2338; nps.gov/acad
Dog-friendly: Leashed dogs permitted

Trail surface: Gravel road, forest floor, sandy trail at end
Land status: Acadia National Park
Nearest town: Bar Harbor
Maps: USGS Acadia National Park and Vicinity; Nat Geo Trails Illustrated Topographic Map: Acadia National Park
Other trail users: Trail runners, dog walkers, local residents
Special considerations: No facilities. An Oldfarm app, produced by the park and Northern Arizona University to educate visitors, is used with an Apple device in tandem with 11 numbered stations along the trail.

FINDING THE TRAILHEAD

From downtown Bar Harbor head south on ME 3 for 1 mile. A small parking lot is located on the left (east) just after Nannau Wood, a private road, and just before Old Farm Road, also private. The trail begins off the parking lot. If the parking lot is full, often the case during peak times, you can park at the town ballfields and walk south just over 0.5 mile along ME 3 to the trailhead. The Island Explorer bus does not have a stop here, although the Sand Beach line goes by; you may be able to ask the bus driver to let you off if it is safe to do so. **GPS:** N44 22.25' / W68 11.51'

WHAT TO SEE

At Compass Harbor you can see where the park's first superintendent, George B. Dorr, took his daily swim in the cold waters of Frenchman Bay or tended to the wide-ranging gardens that once surrounded Oldfarm, his sprawling estate here. The trail begins as a wide gravel road off the parking lot and soon comes to a sign pointing to Compass Harbor. The trail goes left and narrows as it approaches the ocean.

During a hike in 2018, Ranger Maureen Fournier, an authority on Compass Harbor, noted that the trail partly utilizes a roadbed from a formal driveway to the mansion, which she said was considered the first well-built estate in Bar Harbor. "Imagine going back in time one hundred years to see what this was like," said Fournier, now a former ranger who once conducted the park's interpretive program at Compass Harbor.

The Porcupine Islands glow in the setting sun as a cruise ship anchors outside Bar Harbor.

Head out on a sandy trail on a peninsula toward Dorr Point, but stop before an eroded section of the trail. Compass Harbor and Ogden Point are located to the left (north and northwest); Sols Cliff is to the right (southeast). Frenchman Bay is straight ahead. Near the point, look for some old granite blocks that were once part of Dorr's saltwater bathing pool that filled at high tide.

Just before reaching the point, an unofficial trail leads to the ruins of the Dorr manor house, which was built from 1880 to 1881 on land purchased by his father in 1868 and donated to the National Park Service by Dorr in 1942. We counted forty-three granite steps and came upon an aged foundation for the Oldfarm manor house and a brick patio. "It is widely believed this is granite from his own quarry," which was owned by the family and located at the southern end of the estate, Fournier said. "The steps all come from his quarry."

In 2016 the NPS completed a 145-page *Cultural Landscape Inventory and Assessment for Oldfarm*, which recommends management approaches for the 58 acres the park still owns from the original 100-acre estate at Compass Harbor and analyzes the historical significance of the property.

None of Dorr's formal gardens remain, but several plants and shrubs from the historic period can still be found at the manor site, Fournier said, including a large lilac and a prominent vine. An arborvitae hedge, which likely separated a tennis court from the cutting garden, has deteriorated, but about ten to twelve trees still exist, the NPS assessment said.

Acadia National Park Ranger Maureen Fournier leads a tour of park founder George B. Dorr's family homestead at Compass Harbor.

Dorr was adamant that his cherished Oldfarm become part of the park and even offered the property as a summer White House to President Calvin Coolidge in 1928 and then to the executive branch under President Franklin D. Roosevelt in 1940 to garner support. Roosevelt suggested it should be donated to the National Park Service, and the property finally became part of the park two years before Dorr died at Oldfarm. But in 1951, finding the estate too expensive to preserve and maintain, the NPS razed it, Fournier said.

"People are aghast when you tell them what happened with the house, but it was 1951, and the park service had no money," she explained. At that time in the nation's history, in the wake of the Great Depression and World War II, one can imagine that the federal government didn't have the funds to keep up Oldfarm, or many other facilities or programs.

The estate's 1879 Storm Beach Cottage, where Dorr often stayed, is still in good condition and used as park staff housing.

Today the National Park Service calls Dorr the father of the park and credits him for his indefatigable work in leading the effort to create Acadia. There's no better spot to ponder that than Compass Harbor.

Return the way you came.

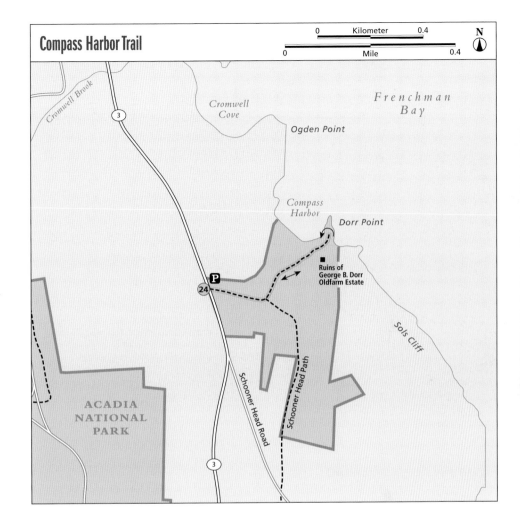

Compass Harbor Trail

Cromwell Brook

3

Cromwell Cove

Frenchman Bay

Ogden Point

Compass Harbor

Dorr Point

Ruins of George B. Dorr Oldfarm Estate

24

Schooner Head Road

Schooner Head Path

Sols Cliff

ACADIA NATIONAL PARK

3

0   Kilometer   0.4

0   Mile   0.4

N

MILES AND DIRECTIONS

0.0 Start at the Compass Harbor trailhead, which leaves from the parking lot on the left (east) side of ME 3, just south of Nannau Wood, a private road.

0.1 Turn left at the junction toward Compass Harbor.

0.4 Approach Dorr Point and the remains of George B. Dorr's Oldfarm estate. Return the way you came.

0.8 Arrive back at the trailhead.

25 SAND BEACH AND GREAT HEAD TRAIL

Enjoy Acadia's only ocean beach, made of sand, tiny shell fragments, quartz, and pink feldspar. Then take a hike along the Great Head Trail for its expansive views of the Beehive, Champlain Mountain, Otter Cliff, Egg Rock, and the Cranberry Isles. Also visible just off the tip of Great Head peninsula is an unusual rock formation called Old Soaker.

Start: Top of the stairs to Sand Beach
Elevation gain: 290 feet
Distance: 1.7-mile lollipop
Difficulty: Moderate
Hiking time: 1–1.5 hours
Seasons/schedule: Open year-round; best spring through fall, particularly early morning or late afternoon in summer to avoid the beach crowds
Fees and permits: Acadia National Park pass required May through Oct
Trail contact: Acadia National Park, PO Box 177, Bar Harbor 04609; (207) 288-2338; nps.gov/acad
Dog-friendly: Dogs prohibited on Sand Beach June 15 through the weekend after Labor Day; leashed dogs permitted other times of year

Trail surface: Sandy beach, rock ledges, forest floor
Land status: Acadia National Park
Nearest town: Bar Harbor
Maps: USGS Acadia National Park and Vicinity; Nat Geo Trails Illustrated Topographic Map: Acadia National Park
Other trail users: Sunbathers on Sand Beach in summertime
Special considerations: Year-round restrooms are available at the Sand Beach parking lot. Bring extra socks or a towel in case your feet get wet when you cross a small channel to get from the beach to the trailhead. A seasonal vehicle registration system is set to start no earlier than 2022. Go to recreation.gov.

FINDING THE TRAILHEAD

From the park's visitor center at Hulls Cove, drive south on the Park Loop Road for about 3 miles; turn left (east) at the sign for Sand Beach. Follow the one-way Park Loop Road for about 5.5 miles, past the park entrance station, to the beach parking lot on the left (east) side of the road. The Island Explorer's Loop Road and Sand Beach lines stop at the beach parking lot. Walk down the stairs at the eastern end of the parking lot and head east across Sand Beach to the Great Head trailhead. **GPS:** N44 19.45' / W68 11.01'

WHAT TO SEE

A hike on the Great Head peninsula is a perfect way to break up a lazy summer afternoon lounging on Sand Beach. Because it is so quintessentially Acadia, it's also a perfect place to bring first-time visitors, as we have with our nieces Sharon, Michelle, and Stacey.

A relatively modest scramble up the rocky slope of Great Head leads to dramatic views of the beach you just left behind, as well as vistas of such other notable park features as the Beehive, Champlain Mountain, and Otter Cliff.

Once, when we hiked Great Head with Sharon and Michelle, the views were made even more dramatic by the fog that first enveloped Sand Beach and the Beehive behind us and then receded like the outgoing tide. "I feel like I'm living in a postcard," said

Climb up Great Head for this view of Sand Beach.

Sharon, 15 at the time. "This is really fun," said Michelle, 12 at the time, as opposed to the "kind of fun" rating she gave to a hike with less-dramatic views the day before.

Since the 1840s and 1850s, Great Head has been a popular destination for artists as well as tourists. A stone teahouse known as Satterlee's Tower once stood on the summit; the ruins of it are still visible.

Once, as we stood by the ruins with Stacey, the ringing of a nearby buoy sounded almost like a clock tower, chiming that it's time for tea. It was one of Stacey's first hikes in Acadia, and she was struck by the contrast of sandy beach and rocky summit. "That's very rare," said Stacey.

From the parking lot, head down the stairs to the beach and walk 0.1 mile to the farthest (easternmost) end. Cross a channel—best at low tide to keep your feet dry—to the Great Head trailhead. Go up a series of granite steps bordered by a split-rail fence. At the top of the steps, at 0.2 mile, turn right (southeast) and follow the blue blazes up the rocky ledges. Views of Sand Beach, the Beehive, and Champlain Mountain are immediately visible.

At the next trail junction, at about 0.3 mile, bear right (south) to head toward the tip of the peninsula, with views of Old Soaker, a nearby outcropping that appears rectangular at low tide, and of Otter Cliff and the Cranberry Isles in the distance. At 0.6 mile the trail rounds the peninsula. At 0.9 mile it reaches the summit of Great Head, where there are views of Frenchman Bay and Egg Rock.

Fall colors and a pink sky are distinctive in autumn at Great Head.

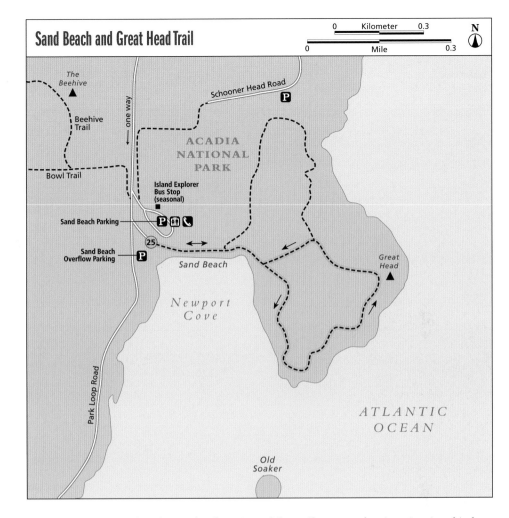

Sand Beach and Great Head Trail

At about 1.2 miles, along a level section of the trail, you reach a junction in a birch grove. Turn left (southwest) and ascend gradually up Great Head ridge, with views of Champlain Mountain, the Beehive, and Gorham Mountain. (**Option:** Go straight [northwest] at this junction to a parking lot near Schooner Head Road and then circle back, adding another 0.8 mile to the loop.)

At the last junction, at 1.4 miles, bear right (northwest) to return to the trailhead and Sand Beach. Head back to the parking lot for a hike of 1.7 miles.

MILES AND DIRECTIONS

- **0.0** Start at the top of the stairs to Sand Beach, and walk east along the beach.
- **0.1** Cross a small channel at the east end of the beach to reach the Great Head trailhead.
- **0.2** Bear right (southeast) at the top of the stairs.
- **0.3** At the junction with the spur trail inland, go right (south) along the shore.

An immature bald eagle lands with its prey on Sand Beach in December at Acadia National Park.

0.4 Reach the south end of the Great Head peninsula and follow the trail as it curves northeast along the shore.

0.9 Arrive on the Great Head summit, where the remnants of a stone teahouse can be found.

1.2 Bear left (southwest) at the junction in the birch grove with the spur trail to Great Head ridge.

1.4 Bear right (northwest) at the junction.

1.6 Arrive back at the Great Head trailhead. Walk west along the beach to the parking lot.

1.7 Arrive back at the parking lot, completing the loop.

26 OCEAN PATH

This easy hike takes you along Acadia's distinct pink granite coast-line, bringing you to Thunder Hole, where you may hear a reverber-ating boom as the surf crashes against a rocky chasm; Otter Cliff, where you may see rock climbers on the 60-foot precipice; and Otter Point, where you may catch a colorful sunset.

Start: Ocean Path trailhead to the right (east), just before stairs down to Sand Beach
Elevation gain: 303 feet
Distance: 4.4 miles out and back
Difficulty: Easy
Hiking time: 2–2.5 hours
Seasons/schedule: Open year-round; best spring through fall, particularly early morning or late afternoon in summer to avoid the crowds
Fees and permits: Acadia National Park pass required May through Oct
Trail contact: Acadia National Park, PO Box 177, Bar Harbor 04609; (207) 288-2338; nps.gov/acad
Dog-friendly: Leashed dogs permitted
Trail surface: Graded gravel path, forest floor, rock ledges, rock steps
Land status: Acadia National Park
Nearest town: Bar Harbor

Maps: USGS Acadia National Park and Vicinity; Nat Geo Trails Illustrated Topographic Map: Acadia National Park
Other trail users: Motorists and tour bus passengers stopping along the Park Loop Road to view Thunder Hole or Otter Point, rock climbers accessing Otter Cliff
Special considerations: Year-round restrooms available at Sand Beach and Fabbri parking lots; seasonal restroom at Thunder Hole parking area. A short part of Ocean Path—just before the first parking lot on the right, 0.3 mile south of Sand Beach—includes a viewing platform that's accessible for visitors with wheelchairs or baby strollers. A seasonal vehicle registration system is set to start no earlier than 2022. Go to recreation.gov.

FINDING THE TRAILHEAD

From the park's visitor center at Hulls Cove, drive south on the Park Loop Road for about 3 miles; turn left (east) at the sign for Sand Beach. Follow the one-way Park Loop Road for about 5.5 miles, past the park entrance station, to the beach parking lot on the left (east) side of the road. The trailhead is on the right (east) just before the stairs to the beach. The Island Explorer's Loop Road and Sand Beach lines stop at the beach parking lot. **GPS:** N44 19.45' / W68 11.01'

WHAT TO SEE

The sounds of the ocean and the views of rocky cliffs and pink granite shoreline are never far from Ocean Path. When the conditions are just right at Thunder Hole, halfway along the path, the surf crashes through a rocky chasm with a thunderous roar. At Otter Point, at trail's end, the sound of a ringing buoy fills the air. Rock climbers can be seen scaling Otter Cliff, one of the premier rock climbing areas in the eastern United States, while picnickers, birders, and sun worshippers can be found enjoying themselves on the flat pink granite slabs that dot the shore here.

First used as a buckboard road in the 1870s, Ocean Path and Ocean Drive were incor-porated into John D. Rockefeller Jr.'s vision of scenic roads, bringing visitors to many of Mount Desert Island's unique features. He began motor-road construction in the park in 1927 and hired landscape architect Frederick Law Olmsted Jr. to lay out many of the routes, including the Otter Cliff section of Ocean Drive. Ocean Path, first described in 1874, was substantially reconstructed by the Civilian Conservation Corps during the 1930s' Great Depression, with funding assistance from Rockefeller.

Because of its ease and accessibility, Ocean Path can be crowded during the height of the tourist season. The best time to walk it is either very early or very late on a summer's day, or in spring or fall. If you explore the shore along Ocean Path, park officials ask that you please stay on designated routes to and from the path.

Ocean Path, often worn from heavy use and storms, was substantially rehabilitated in 2015 and 2016. The work included about 0.5 mile of resurfacing, including 550 feet of paving with a porous compound that binds to gravel and is designed to prevent damage from rain runoff; forty-three new or redone steps; an access trail for the physically disabled from a small parking lot on the right, 0.3 mile south of Sand Beach and across from a rocky island known as Old Soaker (thus leading to the informal name, the Old Soaker lot); and a new viewing platform just north of the Old Soaker lot.

The Ocean Path trailhead is on the right just before the stairs to Sand Beach. Follow the gravel path past the changing rooms and restrooms, up a series of stairs, and then left (south), away from a secondary parking area. The easy trail takes you southwest along the shore, paralleling the Ocean Drive section of the Park Loop Road.

Thunder Hole, a popular destination, is at 1.0 mile. Many visitors driving through the park on calm summer days stop here and cause a traffic jam but go away disappointed. The best time to experience the power of Thunder Hole is after a storm and as high tide approaches, when the surf crashes violently through the chasm, pushing trapped air against the rock and creating a sound like the clap of thunder.

Even when you know the best time to hear Thunder Hole, it can still take a number of visits before you hit it right. On one trip to Acadia, we went with our nieces Sharon

The view along Ocean Path includes Gorham Mountain, the Beehive, Sand Beach, and Great Head.

Ranger Anne Warner leads a guided hike along Ocean Path to this view across Otter Cove to Cadillac and Dorr Mountains.

and Michelle to this spot three times, once late at night with stormy seas, but didn't hear the thundering boom as expected.

If you come to Thunder Hole during stormy conditions, be careful. Visitors have been swept out to sea here and at Schoodic Peninsula, a reminder of how powerful nature can be along Acadia's coast. Watch out for large waves, stay a safe distance away, and don't turn your back on the ocean.

At 1.3 miles on Ocean Path, you pass a short series of stairs on the right (west) that lead across the Park Loop Road to the Gorham Mountain trailhead. Monument Cove, with its startling granite structures, is near this trailhead.

This end of Ocean Path, with boulder after boulder of pink granite on the shoreline, may be the most beautiful. Anne Warner, a longtime seasonal park ranger at Acadia, recommends starting a hike on Ocean Path across from the Gorham Mountain parking lot and heading southwest to Otter Point if you have limited time and can only do part of the path.

During a tour, Warner talked about the beauty of the tide pools, the cliffs, and the ocean waves. She pointed out some subtler parts of the landscape found in a forest that often lines the path, including trees with big root structures growing on rocks, the fragrance of the balsams, the value of deadfall for soils, and strands of old man's beard, among more than 400 species of lichen in the park. "The whole trail is incredibly beautiful," Warner said. "I don't ever get tired of it."

The path's only noticeable elevation gain comes as it rises through the woods toward Otter Cliff, reached at 1.8 miles. On the approach, you can see rock climbers scaling the rock face or waiting at the top of the cliffs for their turn. A staircase leads down on the

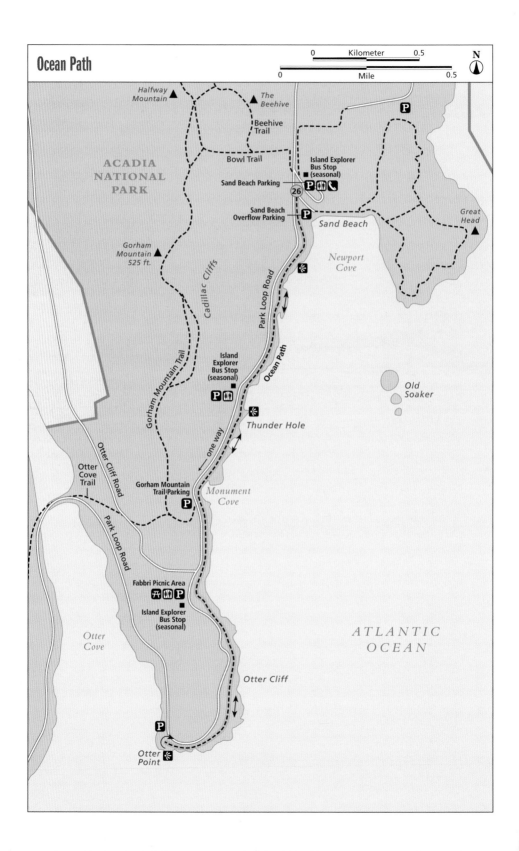

Ocean Path

Kilometer 0 0.5
Mile 0 0.5

N

Halfway Mountain ▲

The Beehive

Beehive Trail

ACADIA NATIONAL PARK

Bowl Trail

Island Explorer Bus Stop (seasonal)

Sand Beach Parking

Sand Beach Overflow Parking

Sand Beach

Great Head ▲

Gorham Mountain ▲ 525 ft.

Cadillac Cliffs

Newport Cove

Park Loop Road

Gorham Mountain Trail

Ocean Path

Island Explorer Bus Stop (seasonal)

Old Soaker

one way

Thunder Hole

Otter Cliff Road

Otter Cove Trail

Gorham Mountain Trail Parking

Monument Cove

Park Loop Road

Fabbri Picnic Area

Island Explorer Bus Stop (seasonal)

Otter Cove

ATLANTIC OCEAN

Otter Cliff

Otter Point

left (east) to the rock climbers' registration board.

Ocean Path ends at 2.2 miles, at Otter Point, where you can watch the sun set over Acadia and find a nearby commemorative plaque dedicated to Rockefeller. A new bronze plaque, financed by contributions to replace the 1960s original, was dedicated in 2016 during a ceremony attended by about twenty Rockefeller family members, including the youngest of Rockefeller's six children, banker David Rockefeller Sr., who died in 2017 at the age of 101.

Return the way you came.

MILES AND DIRECTIONS

0.0   Start at the Ocean Path trailhead, on the right just before the stairs to Sand Beach. Follow the gravel path up a series of stairs and then left (south), away from a secondary parking area.

1.0   Reach Thunder Hole (a viewing platform there may be closed during stormy seas).

1.3   Pass the Gorham Mountain trailhead, which is across the Park Loop Road.

1.8   Reach Otter Cliff, where you can see rock climbers scaling the precipice.

2.2   Arrive at Otter Point, where you can watch the sun set. Return the way you came.

4.4   Arrive back at the trailhead.

A light December snow dusts Monument Cove off Ocean Path in Acadia National Park.

27 GORHAM MOUNTAIN AND CADILLAC CLIFFS TRAILS

This is a classic Acadia hike to a 525-foot peak with sweeping views of Great Head, Sand Beach, Otter Cliff, Champlain Mountain, and the Beehive. The trail, among the most traveled in the park, is also one of the most historic, dating back to the early 1900s and the Great Depression. The hike includes a spur trail to Cadillac Cliffs and an ancient sea cave.

Start: Gorham Mountain trailhead at the Gorham Mountain parking lot on right (west) side of one-way Park Loop Road, south of Thunder Hole
Elevation gain: 445 feet
Distance: 1.8-mile circuit loop
Difficulty: Moderate
Hiking time: 1–1.5 hours
Seasons/schedule: Open year-round; best spring through fall, particularly early morning or late afternoon in summer to avoid the crowds
Fees and permits: Acadia National Park pass required May through Oct
Trail contact: Acadia National Park, PO Box 177, Bar Harbor 04609; (207) 288-2338; nps.gov/acad
Dog-friendly: Leashed dogs permitted (but not on the Cadillac Cliffs Trail, which features a couple of iron rungs)
Trail surface: Forest floor, rock ledges, rock steps
Land status: Acadia National Park
Nearest town: Bar Harbor
Maps: USGS Acadia National Park and Vicinity; Nat Geo Trails Illustrated Topographic Map: Acadia National Park
Other trail users: Campers at Blackwoods Campground hiking up Gorham via Otter Cove Trail
Special considerations: No facilities at trailhead; restrooms at Thunder Hole (seasonal) and Fabbri (year-round) parking areas. A seasonal vehicle registration system is set to start no earlier than 2022. Go to recreation.gov.

FINDING THE TRAILHEAD

From the park's visitor center at Hulls Cove, drive south on the Park Loop Road for about 3 miles; turn left (east) at the sign for Sand Beach. Follow the one-way Park Loop Road for about 7 miles, passing the park entrance station, Sand Beach, and Thunder Hole, to the Gorham Mountain sign and parking lot on the right (west) side of the road. The Island Explorer bus does not have a stop here, although the Sand Beach and Park Loop lines go by; you may be able to ask the bus driver to let you off if it is safe to do so. **GPS:** N44 19.00' / W68 11.28'

WHAT TO SEE

Charlie Jacobi, a retired ranger at Acadia National Park, estimates that he's hiked the Gorham Mountain Trail maybe 300 times over the years, mostly as part of the job. But he says it never gets old. "Every day is different," said Jacobi during a recent hike on a sunny afternoon to the peak of Gorham, noted for some of the most rewarding views in Acadia. The trail is among the most popular in the park, and it's easy to see why. "This whole ridge—Gorham, Champlain, and the Beehive—is close to the ocean," says Jacobi, who retired in 2017 after working thirty-three years at the park. "You're right on top of it— almost. That's what makes it attractive."

Gorham Mountain provides views of Baker Island, the Cranberry Isles, and the Park Loop Road.

The trail, marked by historic-style cairns that Jacobi helped reintroduce to the park, follows the great ridge that runs all the way to Champlain Mountain and is the closest to the ocean of all of Acadia's mountain ridges. An additional bonus, if you choose to take it, is the 0.5-mile spur trail to the once-submerged Cadillac Cliffs and an ancient sea cave, illustrating the powerful geologic forces that helped shape Mount Desert Island.

From the parking lot, bypass the Otter Cove Trail that connects to Blackwoods Campground and comes in on the left (southwest) near the trailhead. Bear right on the Gorham Mountain Trail to climb gradually through an evergreen forest and up open ledges, heading north. Though the trail is often shaded by conifers in this section, the sounds of the ocean surf signal that the shore is nearby.

At 0.2 mile the Cadillac Cliffs Trail leads right (northeast), paralleling and then rejoining the Gorham Mountain Trail at 0.5 mile. Don't miss a bronze memorial at this intersection honoring Waldron Bates, chair of the Roads and Paths Committee of the Bar Harbor Village Improvement Association from 1900 to 1909, who developed the century-old style of cairn now used to mark many Acadia trails. Bates also laid out the Cadillac Cliffs Trail, first noted in 1906.

The Cadillac Cliffs Trail, built in the early 1900s and eligible for the National Register of Historic Places, got a major facelift in 2015 to repair erosion and collapsing stone stairs and retaining walls. The trail work was part of the larger Acadia Trails Forever program, a joint effort with the nonprofit Friends of Acadia to maintain the trails.

Bear right onto the spur to include the Cadillac Cliffs on the way up—it is best to do it on the ascent rather than the descent because of the iron rungs and steep rock face along the way. Start ascending along difficult granite rock and soon come alongside some high cliffs. You'll go under two rock slabs perched against each other. The towering cliffs and prehistoric sea cave soon loom on the left.

Before reaching a boardwalk, peer into the sea cave and look to the left to see a couple of big beach cobblestones wedged inside by the surf many millions of years ago. Cross the short wooden boardwalk to get off the ledge. Look back to see the cliffs at their

The rock face on Gorham Mountain provides good terrain for hikers.

most impressive. The layers of smooth pink granite look like giant blocks stacked neatly atop one another.

The sea now washes against the shore hundreds of feet below the pink Cadillac Cliffs, but the waves once crashed along here. As the glacier that covered the area melted, the sea level rose and the earth's crust rebounded as it was freed from the weight of the ice.

The spur next brings you up a series of iron rungs and mostly stone stairs to rejoin the Gorham Mountain Trail at 0.5 mile. Bear right (northwest) on the ridge trail and ascend moderately as a near-barren island called Old Soaker comes into sight through the trees. All along this portion of the route you will enjoy views south to Otter Cliff, northeast to Great Head and Sand Beach, and north to the Beehive and Champlain Mountain. Frenchman Bay and Egg Rock can be seen in the distance to the east.

We stopped when we spotted a Bates-style cairn in need of repair.

In 2002 Jacobi and Gary Stellpflug, fore-man of the Acadia trails crew, revived the use of the Bates–style cairns, which consist of two to four base stones with a lintel laid across them, capped by a pointer stone. The Gorham Mountain Trail is home to fifty-one such cairns and is part of a research study Jacobi led to test the effectiveness of signs in discouraging people from stacking stone, dismantling, or otherwise damaging the cairns. As one sign near a cairn cautioned, adding or removing rocks misleads hikers, causes erosion or kills plants, and degrades the mountain landscape.

We reached the peak of Gorham Mountain at 0.9 mile. At the 525-foot summit, looking northeast, Jacobi pointed out the back side of the Beehive. To the north, a small hill called Halfway Mountain is situated below Champlain Mountain and Huguenot Head; to the west are Dorr and Cadillac Mountains. On the mainland in the distance is Schoodic Mountain with its radio tower, and then the Schoodic Peninsula to the east. The Cranberry Islands, including Baker Island and its 1855 light tower, are to the south.

Return the way you came.

On the trek down, listen for the sounds of a bell buoy located near an ocean ledge. On a day when the sky is blue and the sun bright, the ocean can appear almost tropical.

"Oh, my God," said Jacobi. "This is spectacular."

No matter how many times you hike the Gorham Mountain Trail, it is always rewarding.

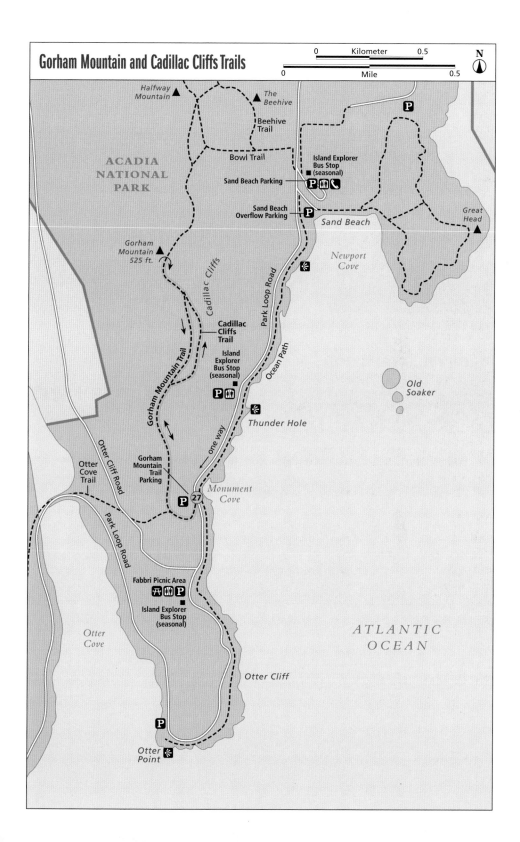

Gorham Mountain and Cadillac Cliffs Trails

Kilometer
0   0.5

Mile
0   0.5

N

Halfway
Mountain ▲

The
Beehive ▲

Beehive
Trail

P

ACADIA
NATIONAL
PARK

Bowl Trail

Island Explorer
Bus Stop
■ (seasonal)

Sand Beach Parking

P 🚻 📞

Sand Beach
Overflow Parking

P

Sand Beach

Great
Head ▲

Gorham
Mountain ▲
525 ft.

Newport
Cove

Park Loop Road

Cadillac Cliffs

Cadillac
Cliffs
Trail

Ocean Path

Old
Soaker

Gorham Mountain Trail

Island
Explorer
Bus Stop
(seasonal)

P 🚻

Thunder Hole

Otter
Cove
Trail

Gorham
Mountain
Trail
Parking

one way

Monument
Cove

P 27

Otter Cliff Road

Park Loop Road

Fabbri Picnic Area

⛬ 🚻 P
■

Island Explorer
Bus Stop
(seasonal)

Otter
Cove

ATLANTIC
OCEAN

Otter Cliff

P

Otter
Point ⚓

The hike to Gorham Mountain features views of Sand Beach, Great Head, and, far in the background, the Schoodic Peninsula.

MILES AND DIRECTIONS

0.0 Start at the Gorham Mountain trailhead, at a parking lot on the right (west) side of the one-way Park Loop Road. Coming in on the left just after the trailhead is the Otter Cove Trail that links to Blackwoods Campground. Bear right at the junction to continue on the Gorham Mountain Trail.

0.2 Reach the junction with the southern end of the Cadillac Cliffs Trail. Bear right (northeast) to take the spur to the ancient sea cave. (**Option:** Stay straight to continue on the Gorham Mountain Trail.)

0.5 Reach the junction of the northern end of the Cadillac Cliffs and Gorham Mountain Trails. Bear right to continue northwest to the Gorham Mountain summit.

0.9 Arrive at the Gorham Mountain summit. Return to the trailhead, bypassing the Cadillac Cliffs Trail and staying straight on the Gorham Mountain Trail.

1.8 Arrive back at the trailhead.

28 CADILLAC SUMMIT LOOP TRAIL

Located at the top of Acadia's highest mountain, this short and easy trail offers perhaps the best views in the park and wayside exhibits that identify more than forty islands, peaks, and other key points that lie off its slopes. On a sunny day this loop is the best place for any hiker to get some bearings before exploring the rest of Acadia. The trail is often busy during peak summer months, since cars and buses can drive up the mountain's access road.

Start: Cadillac Summit Loop paved walkway access on the eastern edge of the summit parking lot, past the gift shop
Elevation gain: 61 feet
Distance: 0.5-mile loop
Difficulty: Easy
Hiking time: About 30 minutes
Seasons/schedule: Cadillac Mountain Road open Apr 15 through Nov 30 (summit loop can be accessed year-round via hiking trails); best spring through fall, particularly early morning or late afternoon in summer, to avoid the crowds that can gather for sunrise, sunset, and even the middle of the day
Fees and permits: Acadia National Park pass required May through Oct
Trail contact: Acadia National Park, PO Box 177, Bar Harbor 04609; (207) 288-2338; nps.gov/acad

Dog-friendly: Leashed dogs permitted
Trail surface: Paved walkway
Land status: Acadia National Park
Nearest town: Bar Harbor
Maps: USGS Acadia National Park and Vicinity; Nat Geo Trails Illustrated Topographic Map: Acadia National Park
Other trail users: Hikers coming from Gorge Path or Cadillac North Ridge and Cadillac South Ridge Trails, visitors with wheelchairs or baby strollers, birders
Special considerations: The walkway is partially accessible for visitors with wheelchairs or baby strollers. Seasonal summit gift shop and restrooms. The paved auto road to the summit is winding and narrow. A seasonal vehicle registration system is set to start in 2021. Go to recreation.gov.

FINDING THE TRAILHEAD

From the park's visitor center at Hulls Cove, drive south on the Park Loop Road for about 3.5 miles; turn left (east) at the sign for Cadillac Mountain. Ascend the winding summit road to the top. The paved walkway begins off the eastern edge of the parking lot, past the gift shop. The Island Explorer bus does not go up Cadillac, but the Loop Road line has a Cadillac North Ridge stop, where the 2.2-mile moderately difficult Cadillac North Ridge Trail takes you to the top and a connection with the Cadillac Summit Loop Trail. **GPS:** N44 21.09' / W68 13.28'

WHAT TO SEE

You gain a new appreciation for 1,530-foot-high Cadillac Mountain on this trail, with wayside exhibits describing the history and features of Mount Desert Island and the panoramic views from the highest point on the East Coast of the United States. The 0.5-mile summit loop trail on the peak includes two viewing platforms and excellent vistas of the Porcupine and Cranberry Islands, Frenchman Bay, Great Head, the Beehive, Otter Point, and Dorr and other mountains.

Fall colors spread all the way to the sea from the summit of Cadillac Mountain.

Near the start of the trail off the parking lot, a bronze memorial plaque, installed in 1933, commemorates Stephen Tyng Mather, a wealthy entrepreneur, leading advocate for the creation of the National Park Service in 1916, and its first director. Newly designed wayside exhibits, erected in 2015 along the trail and the edge of the parking lot, describe significant aspects of the area, including the geological essence of Acadia—the pink granite with its three main minerals; the night sky over Acadia; and the visionaries who helped found the park a century ago, from George B. Dorr to Charles Eliot and John D. Rockefeller Jr.

A top feature of this hike is a circular platform with two exhibits that pinpoint about forty highlights of the sweeping views, allowing anyone to find spots such as Turtle Island, Egg Rock, Schoodic Point, Porcupine Islands, Seawall Campground, Baker Island, Little Cranberry Island, and the Gulf of Maine.

Aside from getting an appreciation of the islands and other sites from the top of Cadillac, you may also hear song sparrows during spring or see bald eagles and turkey vultures soaring above Cadillac, especially during the annual HawkWatch from late August through mid-October, when migrating raptors such as kestrels, peregrine falcons, and sharp-shinned hawks can be spotted.

You may also see three-toothed cinquefoil, lowbush blueberries, a tiny white flower known as mountain sandwort, and the pink blooms of rhodora. Even a couple of small birch trees can be found along the walkway, proof of the success of restoration efforts over the past decade or so. Wooden barricades and signs reminding hikers to stay on the trail and solid rock are part of the continued revegetation program in the wake of

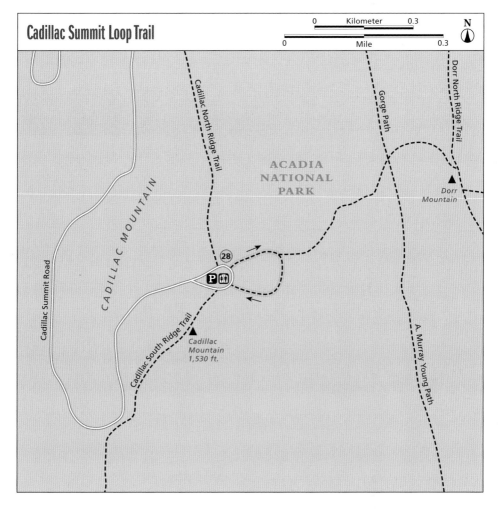

Cadillac Summit Loop Trail

uncontrolled trampling in the past that caused erosion and changed the appearance of the area.

Don't look for a summit marker off the loop trail. The peak of Cadillac, as marked by the US Geological Survey, is actually off the Cadillac South Ridge Trail, near an antenna behind the gift shop. According to Maine's Ice Age Trail map, the summit of Cadillac may have been the first surface of modern Maine to have emerged from the last glaciers, about 17,000 years ago.

There are two access points to the paved summit loop trail off the eastern edge of the parking area. The access point on the left (northeast), near the handicapped parking spots, is also the start of a 2005 paved path that can be used by physically disabled persons and people with baby strollers to reach the main viewing platform without climbing stairs.

The trail, started by the park service in 1932 and completed the following year by the Civilian Conservation Corps—the Depression-era public work relief program—is tinged to match the pink Cadillac granite and features several sets of granite boulders for

A snowy owl settles on a spruce tree on Cadillac Mountain in December in Acadia National Park.

steps. Even though the trail is easy, watch your footing; people have been injured along the walkway, which can be uneven in spots.

The road to the summit, completed in 1932 by the park service, was among the first motor roads built in the park. Before the road was built, an entrepreneur constructed a cog railway in 1883 to the peak from Eagle Lake, but it was dismantled ten years later because people generally preferred to escape the industrial age by hiking or taking a horse-drawn buckboard to the peak.

Because of its grand vistas and easy access, the trail can get very crowded in summer. Early and late in the day are best. But there can be small crowds even before dawn to catch the sunrise, which can be magnificent on Cadillac, the first place in the United States where the sun's rays hit between October 7 and March 6, generally. There can also be a motor brigade heading up for the sunset, as we have found on many days as dusk approached.

MILES AND DIRECTIONS

0.0 Start at the Cadillac Summit Loop trailhead, with two access points located at the eastern edge of the parking lot, past the gift shop. The left (northeastern) trail entrance connects to a ramp that allows wheelchair and baby stroller access to a circular viewing area.

0.5 Arrive back at the trailhead to complete the loop.

PLANTS OF COASTAL MAINE ARE A SMORGASBORD OF DELIGHT

It's not only the ocean views, big sandy beaches, seaside cliffs, and birds that make coastal Maine so beautiful. It's also the wildflowers, trees, shrubs, and other plants. In late May through September, the coastal hikes are brimming with colorful flowers and plants that stimulate the senses.

Look for the purple and pink rhodora that thrive in wetlands in Maine in May; the ground-hugging, greenish white flowers of the bunchberry that fill the sides of trails in late spring and early summer; the bright pink sheep laurel; the blue flag iris that burst on the shores in July; the wild blueberries to pick in August; the asters of September; the apples of fall, and trees like jack pine and pitch pine.

Few people know the plants better than Jill E. Weber, a botanist who consults for Acadia National Park and is helping research how best to restore and protect plants atop Cadillac Mountain. She waxes poetic about some of her favorite plants that can be found along coastal Maine and beyond.

Apple blossom: "Is there a square mile of Maine where one can't find an apple tree?" Weber asks. "Europeans brought apples to North America, and a few centuries later they are completely at home throughout Maine. Seeing them on the landscape makes one imagine that plant's origin: Was this place a family farm? Was it a hard life? Was this place cherished by a family for generations? Or, was this tree planted by a bird or squirrel that had feasted on the fruit? Some folks find these trees and try to identify the

An apple blossom accentuates the beauty of the Giant's Stairs.

heritage variety and propagate it to keep the species alive. And of course some of us gravitate to these flowering trees to become intoxicated by the heady scent of those ephemeral flowers!"

Bunchberry: "Bunchberries are much loved in Maine. They are iconic members of the flora, both when in flower and in fruit. They are close relatives of flowering dogwood, a small tree found in the mid-Atlantic states. When we see what seem to be individual flowers, we are actually looking at many small flowers, surrounded by those obvious petal-like bracts. These bracts are really signals to pollinators to come on in and get a snack. If pollinated, each one of those tiny flowers will mature into what we know in the late summer as one of the red berries that make up the 'bunch' of berries."

Rhodora: "What a striking shrub! Rhodora presents us with magenta flowers before it and other shrubs leaf out. Mainers watch for the appearance of the flowers as a signal that winter has really passed and spring has started."

Sheep laurel: "Ubiquitous in Maine, from shore, to bogs, to fields, and mountaintops, sheep laurel is usually ignored. Look more closely and marvel at the pollination story of this plant. The tops of its pollen-bearing structures—the anthers—are imbedded in the flower petal, and the filaments—the stems that hold the anthers—are attached to the base of the flower. As the pollen ripens and the flower tissues begin to dry and shrink, the anthers are held under tension. If a pollinator lands on the flower, the anthers are released like catapults and batter the unsuspecting insect with pollen. The dazed critter then goes to the next flower and, as it wanders, spreads the pollen where needed."

Blue flag: "Blue flowers are the most unusual in nature. Think about it: We can all name many white, pink, or yellow flowers, but the list of blue ones is shorter. So although blue flag irises are fairly common in early summer along Maine's shores and wet meadows, be sure to notice them. It you are close enough you can check out their unusual form—not the typical petal arrangement."

Jack pine: "Jack pine is a northern species that reaches its southern limit in Maine. Thus it produces a habitat that is somewhat rare here. Look at the branches: You'll likely see many cones attached all the way to the base of the branch. Why? Jack pines depend on fire to release their cones and seeds, and fire is infrequent here. Some still manage to release seed, and jack pines persist in Maine."

Pitch pine: "Pitch pine is a southern species that reaches its northern limit in Maine. Farther south, it takes a treelike form, but here in Maine it often looks like a venerable old bonsai, rendering our wild landscapes like fabulous gardens. Like jack pine, pitch pine depends on fire for release of its seeds. Pitch pine in Maine tends to grow on or next to granite, and research on Maine populations shows that when the granite absorbs the sun, it can generate heat that is sufficient for pitch pines in Maine to release their seeds so that new trees can grow."

A potent pitch pine on Great Head is full of cones set to release pollen to start a three-year process for making mature seeds.

Birch: "A birch is a birch, right? Not in Maine, where we have paper birch, gray birch, yellow birch, mountain paper birch, and even foot-tall dwarf and bog birches. One birch or another grows in almost every habitat. They're harvested to make toothpicks, furniture, and canoes, and wildlife species browse on their tender twigs. What's not to love?"

This hike takes you up the lowest of twenty-six peaks in Acadia, yet it features one of the best panoramas, overlooking Somes Sound, Fernald Cove, and the Cranberry Isles. There are views of Acadia and Norumbega Mountain, as well as excellent access to a large beach under the cliffs at Valley Cove, where you might even see peregrine falcons in flight.

Start: Flying Mountain trailhead, at small parking area off Fernald Point Road, past the St. Sauveur Mountain parking lot south of Somesville on ME 102
Elevation gain: 311 feet
Distance: 1.4-mile loop
Difficulty: Moderate
Hiking time: About 1 hour
Seasons/schedule: Open year-round; best spring through fall, particularly early morning or late afternoon in summer to avoid the crowds
Fees and permits: Acadia National Park pass required May through Oct
Trail contact: Acadia National Park, PO Box 177, Bar Harbor 04609; (207) 288-2338; nps.gov/acad

Dog-friendly: Leashed dogs permitted but not recommended because of some steep sections
Trail surface: Forest floor, rock ledges, gravel road
Land status: Acadia National Park
Nearest town: Southwest Harbor
Maps: USGS Acadia National Park and Vicinity; Nat Geo Trails Illustrated Topographic Map: Acadia National Park
Other trail users: Boaters and kayakers coming ashore in Valley Cove for day hikes, birders
Special considerations: No facilities; park recommends this as an option for young hikers

FINDING THE TRAILHEAD

From Somesville head south on ME 102 for about 4.5 miles, past the St. Sauveur Mountain parking lot. Turn left (east) onto Fernald Point Road and travel about 1 mile to the small parking area at the foot of the gravel Valley Cove Trail, an old fire road. The trailhead is on the right (east) side of the parking area. The Island Explorer bus does not stop here. **GPS:** N44 17.57' / W68 18.55'

WHAT TO SEE

It's easy to see how Flying Mountain got its name from the way the trail ascends swiftly to a bird's-eye view. In just 0.3 mile from the parking area, you reach the 284-foot summit and its dramatic vistas.

The trail, first described in the late 1800s, climbs through deep woods and then up rocky ledges. While in the shade of the woods, hikers should be pleased that the park service improved this old and well-trodden trail several years ago by adding log cribbing, or interlocked logs, to support the steep climb. We counted ninety-three newer log steps right at the start of the ascent. The work helps prevent erosion and makes it an easier climb for children and others. Soon granite ledges serve as stone steps, sometimes interspersed with cribbing.

Once above tree line and at the top of the rock face, you get views to the southeast of Greening Island and the Cranberry Isles. To the northwest are the rocky cliffs of Valley Peak. Dominating the view from the summit is the grassy peninsula known as Fernald

A powerboat leaves a wake in Somes Sound below Flying Mountain.

Point. Across the Narrows at the mouth of Somes Sound is the town of Northeast Harbor. From here you can look down on kayakers rounding Fernald Point or boaters entering and leaving Somes Sound. You may even hear a ferry blow its whistle in Northeast Harbor, as we did on one of our climbs here.

Some hikers turn around here, content with the views on Flying Mountain. But those who go on are rewarded with scenes of Somes Sound; Valley Cove; and Norumbega, Acadia, Penobscot, and Sargent Mountains. Some may even be fortunate enough to see or hear peregrine falcons, which have returned to nesting in the cliffs above Valley Cove, one of Acadia's top conservation accomplishments.

"It's a feel-good story," said Bruce Connery, retired wildlife biologist at Acadia. "It is positive, positive, positive."

Peregrine falcons nearly became extinct in the 1960s, but Rachel Carson's book *Silent Spring* alarmed the public and helped push the federal government to ban the pesticide DDT, which can dangerously thin eggshells, and pass the Endangered Species Act, in 1972. The park reintroduced peregrine falcons, and the first successful nesting in thirty-five years occurred in 1991. Since then, more than 140 peregrine falcon chicks have fledged in the park, mainly at Valley Cove, Jordan Cliffs, and the precipice on the east face of Champlain Mountain. Acadia still runs an active banding program for the chicks.

The Flying Mountain Trail is noted for its birds, including falcons, ospreys, and songbirds. On a recent hike, we took photos of a black-throated green warbler in the woods just off the peak and spotted a falcon soaring high above.

Just beyond the summit of Flying Mountain, at 0.4 mile, you get the first glimpse of the northern reaches of Somes Sound, as well as of Acadia Mountain to the north and Norumbega Mountain on the other side of the sound to the northeast. The ridge of Sargent and Penobscot Mountains is just beyond that of Norumbega. There's a spur to an overlook to the right (east) before the trail begins its steep descent toward Valley Cove.

When the trail reaches the shore of the cove, go left (west). A new wooden bridge with a railing crosses a stream, and separate hard-surface steps on each end converge at

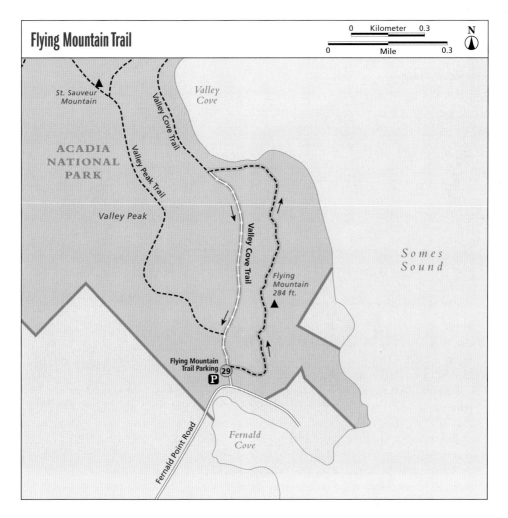

0   Kilometer   0.3

0   Mile   0.3

N

St. Sauveur
Mountain

*Valley
Cove*

Valley Cove Trail

ACADIA
NATIONAL
PARK

Valley Peak Trail

Valley Peak

Valley Cove Trail

*S o m e s
S o u n d*

Flying
Mountain
284 ft.

Flying Mountain
Trail Parking (29)

P

Fernald Point Road

*Fernald
Cove*

a short, wide stairway that provides excellent access down to the rocky cove and pebble beach. There's lots of room, especially at low tide, and great views of steep, dark cliffs rising above the sound and of herring gulls soaring nearby.

The beach access was part of a rehabilitation in 2016 after the trail was damaged during the winter. In addition to two new wooden bridges, the work included more than 425 feet of new tread surface on the Flying Mountain Trail and new stone and log retaining walls.

At about 0.9 mile you reach the junction with the gravel Valley Cove Trail, an old fire road. Turn left (south) onto the old fire road and loop back to the parking area at 1.4 miles. Hardy hikers can stay straight along the rocky shores of Valley Cove and add a more challenging 1.0-mile section of the Valley Cove Trail that heads north, if it's not closed for peregrine falcon nesting season. A major upgrade of the Valley Cove Trail was completed in 2019.

Left: Birders look for peregrine falcons above Valley Cove during the Acadia Birding Festival.
Right: Steps provide Valley Cove beach access off the Flying Mountain Trail.

MILES AND DIRECTIONS

0.0 Start at the Flying Mountain trailhead, on the east side of the parking area at the foot of the gravel Valley Cove Trail (an old fire road).

0.3 Reach the summit of Flying Mountain.

0.9 Turn left at the junction with Valley Cove Trail to loop back to the parking area.

1.4 Arrive back at the trailhead.

30 WONDERLAND

This easy trail along an old road brings you to pink granite outcrops along the shore and tide pools at low tide. You will see skunk cabbage, pitch pine, and wild sarsaparilla along the way, and ponder why broken mussel shells are found inland along the trail rather than on the coastline.

Start: Wonderland trailhead on ME 102A, about 1 mile southwest of Seawall Campground and picnic area
Elevation gain: 77 feet
Distance: 1.4 miles out and back
Difficulty: Easy
Hiking time: About 1 hour
Seasons/schedule: Open year-round; best spring through fall, particularly early morning or late afternoon in summer to avoid the crowds; low tide for tide pool exploration
Fees and permits: Acadia National Park pass required May through Oct
Trail contact: Acadia National Park, PO Box 177, Bar Harbor 04609; (207) 288-2338; nps.gov/acad

Dog-friendly: Leashed dogs permitted
Trail surface: Graded gravel road, rocky shore
Land status: Acadia National Park
Nearest town: Southwest Harbor
Maps: USGS Acadia National Park and Vicinity; Nat Geo Trails Illustrated Topographic Map: Acadia National Park
Other trail users: Birders
Special considerations: Wheelchair accessible with assistance. Closest facilities at Seawall picnic area or Ship Harbor Trail. Park recommends this as a family-friendly trail.

FINDING THE TRAILHEAD

From Southwest Harbor head south about 1 mile on ME 102. Bear left (southeast) on ME 102A, passing the town of Manset in about 1 mile and Seawall Campground and picnic area in about 3 miles, reaching the Wonderland trailhead in about 4 miles. Parking is on the left (southeast) side of the road. The trail heads southeast along an abandoned gravel road toward the shore. The Island Explorer's Southwest Harbor line stops at Seawall Campground, a mile away, and passes Wonderland on the way to Bass Harbor Campground. If asked, the bus driver may let you off at the Wonderland parking area if it is safe to do so. **GPS:** N44 14.01' / W68 19.12'

WHAT TO SEE

Walk through the diverse forest, see the smooth pink granite along the shore, see the birds, smell the salty sea, and explore the tide pools and you will know why they call this Wonderland.

The easy trail along an old gravel road starts by winding through dark woods, including tall and feathery tamarack, a deciduous conifer that loses its needles in the fall, and then by wild sarsaparilla, which is thick in the ground cover, and cinnamon fern. At about 0.1 mile go up a slight hill and make your way carefully among some roots and rocks. This is the toughest part of an otherwise gentle, well-graded trail.

During a "Birds and Botany of Wonderland" tour, Susan Hayward, a founder of the Maine Master Naturalist Program, pointed out flowers such as beach pea and black chokeberry, and woody plants like alder, shadbush, and a large mat of broom crowberry.

From the Wonderland Trail you can look over Bennet Cove back toward the east side of Mount Desert Island.

She stopped next to some tall pitch pine, which is uncommon farther north of Acadia and has more needles per cluster and larger cones than jack pine, fairly common south and west of Acadia. "Pitch pine is rare in this part of the woods," Hayward said. "It has a bundle of three needles per cluster," while jack pine has two.

Through the trees you begin to see the ocean on the right (southeast). At 0.7 mile the trail brings you to the shore, where pink granite dramatically meets the sea. Tectonic plates collided here hundreds of millions of years ago, creating tremendous pressure and heat, and the pink granite is a result of the cooled-off magma, according to a Maine Natural Heritage Hikes brochure for the Wonderland Trail. You can spend hours exploring here, especially when low tide exposes a bar to Long Ledge and tide pools with their diverse marine life, from rockweed to barnacles to green crabs. Be careful of wet rocks, slick seaweed, and sudden waves.

Attending the annual Acadia Birding Festival, we were amazed to look through a scope and watch a flock of about three dozen black scoters diving headfirst into the ocean for food and then fluttering their wings upon emerging. We also spotted an adult bald eagle, with its trademark white head and tail; a red-breasted nuthatch hopping on limbs; and songbirds such as a black-throated green warbler and a yellow-rumped warbler.

You can also take forever and a day to explore inland along the trail, as our nieces Sharon and Michelle did when we hiked this together, wondering about cracked-up seashells and seaweed found far from shore. We theorized that gulls must have dropped the

Above: A black-throated green warbler is a favorite sighting of birders at Acadia National Park.
Below: A black-masked cedar waxwing rests on a limb at Acadia National Park.

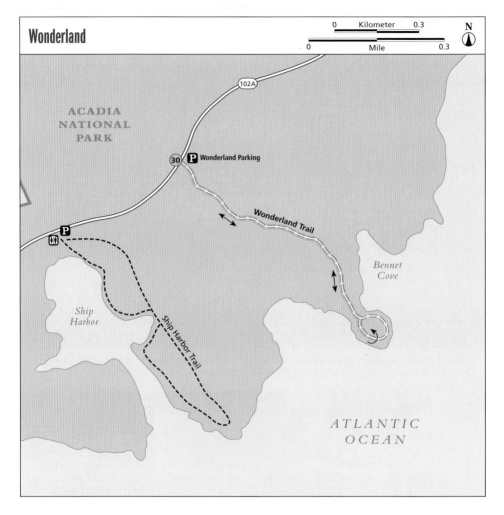

Wonderland

0 — Kilometer — 0.3

0 — Mile — 0.3

N

ACADIA
NATIONAL
PARK

102A

30 **P** Wonderland Parking

P

Wonderland Trail

Bennet
Cove

Ship
Harbor

Ship Harbor Trail

ATLANTIC
OCEAN

mussel shells from the air to open them for food. That was proven later in the trip when we hiked the Bar Island Trail at low tide and witnessed that same gull-feeding activity. There are many things to wonder about along Wonderland.

Return the way you came.

MILES AND DIRECTIONS

0.0   Start at the Wonderland trailhead, on the southeast side of ME 102A, at the edge of the parking area.

0.1   The trail heads slightly uphill.

0.7   Reach the shoreline. Return the way you came. (**Option:** Add on a loop to explore the rocky outcroppings.)

1.4   Arrive back at the trailhead.

31 SHIP HARBOR TRAIL

With a maritime mystery in its past, a huge undeveloped harbor, and sprawling pink granite, the Ship Harbor Trail epitomizes a lot about hiking the coast of Acadia National Park. President Barack Obama chose the trail as one of only a few he hiked with his wife and daughters during a visit in July 2010.

Start: Ship Harbor trailhead on ME 102A, about 1.2 miles southwest of Seawall Campground and picnic area
Elevation gain: 20 feet
Distance: 1.3-mile figure-eight loop
Difficulty: Easy
Hiking time: About 1 hour
Seasons/schedule: Open year-round; best spring through fall, particularly early morning or late afternoon in summer to avoid the crowds; low tide for tide pool exploration
Fees and permits: Acadia National Park pass required May through October
Trail contact: Acadia National Park, PO Box 177, Bar Harbor 04609; (207) 288-2338; nps.gov/acad

Dog-friendly: Leashed dogs permitted
Trail surface: Graded gravel path, forest floor, rocky shore
Land status: Acadia National Park
Nearest town: Southwest Harbor
Maps: USGS Acadia National Park and Vicinity; Nat Geo Trails Illustrated Topographic Map: Acadia National Park
Other trail users: Visitors with wheelchairs or baby strollers, birders
Special considerations: The first 0.25 mile of the trail is on a hard-packed surface, making it accessible to visitors with wheelchairs or baby strollers. There is a chemical toilet at the trailhead. Park recommends this as a family-friendly trail.

FINDING THE TRAILHEAD

From Southwest Harbor head south about 1 mile on ME 102. Bear left (southeast) on ME 102A, passing the town of Manset in about 1 mile, Seawall Campground and picnic area in about 3 miles, and the Wonderland Trail parking area in about 4 miles. The Ship Harbor trailhead is about 0.2 mile beyond Wonderland. The trailhead parking lot is on the left (south) side of ME 102A. The Island Explorer's Southwest Harbor line stops at Seawall Campground, more than a mile away, and passes by Ship Harbor Trail on the way to Bass Harbor Campground. If asked, the bus driver may let you off at the Ship Harbor Trail parking area if it is safe to do so. **GPS:** N44 13.54' / W68 19.31'

WHAT TO SEE

The trail is one of the easiest and most popular in Acadia, maybe because it offers so much: a thick spruce forest, wildflowers and lowbush blueberries in season, expanses of flat granite for relaxing next to the surf, intimate views of the islands, and the drama of the sea crashing against immense cliffs. Located on the southern shore of the west side of Mount Desert Island, the hike is composed of two loops, or a figure eight, totaling 1.3 miles with colorful, new wayside exhibits that explain sea life in the flats and tide pools.

The history of Ship Harbor and the trail is also fascinating. The name of the harbor may stretch back to the fall of 1739, when some believe it was the site of the wreck of the *Grand Design*, an English vessel carrying Irish immigrants to Pennsylvania. A park-wide

The Ship Harbor Trail affords some close-up views of islands.

archaeological study in 2004 found evidence that suggests the name of the harbor may stem from that disaster, though there is no definitive proof.

The trail itself took decades to reach fruition.

Park pioneers George B. Dorr and John D. Rockefeller Jr. worked to provide roadside access to Ship Harbor as early as the 1930s, and it was queued up to be completed by the Civilian Conservation Corps. But the work was left undone when the Corps disbanded in the park at the onset of World War II. It was finally completed in 1957 as part of a national program to improve the National Park System in time for its fiftieth anniversary in 1966. Important new work was finished in 2015, when the entire first, or inner, 0.6-mile loop was improved and regraded to comply with access standards for physically disabled persons, said Gary Stellpflug, Acadia trails foreman.

During the hike, when you reach the first fork, at 0.1 mile at the base of the figure-eight loop, bear right (south), following the hard-packed surface to the edge of the Ship Harbor channel and the mudflats, which can be viewed at low tide. The trail now begins to get rocky and uneven as it approaches an intersection at 0.3 mile, in the middle of the figure-eight loop. Bear right along the graded surface to the edge of the Ship Harbor channel. Common eiders are often seen floating at the mouth of Ship Harbor, and it's possible to catch glimpses along the trail of a bald eagle or osprey, or even such uncommon birds as a palm warbler or an olive-sided flycatcher. During a tour as part of the Acadia Birding Festival, guide Tom Hayward identified three laughing gulls, which have black heads and are smaller, with more narrow wings than herring gulls; three common terns; a double-crested cormorant with its yellow face and black body; and a northern parula, a common warbler, among other birds.

At 0.7 mile, near the mouth of Ship Harbor, you reach the rocky shore along the Atlantic. Here you can admire the dramatic pink cliffs or explore tide pools at low tide, when barnacles, rockweed, snails, and other sea life are exposed by the receding waters. Granite cliffs stretch to the edge of the ocean shore at the tip of this loop. You can get some great close-up views of islands at the end of this loop, from left to right facing the

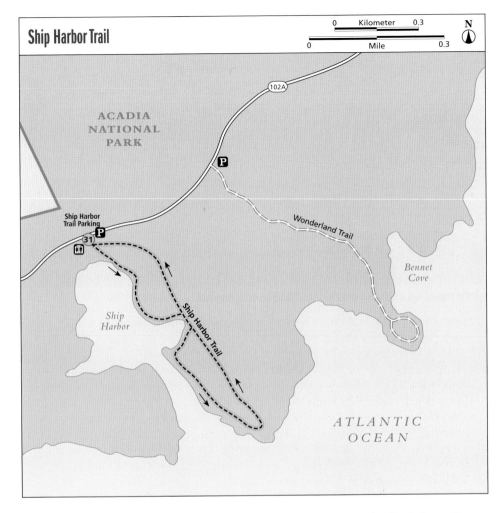

Ship Harbor Trail

0   Kilometer   0.3

0   Mile   0.3

N

ACADIA
NATIONAL
PARK

P

Ship Harbor
Trail Parking

P

31

Wonderland Trail

Bennet
Cove

Ship
Harbor

Ship Harbor Trail

ATLANTIC
OCEAN

ocean (or southeast to southwest): Little Duck Island, Great Duck Island, Great Gott Island directly in front (or south), then Placentia and, behind it, Swan's Island.

Turn left to circle back along the remaining section of the figure-eight loop. When you reach an intersection at 1.0 mile, back at the center of the figure eight, bear right (northwest) to continue along the hilly inland section of the loop, which is now well-graded and accessible. (**Option:** To return along the Ship Harbor channel, bear left at this intersection to retrace your steps along the channel northwest back to the trailhead.)

At a fork at the base of the figure-eight loop, bear northwest for 0.1 mile to return to the parking lot. You will walk over almost 300 feet of bogwalk, constructed with three planks instead of the usual two, to help protect the fragile area from heavy use.

MILES AND DIRECTIONS

0.0 Start at the Ship Harbor trailhead, on the left (south) side of ME 102A.

The sun accents the pink granite at the Ship Harbor Trail at Acadia National Park.

0.1 Bear right (south) at the fork, at the base of the figure-eight loop, and head along the edge of the Ship Harbor channel.

0.3 At the intersection in the middle of the figure-eight loop, bear right again to continue along the edge of the Ship Harbor channel.

0.7 Reach the rocky shoreline along the Atlantic and turn left (northwest) to circle back along the hilly inland section of the figure-eight loop.

1.0 At the intersection in the middle of the figure-eight loop, bear right (northwest) to continue along the hilly inland section.

1.2 Reach the fork at the base of the figure-eight loop; bear right (northwest) to head back to the parking lot.

1.3 Arrive back at the trailhead.

32 BAKER ISLAND (ACADIA— CRANBERRY ISLES)

One of the more remote parts of Acadia National Park, accessible only by boat, Baker Island offers mystical views back toward the park's mountain skyline and the opportunity to see the region's first lighthouse. You can also trek to the "dance floor," the giant flat slabs of pink granite on the south shore. Baker Island boasts a 200-plus-year history, led by the original settlers, William and Hannah Gilley, who moved there around 1806 and had twelve children, including nine born on the island. Pay your respects at the island cemetery.

Start: Baker Island trailhead on the north shore, where the boat launch lets you off
Elevation gain: 118 feet
Distance: 2.0 miles out and back
Difficulty: Easy to moderate
Hiking time: 1–1.5 hours
Seasons/schedule: Ranger-narrated boat cruise operates from mid-June through at least the end of Aug.
Fees and permits: Acadia National Park pass required May through Oct; separate fee for boat cruise
Trail contact: Acadia National Park, PO Box 177, Bar Harbor 04609; (207) 288-2338; nps.gov/acad
Dog-friendly: No dogs allowed
Trail surface: Forest floor, granite ledges
Land status: Island mostly owned by Acadia National Park, with some private houses and land dotting the landscape

Nearest town: Off-island; best to stock up on supplies before boarding boat cruise
Maps: USGS Acadia National Park and Vicinity; Nat Geo Trails Illustrated Topographic Map: Acadia National Park
Other trail users: Baker Island property owners, passengers from private boats, trail runners
Special considerations: No facilities. Acadia National Park does not recommend the Baker Island cruise for young children. No pets or strollers. There is no deepwater dock on the island; visitors must be mobile enough to get to shore via a small boat launch. The park has historically contracted with Bar Harbor Whale Watch Co. to provide passage to Baker Island for the up to 5-hour ranger-narrated cruise and hike, but check with the park for any changes. Respect the rights of private property owners.

FINDING THE TRAILHEAD

The boat launch lets you off at the trailhead on the north shore of Baker Island. **GPS:** N44 14.42' / W68 12.07'

WHAT TO SEE

With its ancient lighthouse, storied past, incredible views of the Acadia skyline, and massive granite "dance floor," Baker Island is a powerful draw. Located a little more than 3 miles south of Mount Desert Island, with no public ferry, Baker is almost entirely owned by the National Park Service. It can be a hurdle to reach, but its history and shoreline of sand, granite, and cobblestones make it well worth the effort.

From the north shore of Baker Island, Jack Russell points out the skyline of Mount Desert Island to coauthor Dan Ring, while Barbara Hopp Linton, seated to the left, and Robin Emery, standing to the right, soak up the afternoon sun.

The history of the circular island is topped by the original settlers, William and Hannah Gilley, who moved to the island around 1806 with three children and then had nine more after arriving on the island.

Charles W. Eliot, youngest-ever president of Harvard, who helped create Acadia National Park, was so intrigued by the family and its hardscrabble island existence that he wrote *John Gilley, One of the Forgotten Millions*, a little tome first published in 1899. As Eliot wrote, William Gilley was appointed the first keeper of the Baker Island Light Tower in 1828 for $350 a year, free occupation of the house, and all the sperm oil he could use in the household. Gilley was followed by at least seventeen other keepers, including one who claimed to have been visited by armed Germans, who stole fuel from the light station drums after surfacing in one of the U-boats patrolling Frenchman Bay during World War II.

It was often a difficult and stark existence, but the Gilleys and their descendants toughed it out on Baker Island, living off the sea along with their cows, oxen, hogs, sheep, and vegetable farm. The tenth child and youngest son, John Gilley, made money as captain of a schooner noted for carrying 100-ton cargos of smooth, hand-picked cobblestones off neighboring island beaches to Boston to be used for paving. Among the last of the family to live on the island was Phebe Jane Gilley, a granddaughter of the original couple, who never left the island the last thirty-six years of her life before dying in 1929 at age 87.

The lighthouse of Baker Island, one of the five Cranberry Isles, is listed on the National Register of Historic Places.

The best way to reach Baker is on the Acadia National Park ranger-narrated cruise, available from mid-June to at least the end of August. A fee and reservation are required for a ticket on the cruise. The park has historically contracted with Bar Harbor Whale Watch Co. to provide passage to Baker Island, but check the park calendar for any changes: nps.gov/acad/planyourvisit/calendar.htm.

We hiked the island twice over the years, including most recently on a sunny early September day with four people from the region: Jack Russell, who grew up on Mount Desert Island and was cochair of the Acadia Centennial Task Force; Tim Henderson of Castine, a volunteer at the park; Robin Emery of Lamoine; and Barbara Hopp Linton of Sullivan. We took a private Cadillac Water Taxi from Northeast Harbor on Mount Desert Island and landed in a dinghy in a cove on the north shore of Baker Island, a southwest wind from the shore providing us with calm waters.

The 2.0-mile round trip hike starts at this cove. As the waves fell gently on shore, Russell, a former nine-year board member of the nonprofit Friends of Acadia and now honorary trustee, pointed out the peaks of the Acadia skyline and other landmarks at sea. We saw Little Cranberry Island, also known as Islesford, about a mile to the northwest, with a small island known as the Green Nubble about halfway in between. At low tide, a massive rocky bar and mudflats become exposed between Baker and Little Cranberry.

Beyond Little Cranberry, we had a spectacular view of the skyline of just about all the high peaks of Acadia National Park on Mount Desert Island. Looking east to west on Mount Desert, Great Head looms first above the sea and then Sand Beach, followed by the peaks of Gorham, Champlain, Huguenot Head, Dorr, Cadillac, Pemetic; one of the two Bubbles; the massive shape of Sargent; then Parkman, Norumbega (which looks like a long bread loaf from the north shore of Baker), Acadia, St. Sauveur, and Western Mountain, which includes Mansell.

From the trail at the cove, we hiked toward the light tower, and our first stop was to pay our respects at the historic cemetery. The cemetery, restored by the Keepers of Baker Island, a nonprofit group that works with the park to protect the island, and the Islesford Historical Society, includes thirteen plots with stones, including those of descendants of the Gilley family, and one unmarked grave of an infant.

Upon landing on Baker Island, Jack Russell, an honorary trustee of the nonprofit Friends of Acadia and a regional historian, picks up some rocks from different geologic eras. Ellsworth schist, with gray and white bands, is the oldest, at between 505 and 510 million years old. The dark gray rock is gabbro, dating from about 425 million years ago.

Only two homes on the island are private, and both are painted red. The first off the trail is the former home of Phebe Jane Gilley Stanley, now owned by the Pearson family. The second is the old schoolhouse, owned by the family of Cornelia J. Cesari,

Hikers ascend to the Baker Island Light Tower and keeper's quarters at Acadia National Park.

author of the first comprehensive history of the island, *Baker Island*, published in 2018. As you walk past the homes along "Main Street," you can see why Cesari in her book calls Baker "an out-of-worldly experience, a timeless Brigadoon."

Please respect the homeowners' privacy, or say hello if the opportunity arises.

Between the two red buildings, before you reach the light station, stands a white, wood-framed house, built in 1840 by William Gilley for his oldest daughter, Hannah, and her husband, Joseph Stanley. It was later inhabited by a son, Elisha Gilley, after his sister moved off-island.

Continue up the hill to a wooden sign at 0.4 mile describing a little history of the lighthouse. You will return to this sign before heading down the trail to the south side of the island. It's fun to explore and photograph the light station from different angles. The original light tower and light-keeper's quarters were both built of rubble-stone in 1828 but were replaced in 1855 by the brick tower and wooden house still standing today.

The 10-acre Baker Island Light Station includes the keeper's dwelling, light tower, oil house, and garage and is under the jurisdiction of Acadia National Park, having been acquired from the US Coast Guard, which has employed it as an automatic aid to navigation since 1957. The Coast Guard uses an easement to maintain the automated light in the 1855 light tower.

From the lighthouse, walk back down to the wooden Baker Island lighthouse sign at 0.5 mile; turn left (south), following a trail heading behind a 1942 US Coast Guard garage to continue through the woods in a southwesterly direction toward the "dance floor" granite formations. The dance floor was probably named by late nineteenth- and early twentieth-century visitors to the island, who would twirl and frolic on the rocks' giant flat faces.

At 0.8 mile reach the dance floor on the south shore of the island, with Great Duck and Little Duck Islands the two prominent islands to the southwest. Turn left (east) to explore the enormous rock slabs. Even on a nice day, the sea surges and crashes against the rocks, while big flocks of herring gulls perch on the edges of the granite. Be careful—it can be dicey to walk on this granite, as is the case virtually anywhere on the granite of Acadia.

Be grateful for the extensive work of the Keepers of Baker Island and the park service over the past decade or so to clean and clear the island of debris, waste, and overgrowth.

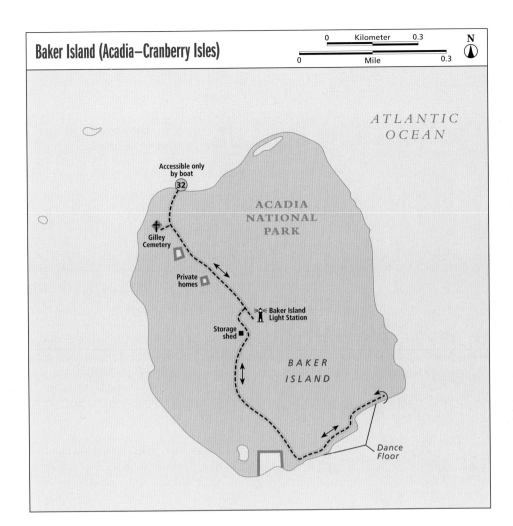

Baker Island (Acadia–Cranberry Isles)

Accessible only
by boat

32

Gilley
Cemetery

Private
homes

ACADIA
NATIONAL
PARK

ATLANTIC
OCEAN

Baker Island
Light Station

Storage
shed

BAKER

ISLAND

Dance
Floor

Their hard work each year immensely improves and maintains the island's access and views, for everyone's enjoyment.

At 1.0 mile, return the way you came. (**Option:** If you skip the cemetery and the lighthouse on the way back, you'll save about 0.1 mile on the round-trip.)

MILES AND DIRECTIONS

0.0 Start at the Baker Island trailhead and follow the path toward the lighthouse, turning right (west) at the first junction to Gilley Cemetery.

0.1 Pay your respects at the cemetery, then return to the main trail and turn right (southeast) to continue to the lighthouse.

0.2 Walk by the Phebe Jane Gilley Stanley house, now a privately owned residence, on the right.

0.3 Walk by the old schoolhouse, now a privately owned residence, on the right.

Acadia National Park volunteer Tim Henderson runs the pink granite of the "dance floor" on Baker Island.

0.4 Pass a wooden Baker Island lighthouse sign and ascend the hill to explore the lighthouse.

0.5 Return to the wooden sign below the lighthouse and turn left (southwest), following a trail heading behind a 1942 US Coast Guard garage to continue through the woods in a southwesterly direction toward the dance floor.

0.8 Reach the dance floor; turn left (east) along the shore to explore the pink granite slabs.

1.0 Turn around and retrace your steps.

2.0 Arrive back at the trailhead.

33 SUNDEW TRAIL (ACADIA—SCHOODIC PENINSULA)

For a short hike, the Sundew Trail packs in a lot. There are three different spurs to some tremendous Schoodic shoreline, offering views of Cadillac Mountain across Frenchman Bay in the distance, dramatic granite gorges, and then a quiet cove.

Start: Sundew trailhead, at the northwest corner of the parking lot near Eliot Hall and the water tower
Elevation gain: 81 feet
Distance: 1.8 miles out and back, including three short spurs to the shore
Difficulty: Easy
Hiking time: 1–2 hours
Seasons/schedule: Open year-round; best spring through fall, late June through Aug if you're taking the Bar Harbor-Winter Harbor ferry and the Island Explorer's Schoodic line; low tide for tide pool exploration
Fees and permits: Acadia National Park pass required May through Oct
Trail contact: Acadia National Park, PO Box 177, Bar Harbor 04609; (207) 288-2338; nps.gov/acad
Dog-friendly: Leashed dogs permitted

Trail surface: Forest floor, rock ledges, graded gravel, bogwalks
Land status: Acadia National Park
Nearest town: Winter Harbor
Maps: USGS Acadia National Park and Vicinity; Nat Geo Trails Illustrated Topographic Map: Acadia National Park
Other trail users: Participants in Schoodic Education and Research Center programs; Acadia artists-in-residence
Special considerations: No facilities at the trailhead; restrooms and a picnic area near the start of the one-way Schoodic Loop Road; restrooms and ranger station at the day-use parking area of Schoodic Woods Campground. Picnic pavilion near the hike turnaround point off Alvey Drive. Three short spurs off the main trail lead to benches with views.

FINDING THE TRAILHEAD

From the Schoodic park entrance off ME 186, head south on the one-way loop road for 3.5 miles; bear right (southwest) onto the two-way road to Schoodic Point. Turn at your first right (west) onto Acadia Drive and into the Schoodic Education and Research Center campus. Drive straight past the entrance gatehouse and Rockefeller Hall and follow signs for campus parking, meeting halls, and administration. Pass Jacobson Drive and bear right on Musetti Drive, following signs to campus parking and meeting halls. Go straight past Eliot Hall on the right, and park. Walk toward the northwest corner of the parking lot (as if you're heading to the water tower) and find the Sundew trailhead at the edge of the lot, before the tower. The Island Explorer's Schoodic line does not have a stop here; ask the bus driver to let you off at the entrance to the Schoodic Education and Research Center campus if it is safe to do so. **GPS:** N44 20.13' / W68 03.45'

WHAT TO SEE

The Sundew Trail, named for the sticky, insect-eating plants at Acadia, starts over graded gravel and brings you through a shady spruce forest to some fantastic views of the Acadia skyline and nearby islands in Frenchman Bay.

The sun sets behind Cadillac Mountain, adorning Frenchman Bay and the white granite of the Sundew Trail in Acadia National Park.

The trail used to be little more than a jogging path, built in the late 1980s by several sailors at the former US Navy base on the Schoodic Peninsula. The base, acquired by the National Park Service in 2002, was converted into the $18 million Schoodic Education and Research Center in 2011 with the help of $9.3 million in federal dollars to stimulate the economy following the 2009 recession, park user fees, and other federal monies.

The Sundew Trail is used by the research center for interpretive hikes. The trail was extensively rehabilitated and redesigned in 2013 in a project by the Acadia trails crew with help from the Acadia Youth Conservation Corps. In all, 2,350 feet of gravel surface and twenty-five culverts for drainage were constructed over what used to be a natural wood path that turned into a muddy mess at certain times and could barely be used in spring and fall.

At 0.2 mile, at the first of three junctions with short spurs to the shore, turn left (west) at a sign to ocean benches and start a mild descent. Listen for the sounds of waves hitting the shore. The park did not have the funds to grade the entire trail in 2013, so some sections, including the side trails and about 0.25 mile in the middle of the main trail, remain forest floor that can sometimes be rocky with roots.

A juvenile double-crested cormorant uses its webbed feet to grip a ledge off the Sundew Trail at Acadia National Park.

In no time, reach the rocky coast of Schoodic and the ocean, with a spectacular view of the Acadia skyline, topped by Cadillac Mountain straight ahead (west), with the east face of Champlain Mountain in the foreground, below Cadillac, along with the Beehive, Gorham Mountain, and Otter Cliff, just to the south.

Face Frenchman Bay, and Ironbound is the big island to the right (northwest), with a couple of the Porcupine Islands to the west of Ironbound and Egg Rock, with its lighthouse, visible in the middle of the bay in front of Champlain. Looking to the left (south) of the mountain skyline, you can see, from right to left (north to south), Little Cranberry Island and then rounded Baker Island, as well as Little Duck and Great Duck Islands. This outpost on the bay also provides some stunning sights of the rocky shore and some large mats of black crowberry growing among the rocky surface.

Located in a little-visited corner of Acadia, the Sundew Trail is often bypassed by people. Robin Emery, a Lamoine resident who has hiked in Acadia for more than fifty years, walked the Sundew Trail for the first time in her life after agreeing to meet us at the trailhead. Emery said she was amazed by the trail's beauty on a pleasant late-October afternoon. "It is so quiet and peaceful here," she said.

You might also meet an artist-in-residence on the Sundew Trail. Each year, in a competitive application process, the Acadia National Park Artist-in-Residence Program selects a certain number of professional artists to serve fourteen-day residences. Artists

A hiker off the Sundew Trail uses binoculars to get a closer look at Egg Rock in Frenchman Bay.

often paint or photograph the rocky coast of the Sundew Trail because there's a housing option nearby on the Schoodic campus. Artists lead one public outreach presentation and donate within a year one finished work of art with a fresh perspective of Acadia drawn from their experience.

Back to the main trail, turn left and then take the next spur off the Sundew Trail to reach two more benches on this great and rocky Atlantic shoreline.

Return to the main trail and take another spur to the left. Here, at the third and final side trail to the shore, the trail reaches the sprawling and calm West Pond Cove, with two benches and views of wooded and marshy Pond Island to the west and Schoodic Head rising over the trees to the northeast. While walking the trail with Emery, we spotted a lone juvenile double-crested cormorant perched on a ledge, its dark legs and webbed feet providing a good grip.

Return to the main trail again and turn left to hike to the northern end of the trail. Along the way, cross a 150-foot-long elevated boardwalk built in 2013 by the trails crew. Reach a pavilion at the end with an older map of the trail and then return the way you came, skipping the shoreline spurs on the way back.

MILES AND DIRECTIONS

0.0   Start at the Sundew trailhead, the southern end of the trail, at the northwest corner of the parking lot near Eliot Hall and the water tower.

Sundew Trail (Acadia–Schoodic Peninsula)

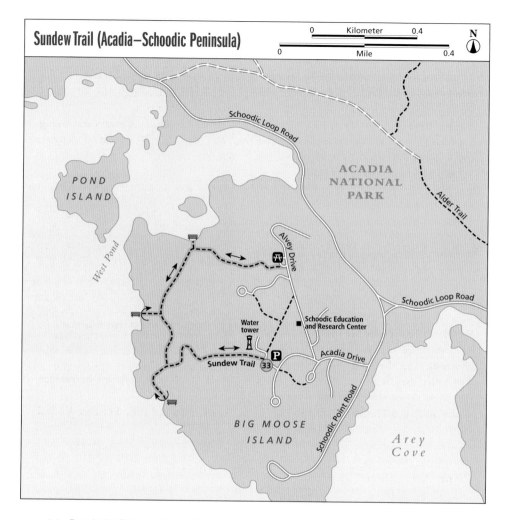

0.2   Reach the first junction with a spur to the shore. Turn left (southwest) onto the spur.

0.3   Return to the junction; turn left (north) to continue on the main Sundew Trail.

0.5   Turn left (west) at the next junction onto the second spur to the shore.

0.6   Return to the junction; turn left (northeast) to continue on the main Sundew Trail.

0.8   Turn left (north) at the third junction with a spur to the shore.

0.9   Return to the junction; turn left (east) to continue on the main Sundew Trail.

1.1   Arrive at the eastern end of the trail near a heliport and picnic pavilion.

1.8   Arrive back at the trailhead, skipping the shoreline spurs and staying on the main Sundew Trail.

MORE IN ACADIA NATIONAL PARK AND BAR HARBOR

BREWERIES, EATS, AND SLEEPS

Atlantic Brewing Company, with two locations, 15 Knox Rd. and 52 Cottage St., Bar Harbor 04609; (207) 288-2326; atlanticbrewing.com. The Cottage Street location has a restaurant, and offerings include such classics as Cadillac Mountain Stout, Thunder Hole Ale, and Bar Harbor Blueberry Ale, as well as small-batch beers. The brewery and tasting room on Knox Road in Bar Harbor is open from late May to mid-Oct and offers tours; the downtown location is open year-round.

Jordan's Restaurant, 80 Cottage St., Bar Harbor 04609; (207) 288-3586; jordansbarharbor.com. Eat where the locals do. Known for its wild Maine blueberry products, from muffins to pancakes; also featuring lobster rolls and clam chowder. All-day breakfast, convenient early open for visitors catching the sunrise on Cadillac Mountain, plus lunch; no dinner. Open Apr through late Nov.

Mt. Desert Island Ice Cream, 7 Firefly Ln., Bar Harbor 04609; (207) 801-4006; mdiic.com. President Barack Obama had the toasted coconut ice cream, First Lady Michelle Obama opted for the chocolate, and their daughters enjoyed the candy

A lobster roll, served at Jordan's Restaurant, is vintage Maine fare.

shop when they vacationed in Acadia in July 2010 and sampled this premium homemade ice cream. Open seasonally.

Jordan Pond House, 2928 Park Loop Rd., Acadia National Park, PO Box 40, Seal Harbor 04675; (207) 276-3316; jordanpondhouse.com. The only restaurant in the park; known for its popovers and view of Jordan Pond and the distinctive twin mountains known as the Bubbles. Open seasonally.

The Pickled Wrinkle, 9 East Schoodic Dr., Birch Harbor 04613; (207) 963-7916; thepickledwrinkle.com. Located just outside the Schoodic section of Acadia National Park and named for a Downeast Maine delicacy, this local favorite serves seafood, steaks, pizza, and burgers and features live entertainment. Near Sundew Trail and Petit Manan National Wildlife Refuge. Open year-round.

Atlantic Oceanside Hotel and Event Center, 119 Eden St., Bar Harbor 04609; (800) 336-2463; barharbormainehotel.com. Set on 12 acres of waterfront and offering modern suites to rooms in a historic mansion known as the Willows, the Atlantic Oceanside often hosts weddings and such annual events as the Mount Desert Island Marathon & Half expo. On-site Bistro restaurant. Open year-round.

Acadia Hotel, 20 Mount Desert St., Bar Harbor 04609; (888) 876-2463; acadiahotel .com. A boutique hotel across from the Village Green, the Acadia Hotel offers guests complimentary bicycles and the convenience of being able to walk to shops and restaurants. Open year-round.

CAMPING

Acadia National Park, with these campgrounds: **Blackwoods Campground** and **Seawall Campground** on Mount Desert Island and **Schoodic Woods Campground** on the Schoodic Peninsula; nps.gov/acad/planyourvisit/camping.htm. Leashed dogs permitted; ranger-led programs available; no showers. **Blackwoods** is 5 miles south of Bar Harbor on ME 3; (207) 288-3724; 281 sites, some of which can accommodate RVs; open seasonally, May to late Oct, then on a limited self-registration basis into early Nov. **Seawall** is 4 miles south of Southwest Harbor on ME 102A; (207) 244-3600; 202 sites, some of which can accommodate RVs; open seasonally, late May through mid-Oct. **Schoodic Woods**, opened in late 2015 with easy access to hiking trails and bike paths styled after the carriage roads on Mount Desert Island, is at 5 Farview Dr., Winter Harbor, on the park's Schoodic Loop Road; (207) 288-1300; 94 sites, including 33 RV sites with water and power, 50 car tent sites with electric, 2 group sites, and 9 private hike-in sites with no electric and no open fires allowed; open seasonally, late May until second Monday in Oct. Campground reservations can be reserved up to 6 months in advance; there are no first-come, first-serve basis sites. Online reservations at recreation.gov.

   Mount Desert Campground, 516 Sound Dr., Mount Desert 04660; (207) 244-3710; mountdesertcampground.com. A total of 157 sites, including 36 waterfront and an additional 12 with water view. No dogs during peak season, late June to early Sept, but allowed at other times. No RVs/trailers longer than 20 feet. Kayak, canoe, and stand-up paddleboard rentals; boat launch; saltwater swimming and fishing. Open seasonally, late May to mid-Oct.

LIGHTHOUSES, MUSEUMS, AND HISTORIC SITES

Bass Harbor Head Light, Lighthouse Road off ME 102A, Bass Harbor; nps.gov/acad/planyourvisit/placestogo.htm. Part of Acadia National Park and the only lighthouse on Mount Desert Island, Bass Harbor Head Light was built in 1858 and still guides mariners in and out of Bass Harbor and Blue Hill Bay with a light that was automated in 1974. A paved path off the southwestern side of the parking lot allows you to stand under the lighthouse and touch the white brick exterior while taking in some breathtaking ocean views. On the southeastern side of the lot, you can take a stairway down to a picture postcard–perfect view of the lighthouse. Grounds open year-round, weather permitting.

   Abbe Museum, with two locations, 26 Mount Desert St. and 49 Sweetwater Circle at the Sieur de Monts entrance to Acadia National Park, Bar Harbor 04609; (207) 288-3519; abbemuseum.org. The first and only Smithsonian affiliate in the state of Maine, the Abbe Museum focuses on the history and culture of Native Americans in Maine. The Mount Desert Street location is open year-round; the one at Sieur de Monts Spring is open seasonally.

COASTAL ATTRACTIONS

Acadia Night Sky Festival, acadianightskyfestival.org. Held annually in mid-Sept to celebrate the dark, starlit skies above the Acadia region, with such events as the Cadillac Mountain Star Party, night-sky photography, and art workshops, lectures, boat cruises, and bioluminescent paddles.

   The Museum in the Streets, barharborvia.org/museum-in-the-streets. A project of the Bar Harbor Village Improvement Association, this series of signs throughout Bar Harbor can be found along the waterfront, explaining the history of Bar Island, sites along the Shore Path, and other coastal attractions.

DOWNEAST

The Downeast section of Maine offers some of the wildest and most magnificent coastline in the state, including the white and pink granite on the shores of Great Wass Island, the lofty cliffs of the Bold Coast, and the endless low-tide flats of Lubec.

"Downeast," a maritime term to describe sailing downwind to head east, generally refers to the coastline east of Penobscot Bay, including Acadia and Bar Harbor, but we include only the less-discovered parts of the region in this section.

Considering their special natural and historical features, many hikes included in this section rival the beauty of Acadia, particularly the Bold Coast section from Cutler to West Quoddy Head. In fact, there was a serious discussion in the 1980s about creating a "Bold Coast National Park," but it faded amid local opposition to federal control over assets such as timber, fish, and lands.

The setting sun spreads crimson, red, and yellow over Sally Island at Petit Manan Point in Steuben.

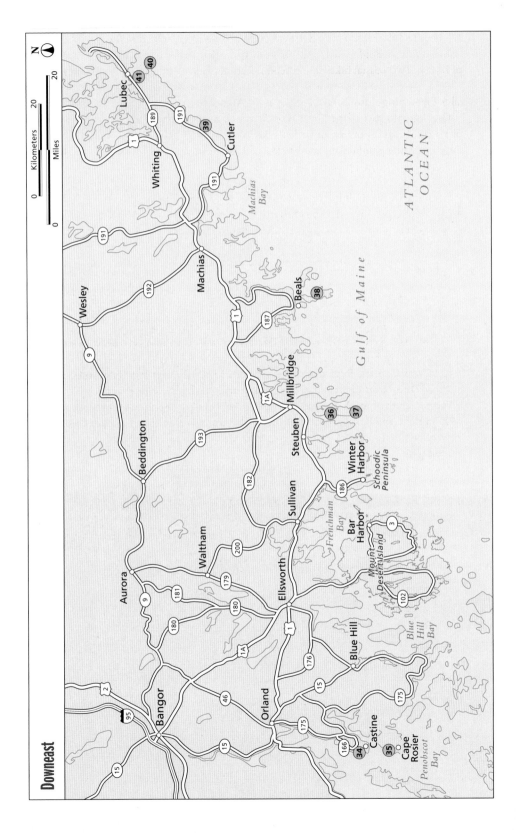

Downeast

The 125-mile Bold Coast Scenic Byway includes roads from Milbridge to Eastport, but the intense Bold Coast hiking is from Cutler north to the funky and friendly town of Lubec. Two coastal hikes in this region feature islands—the Great Wass Island Preserve and Sally Island, an optional low-tide hike on the Petit Manan Point peninsula, open only after the nesting season of bald eagles ends, August 31.

Great Wass is part of the Great Wass Archipelago, more than forty islands off the coast of Jonesport, and is unlike any other hike in this section because of its long shoreline of pink and white granite slabs and boulders, island views, colorful cobble and sand beaches, and big stands of jack pine.

Head "way Downeast" to reach three of the destinations in this guide to coastal trails. From south to north, they begin with the Cutler Coast Public Reserved Land, with its 4.5 miles of coastline and some cliffs that rise more than 100 feet above the sea.

After Cutler, stop at Quoddy Head State Park, located on the easternmost point of the US mainland, with its historic West Quoddy Head Light and the chance to watch whales and seals in the Grand Manan Channel at the mouth of the Bay of Fundy from the lawn of the lighthouse.

Near downtown Lubec, the boardwalk of Mowry Beach Preserve provides vital public access to a long sandy and stony beach with wide, expansive space for a hike at low tide and views to Campobello Island in Canada and Lubec Channel Light.

The eastern section of Penobscot Bay, one of the great bays of Maine, provides the coastline for two more hikes: Holbrook Island Sanctuary and Witherle Woods Preserve.

A 2.9-mile circuit loop in Witherle Woods in Castine on the Blue Hill Peninsula includes Dice Head Light and history dating back to the Revolutionary War.

Farther south along East Penobscot Bay is Holbrook Island Sanctuary, a tranquil state park on the Cape Rosier section of Blue Hill Peninsula that features the opportunity to see reversing falls, a phenomenon unique to Maine along the US East Coast, during an outgoing tide.

The peninsula of Petit Manan Point, one of four mainland divisions of the Maine Coastal Islands National Wildlife Refuge, includes two distinct and beautiful hikes: The Birch Point Trail, which heads north on the peninsula to Dyer Bay, and the John Hollingsworth Memorial Trail, which goes south along Pigeon Hill Bay.

With its vistas of islands and open ocean, cliffs, and variety of beaches, Downeast Maine is a trip you will treasure forever.

34 WITHERLE WOODS PRESERVE

Imagine the battles fought here during the Revolutionary War and War of 1812, and appreciate the wildlife that flourishes on what is now Maine Coast Heritage Trust land. Take in grand views of Penobscot Bay, Maine's largest, from a couple of well-placed benches. On the return, loop by Dice Head Light and a marker commemorating the ill-fated Penobscot Expedition of 1779, which led to the loss of about forty American ships and the court-martial of Paul Revere.

Start: Gravel road at the far (northwest) end of the parking area
Elevation gain: 483 feet
Distance: 2.9-mile circuit loop
Difficulty: Moderate
Hiking time: 1.5–2 hours
Seasons/schedule: Open year-round during daylight hours; best spring through fall
Fees and permits: No fees or permits
Trail contact: Maine Coast Heritage Trust, 1 Bowdoin Mill Island, Ste. 201, Topsham 04086; (207) 729-7366; mcht.org
Dog-friendly: Dogs permitted, leashed or otherwise under control
Trail surface: Gravel road, forest floor, grassy path, bogwalks, paved road
Land status: 185 acres owned and maintained by the nonprofit Maine Coast Heritage Trust. The Town of Castine owns the nearby Dice Head Light and 0.3 acre to manage the underground municipal water supply.
Nearest town: Castine
Maps: USGS Castine; Maine Coast Heritage Trust trail map
Other trail users: Local residents, dog walkers, mountain bikers; bow hunters in season; cross-country skiers in winter
Special considerations: No facilities; no removal of historical artifacts or use of metal detectors permitted; no camping or fires permitted. No mountain bikers allowed on the Indian Trail but permitted on other trails; respect abutting private property. Ticks can be a problem on the grassy path down to the lighthouse. Do not use trails marked off-limits during the spring's critical nesting period for ospreys and other sensitive birds.

FINDING THE TRAILHEAD

From the junction of ME 166 and 166A in Castine, head south on ME 166, following the main road as it crests a hill and turns sharply right (southwest) onto Battle Avenue. Travel another 0.8 mile, passing a golf course, Fort George Park, and the Maine Maritime Academy campus; turn right (northwest) into the Witherle Woods parking area. The trail begins on the gravel road at the far (northwest) end of the parking area. **GPS:** N44 23.11' / W68 48.41'

WHAT TO SEE

One of American history's most contested pieces of land, this strategically positioned promontory overlooking Penobscot Bay changed hands eighteen times between 1613 and 1815 and was the backdrop for the worst American naval disaster before Pearl Harbor, according to various reports about this storied area. But the place is now so peaceful, you may catch a porcupine napping in a tree, hear a downy woodpecker, or stir a nesting osprey, as we did one fine June day.

A side trail at Witherle Woods leads to Dice Head Lighthouse, at the entrance to Castine Harbor.

For that peacefulness, we have the area's history of conservation to thank, from George Witherle's creation of community carriage roads in the 1870s to the private donation or sale of land to Maine Coast Heritage Trust (MCHT) starting in 1985, making this the statewide land conservation organization's first preserve.

Son of a wealthy Castine merchant and shipowner, George Witherle established Witherle Park for residents and "rusticators"—well-off city dwellers spending summers in the countryside—as a place to walk, picnic, or take carriage rides. In fact, his carriage roads became a model for John D. Rockefeller Jr.'s system of roads on Mount Desert Island, much of which is now part of Acadia National Park.

Witherle shared his love of the outdoors with his daughter Amy, who accompanied him on some of his many trips to Katahdin (a ravine west of Maine's highest peak is named for him) and who continued his stewardship when she inherited Witherle Park in the early 1900s. Upon her death in 1949, she passed the land to her cousin, who then sold it to the Hatch family, which ultimately deeded the first 96.5 acres to MCHT in 1985. Now under MCHT's stewardship, Witherle Woods is "a public preserve where wildlife can thrive and visitors can enjoy its natural beauty and fascinating history."

Among the natural beauty and history documented in the preserve are 48 species of birds, including black-throated green warbler and winter wren; 195 species of plants, including a forest composed primarily of red and white spruce, balsam fir, and white pine; and remnants of fortifications from both the Revolutionary War and the War of 1812.

MCHT's preserve brochure highlights more than half a dozen historic sites, including Trask Rock, featured on an early 1900s Castine postcard. The glacial erratic is named for

A porcupine displays its sharp quills from high atop a tree in the Witherle Woods.

Israel Trask, a 14-year-old fifer during the Penobscot Expedition who later claimed he found shelter here from British musket fire so that he could keep playing to encourage colonial troops.

To start the circuit hike, much of which follows the old Witherle Park carriage roads, head northwest on the gravel road at the far end of the preserve parking area. Reach an information kiosk at the top of the hill at 0.2 mile and turn right (northeast). Pass the first two junctions on the left. No signs mark it, but in the woods between these two junctions, remnants have been found of Forward Battery, dug by American forces in 1779 during the failed attempt to capture nearby Fort George from the British.

At the third junction at 0.4 mile, turn left (northwest) to head toward Blockhouse Point and sites of two War of 1812 batteries, staying straight past two side trails on the left at 0.7 mile and 0.8 mile. At 1.0 mile reach a sign marking Furieuse Battery No. 1, named for a French naval ship captured by the British.

Turn left (southeast) at a sign marked "Lookout" to ascend quickly to a high point used by the British to watch for enemy forces coming by sea or land. Take in the best views of the hike from a conveniently placed bench, northeast to nearby Wadsworth Cove and the Castine peninsula isthmus, northwest across Penobscot Bay to Searsport and Stockton Springs, and southwest to Islesboro Island and the Camden Hills on the mainland beyond.

Head back downhill and at 1.1 miles turn left (southwest) on the main trail, reaching Blockhouse Point and the site of Furieuse Battery No. 2 at 1.2 miles. Turn right (northwest) onto a short spur trail marked "Blockhouse Point Lookout" and enjoy a similar view to what you had from the first vantage point, just a little more limited and closer to the bay, again from a handy bench.

Back on the main trail, turn right (south) and then quickly bear right (southwest) at the next junction to take the rugged Indian Trail as it descends toward the waters of Penobscot Bay. At 1.3 miles at another junction, bear right (south) to continue on the Indian Trail. Near here we heard the sound of an osprey and, looking up, saw it circling its nest. Fortunately, we visited outside the critical nesting period, and there were no signs restricting access.

As you continue along the western edge of the preserve along the Indian Trail, you'll get glimpses of Penobscot Bay through the trees. Although Trask Rock is marked on the MCHT map as being along this stretch, we found no obvious place to get a view of the once picture postcard–perfect rock along the shore. But in looking around the woods here, we instead found something so unusual

Bunchberry's white flowers often enhance the trails of coastal Maine in June.

you're unlikely to see it on a postcard: a porcupine roosting high up in a tree.

At 1.6 miles follow the Indian Trail sharply left (northeast), away from private property, and ascend via switchbacks. As the switchbacks level off at 1.7 miles at a junction, turn right (south). At 1.9 miles continue straight past a side trail coming in on the left.

At 2.0 miles, where a preserve trail map is secured to a tree, turn right (southwest); cross over a stone wall and a dirt road to head down a grassy path (beware of ticks) on the way to Dice Head Light. At 2.1 miles turn right (west) onto a gravel road, away from private property, and exit Witherle Woods Preserve onto paved Dyces Head Road. Turn right (west) on the road to explore the town-owned Dice Head Light at 2.4 miles.

Built in 1828, the lighthouse was decommissioned in 1937 and its light moved to a nearby tower. But after a

This hill was used by the British during the War of 1812 as a lookout over Penobscot Bay.

microburst knocked over the tower in 2007, the lighthouse was reactivated in 2008 and shines again. You can explore the grounds, but as the keeper's house is rented out by the town to help cover costs, please respect the tenants' privacy.

Walk back east on Dyces Head Road, past the gated gravel road where you exited the preserve, and continue straight on the paved road as it becomes Battle Avenue. There are no sidewalks; stay on the left (north) side of the road to watch for any oncoming traffic.

As you head back to the preserve parking area, you'll see a hand-painted Castine historical sign marking a July 28, 1779, dawn attack by American forces, the start of the ill-fated Penobscot Expedition.

Massachusetts sought to drive the British out of what was then the province of Maine, but it was nearly bankrupted by the failed mission. The fleet of about forty ships were either captured or sunk to prevent capture, and survivors fled on foot through the Maine woods. Charges of cowardice were brought against artillery commander Paul Revere and others. Revere had shown his patriotism during the Revolutionary War's first battle in April 1775, but "Paul Revere's Ride" wasn't to be immortalized in Henry Wadsworth Longfellow's poem until 1863. Revere requested a court-martial to clear his name and was finally acquitted of all charges in 1782.

As you reach the preserve parking area off Battle Avenue at 2.9 miles, ponder the natural beauty and fascinating history of Witherle Woods.

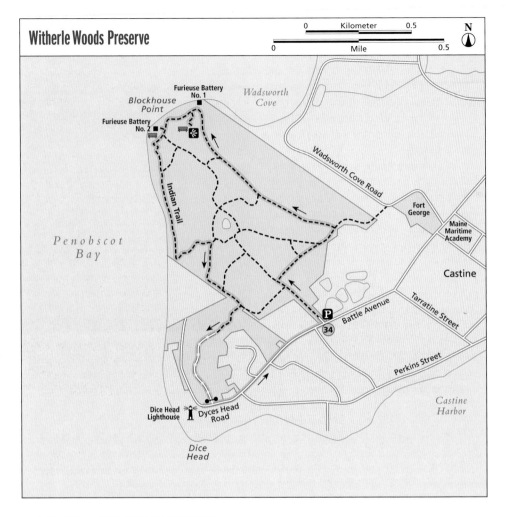

Witherle Woods Preserve

0   Kilometer   0.5
0   Mile   0.5

N

Furieuse Battery No. 1

Blockhouse Point

Furieuse Battery No. 2

Wadsworth Cove

Wadsworth Cove Road

Indian Trail

Penobscot Bay

Fort George

Maine Maritime Academy

Castine

Battle Avenue

Tarratine Street

34

Perkins Street

Castine Harbor

Dice Head Lighthouse

Dyces Head Road

Dice Head

MILES AND DIRECTIONS

0.0 Start at the gravel road at the far (northwest) end of the parking area.

0.2 Reach an information kiosk at the top of the hill and turn right (northeast), staying straight past two side trails that come in on the left.

0.4 Turn left (northwest) at the third junction and head toward Blockhouse Point, staying straight past two side trails that come in on the left.

1.0 Reach the site of Furieuse Battery No. 1; turn left (southeast) at a sign marked "Lookout" to climb quickly up to a vantage point the British used during the War of 1812.

1.1 Descend back to the main trail and turn left (southwest).

1.2 Reach Blockhouse Point and the site of Furieuse Battery No. 2; turn right (northwest) onto a spur trail marked "Blockhouse Point Lookout." Return to the main trail and turn right (south), then quickly bear right (southwest) again to take the Indian Trail.

1.3 Bear right (south) at a junction to continue on the Indian Trail.

Coauthor Dan Ring focuses on the Camden Hills from the Blockhouse Point Lookout at Witherle Woods.

1.6 Turn sharply left (northeast) and ascend switchbacks.

1.7 Turn right (south) at a junction at the top of the switchbacks, staying straight past a side trail that comes in on the left.

2.0 At a trail map secured to a tree, turn right (southwest); cross over a stone wall and a dirt road, and head down a grassy path on the way to Dice Head Light.

2.1 Turn right (west) onto a gravel road.

2.4 Exit the preserve and turn right (west) on paved Dyces Head Road to explore the lighthouse. Head back east on Dyces Head Road, past the gated gravel road where you exited the preserve, and follow the road as it becomes Battle Avenue.

2.9 Arrive back at the preserve parking area.

35 HOLBROOK ISLAND SANCTUARY

Holbrook Island Sanctuary, a quiet preserve on the Cape Rosier peninsula in Brooksville, offers some of the most faraway hiking in coastal Maine. The Goose Falls Trail provides some expansive views across sublime Penobscot Bay to the Camden Hills and ends at one of the top-eight reversing falls in Maine, a phenomenon that occurs at ebb tide.

Start: Goose Falls trailhead, at the west end of the main dock parking area
Elevation gain: 83 feet
Distance: 1.0 mile out and back
Difficulty: Easy
Hiking time: 30 minutes–1 hour
Seasons/schedule: Open year-round 9 a.m. to sunset; best spring through fall, at ebb tide to view the reversing falls
Fees and permits: No fees or permits
Trail contact: Holbrook Island Sanctuary, PO Box 35, Brooksville 04617; (207) 326-4012; maine.gov/holbrookisland
Dog-friendly: Leashed dogs permitted
Trail surface: Forest floor, rock ledges, footbridges
Land status: 1,345-acre park owned and maintained by the State of Maine
Nearest town: Brooksville

Maps: USGS Cape Rosier; Holbrook Island Sanctuary brochure
Other trail users: Trail runners, dog walkers, local residents, birders; cross-country skiers and snowshoers in winter
Special considerations: Facilities include chemical toilets near dock and park headquarters; picnic area and beach near park headquarters. Dock for canoes and kayaks (no boat rental) allows access to Holbrook Island. Network of more than 10 miles of trails goes through diverse habitat, from rocky coast to the tops of steep hills that are actually ancient volcanoes. Parking areas plowed in winter. Park roads are unpaved and may be rough in spots. Bring insect repellent, as mosquitoes can be a problem. To time a visit during ebb tide to view reversing Goose Falls, check the tide chart for nearby Castine: usharbors.com/harbor/maine/castine-me/tides/.

FINDING THE TRAILHEAD

From US 1 in Orland, head south on ME 15 for 3.7 miles to the junction with ME 199. Turn right and follow ME 199 south for 5 miles to the junction with ME 175 in Penobscot. Turn left (south) on ME 175 and continue for 4.8 miles to a junction with ME 176. Turn right after the gas station and farm stand to head west on ME 176 to a stop sign at 1.1 miles. Turn right (northwest) toward West Brooksville to continue following ME 176 for 5.6 miles; turn right (west) after the Holbrook Island Sanctuary sign onto Cape Rosier Road. Follow Cape Rosier Road for 1.6 miles and turn right (northwest) onto unpaved Back Road. At 0.8 mile in on Back Road, pass Indian Bar Road, where the park headquarters, picnic area, and beach are located. At the next intersection, in another 0.6 mile, turn right (north) onto Dock Road. Follow Dock Road for 0.2 mile to the main dock parking area on the left (west). Goose Falls trailhead is at the west end of the main dock parking area. **GPS:** N44 21.31' / W68 48.17'

WHAT TO SEE

The isolated Goose Falls Trail takes you right next to the waters of Penobscot Bay and offers great views of Holbrook Island and 14-mile-long Islesboro Island while going along volcanic rock and ledges that are millions of years old. Along the trail, hikers can look west to southwest across the giant bay and see a long stretch of the Camden Hills, including the hulking mass of Mount Megunticook, farthest to the southwest.

Charles Cannon, manager of Holbrook Island Sanctuary, said the Goose Falls Trail is one of his favorites in the park. "I like the views," he said. "I also like the different ledges and the granite outcrops." Cannon added that he is grateful to the late Anita K. Harris, who donated virtually all the land for the 1,345-acre state park, situated on the Cape Rosier peninsula south across Castine Harbor.

The park also includes 115-acre Holbrook Island, located about 0.5 mile offshore and site of the family home of Harris, who was single with no children. Her family wealth stemmed from her grandfather, founder of the Plymouth Cordage Co. of Massachusetts, a big manufacturer of rope for large sailing vessels. Her father, Edward K. Harris, the largest stockholder in Plymouth Cordage, bought Holbrook Island for $500 in 1891, launching a long family history in the area. In the 1890s he built an estate and farm buildings, and the family began spending summers there.

Anita Harris was a free spirit who loved dogs and horses and worldwide travel. She lived summers in the sixteen-room family home on Holbrook Island until World War II, when she changed her way of life and spent the whole year there. She quietly began buying land on the mainland after her parents died.

In 1971, when she was 77, she donated 1,230 acres to the State of Maine to "preserve for the future a piece of the unspoiled Maine that I used to know," according to the book *Anita's Island*, a history of Holbrook Island by Reta Farnham Hunter. Hunter's father, Capt. Brainard Farnham, operated the Harris family's triple cockpit mahogany speedboat

On the Goose Falls Trails, you can look across Penobscot Bay and view a stretch of the Camden Hills on the mainland.

and did other work for the family. Since she was a little girl, Hunter spent much time on the island and was close to Anita Harris and her younger sister, Marian, a graduate of Radcliffe College, who died in 1962.

Maybe it seemed an idyllic island existence, but there were Harris family tensions. A young son died, and Anita Harris believed her parents favored her other sister. She later disliked her brother-in-law, calling him "old fanny pincher," and he usually stayed on the mainland when her younger sister visited the island.

Anita Harris's estate donated Holbrook Island to the state in 1985 after she died on the island at age 92. She willed money for operation and maintenance of the park, with some restrictions to help keep the land wild. The large Harris family home on Holbrook Island was taken down in 1986 and some parts, such as doors and windows, were sold. A painting of Harris was preserved by the state, but the building's furnishings were auctioned off at the Maine Maritime Academy in Castine.

This guide focuses on the Goose Falls Trail, but the state park offers far more for visitors and hikers, including at least nine other trails, such as the Back Shore Trail, which is full of old foundations, cellars, and gardens from the once-magnificent Hutchins estate, where the Harris family lived while their sixteen-room home was being built on Holbrook Island. The Back Shore Trail leads to a remote pebble and stone beach that we enjoyed. We also spent time at the sand beach and picnic area near the park headquarters, where we saw a bald eagle.

The Goose Falls Trail, marked by orange blazes on trees, starts at the dock parking area near the end of Dock Road and is just about 1.0 mile round-trip.

Narrow at the beginning, the trail quickly takes you through birch trees and along thick ferns to the shore at 0.1 mile. Soon you reach a rocky ledge with an old tree stump for sitting, as well as a view of Holbrook Island and, behind it, a section of Islesboro Island across Penobscot Bay. Looking to the west and southwest, you can see the hills of Northport and Ducktrap Mountain on the mainland.

On a sunny day in early September, the waters of Penobscot Bay were silent and peaceful, hallmarks of the park as a whole, according to the park manager. The park has only 10,000 to 12,000 visits a year, Cannon said. "It is quiet. If people like solitude and seclusion and trails with no crowds, it's a good place." The sanctuary can have a lot of biting bugs, including mosquitoes, but an over-the-counter repellent usually provides enough protection, he noted.

At various points, the trail is lined with deciduous trees such as maples and oaks and also conifers like spruce and cedar. From much of the trail, you can get good distant views of Islesboro Island in the northern part of Penobscot Bay beyond Holbrook Island. Islesboro Island lies about 3 miles offshore, and it splits Maine's largest bay, Penobscot Bay, into two sections—an east and west passage.

As you continue along the trail, you step over a lot of roots and reach a stony beach with views of hills to the west on the mainland. After this spot, ascend slightly along a rock face and then up and down along roots and granite to an informal trail at 0.3 mile that takes you to a viewpoint about 20 feet above the water. Some huge boulders and a private dock are visible to the southwest, on the other side of Goose Falls Cove.

From here you can look across the bay beyond Islesboro to the mainland and see big sloping Mount Megunticook to the southwest then—south to north on the skyline—Bald Rock Mountain, Frohock Mountain in a low point in Lincolnville, the rising Ducktrap Mountain, and then the hills of Northport. After taking in the views from the

A boat motors betw
the Goose Falls Trail
Holbrook Isl

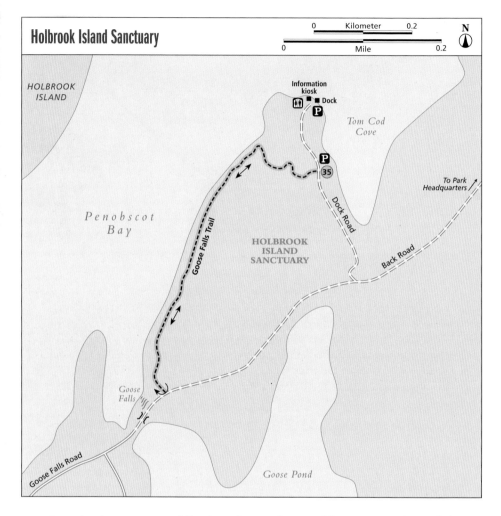

0   Kilometer   0.2

0   Mile   0.2

N

HOLBROOK
ISLAND

Information
kiosk

Dock

Tom Cod
Cove

P

P
35

To Park
Headquarters

Penobscot
Bay

Dock Road

HOLBROOK
ISLAND
SANCTUARY

Back Road

Goose Falls Trail

Goose
Falls

Goose Falls Road

Goose Pond

rocky, volcanic promontory, hike through a nearly untrodden mossy section and then across a 5-foot-long wooden footbridge over a creek with rocky ledges.

The trail ends at Back Road at 0.5 mile just northeast of Goose Falls, where you can see the reversing falls during an outgoing tide. Special to Maine along the US Atlantic seaboard, reversing falls are created by changing tides, bedrock just below the surface of the water, and a narrow, constricting channel, according to the University of Maine's Sea Grant program.

Goose Falls drains Goose Pond in a rush of whitewater during ebb tide through a tight opening in the subsurface bedrock. "It's not like a waterfall," Cannon explained. "It's more like a rapids."

Goose Pond was actually drained in 1968 as part of the old Callahan mining operation, but a local reclamation group worked with a mining representative to revive the pond with tidewater in the early 1970s.

Looking southwest, you can also see a dam at Goose Falls that is a legacy of the Callahan ore mine, which was under Goose Pond and next to it.

The wooded Holbrook Island was home to Anita Harris, who donated the land for Holbrook Island Sanctuary State Park.

Fearful that the old mining operation was contaminating the cove, Anita Harris moved her boat float on the mainland from Goose Falls Cove about 1 mile to the northeast to Tom Cod Cove and also began using Castine Harbor more often.

The Callahan mine closed in 1972, but it has been designated a federal Superfund site. The initial cleanup of PCBs and other contamination was completed in 2013, but ongoing cleanup will continue for many years.

Turn around and return the way you came.

MILES AND DIRECTIONS

0.0   Start at the Goose Falls trailhead, at the west end of the main dock parking area.

0.1   Reach the coast and a view of nearby Holbrook Island and Castine across Penobscot Bay.

0.3   Informal spur trail to rocky promontory.

0.4   Cross a wooden footbridge.

0.5   The trail ends at Back Road, just northeast of Goose Falls. Retrace your steps.

1.0   Arrive back at the dock parking area.

36 PETIT MANAN NATIONAL WILDLIFE REFUGE—BIRCH POINT

Hikers on the Birch Point Trail first pass impressive Carrying Place Cove and then Dyer Bay, where you can watch bald eagles near Sally Island and possibly catch the start of a brilliant sunset. You can get views of lobster boats in action, walk along well-maintained board-walks, and learn a lot about wildlife, plants, and geography from interpretive signs. You can also spend a lot of time picking wild Maine blueberries in August.

Start: Birch Point trailhead, at the southwest end of the refuge's first parking lot
Elevation gain: 358 feet
Distance: 4.2-mile circuit hike, not including an optional 0.2-mile round-trip low-tide walk to Sally Island
Difficulty: Moderate
Hiking time: 2.5–3.5 hours
Seasons/schedule: Open year-round during daylight hours; best spring through fall, late July through early Aug for blueberry picking
Fees and permits: No fees or permits
Trail contact: Maine Coastal Islands National Wildlife Refuge, PO Box 1735, Rockland 04841; (207) 594-0600; fws.gov/refuge/Maine_Coastal_Islands/
Dog-friendly: Dogs permitted on a hand-held leash no longer than 10 feet
Trail surface: Forest floor, footbridges, bogwalks, boardwalks, sandy and rocky beach; rocky tidal flats to Sally Island if visiting at low tide after eagle nesting season ends (Aug 31)
Land status: 2,195-acre mainland Petit Manan refuge; part of the Maine Coastal Islands National Wildlife Refuge, owned and maintained by the US Fish and Wildlife Service
Nearest town: Steuben
Maps: USGS Petit Manan Point; Maine Coastal Islands National Wildlife Refuge trail map
Other trail users: Birders, local residents, trail runners, dog walkers, blueberry pickers
Special considerations: No facilities. No camping, fires, bicycles, horses, or motorized vehicles. Open to deer hunting during Maine's muzzleloader season in December. Hand-picking of wild Maine blueberries only. Benches and Adirondack-style chairs available at select viewpoints. Trail map can be downloaded at fws.gov/uploadedFiles/Region_5/NWRS/North_Zone/Maine_Coastal_Islands/Maine%20trails.pdf. *Note:* If planning on the low-tide walk to Sally Island after eagle nesting season ends Aug 31, check the tide for nearby Prospect Harbor: usharbors.com/harbor/maine/prospect-harbor-me/tides/. It's only safe to cross within 1.5 hours on either side of low tide.

FINDING THE TRAILHEAD

 From US 1 in Steuben at the refuge's brown Petit Manan Point Division sign, turn south on Pigeon Hill Road. Follow the road 5.7 miles into the refuge and park at the first parking lot on the right (west). The Birch Point trailhead is at the southwest end of the lot. **GPS:** N44 26.21' / W67 53.37'

WHAT TO SEE

The Birch Point Trail heads north on the Petit Manan Point peninsula and offers side trails to Carrying Place Cove and views of a massive salt marsh on the eastern shore of the peninsula. The trail then swings toward Birch Point to the northwest for the chance to watch bald eagles in Dyer Bay. You can also complete a short low-tide walk to Sally Island if it is after August 31, when the eagle nesting season is over and the island is again open to the public. Along the way, you can stop and read interpretive signs with sliding panels that explain the importance of fields, plants like sphagnum moss, coves, salt marshes, cobble beaches, bald eagles, and forests.

The Birch Point Trail is one of two hiking trails in the 2,195-acre mainland Petit Manan refuge. Part of the 8,287-acre Maine Coastal Islands National Wildlife Refuge, Petit Manan is one of four mainland divisions. The coastal refuge complex also includes Petit Manan Island and more than sixty other islands.

The 4.2-mile round-trip starts at the trailhead at the southwest end of the parking lot and heads west to northwest through a blueberry field along an old cart path. The trail enters woods at 0.1 mile and, over the next 0.5 mile, passes a couple more fields with blueberries and benches at each field. The trail goes over a wooden footbridge at 0.8 mile and reaches a junction where you turn right (northeast) onto a short spur to head to an overlook with views of Carrying Place Cove.

At 0.9 mile reach the overlook at the midpoint of Carrying Place Cove, where four Adirondack-style chairs offer sweeping views of the cove and Pigeon Hill (northeast) across the water. During a mid-October hike, across the cove, the sun exposed plenty of

An eagle's nest, seen on the north shore of Sally Island in Petit Manan, will often be reused for years by breeding pairs.

Hikers get this view from Lobster Point in the
Petit Manan National Wildlife Refuge.

nice fall colors, with some hardwoods such as red maples and yellow birch among the dominant green conifers.

Retrace your steps to the junction and turn right (northwest) to continue on the main trail.

Affirming an interpretive sign about the coniferous forest, the aroma of balsam fills the air. Balsam needles are soft and flat, not pointy like those of its fellow conifer, spruce.

At 1.1 miles ascend a little and then walk over a series of boardwalks, all less than 100 feet long, to reach an interpretive sign about sphagnum moss, with some samples thriving amid the moist coastal peat in the area. Like with the other signs along this trail, look at the bottom of a wooden case and slide the colored end of a handle up to the right to read the exhibit. Each case has three white, gray, and black handles at the bottom.

Reach a side trail at 1.5 miles to Lobster Point on Carrying Place Cove; turn right (northeast) to head to the point. Soon pass an expansive salt marsh, rimmed by a distant forest. The salt marsh is an incredibly important part of the ecosystem, partly because it supports birds for nesting and migration and filters nutrients and other runoff from higher areas.

At 1.7 miles reach a cobble beach on the left (northwest) and bear right (east) to loop around Lobster Point, with four Adirondack-style chairs facing the shore. If the sun is out and you're visiting in the fall, you can get some nice colors on the shore to the north and northwest while looking over brown rocky ledge in front of the chairs. About fifteen buoys bobbed in the water off the point, and the call of a pileated woodpecker echoed nearby.

Return to the start of the Lobster Point loop at 1.8 miles and bear right (southwest) across the boardwalk to return to the main trail. At 2.0 miles, back at the junction with the Birch Point Trail, bear right (northwest) and continue on the main trail. At 2.1 miles reach a series of bogwalks that go around the Birch Point Loop, bearing right (north) to go counterclockwise to reach the shore more quickly.

There is a tricky left at a point at 2.3 miles, with a white arrow painted on a wooden sign.

Look to the west off the point in Dyer Bay for a clear view of Sally Island, just 1 acre and home to nesting bald eagles, the US national bird. Sheep Island is larger and just to the north of Sally. Sally Island is marked by thick, tall spruce. The island was donated to the refuge in 1996 by The Conservation Fund, headquartered in Arlington, Virginia.

On our first hike here, the setting sun was spectacular as it reflected off the shallow pools of water between Sally Island and a cobble beach on Birch Point. The sky and clouds above the island turned yellow, pink, and dark gray. We saw at least two bald eagles fly just above the treetops on the island, near a large nest. We heard a high-pitched call, almost like a gull. An interpretive trail sign about bald eagles later described the eagle's call and noted that an average eagle's height is 34 inches.

Bald eagles were one of the first species protected under the 1973 Endangered Species Act. They made a strong comeback following a ban on DDT and were removed from the federal endangered list in 2007. They were first observed nesting on Sally Island in 1985. The island can be reached from this stretch of the Birch Point Trail at low tide, but it is closed to the public February 15 to August 31 during eagle nesting season.

On a second hike to this same point, at low tide in early September, we walked across the rocky tidal flats to Sally Island. If you attempt the low-tide walk, be careful—the rocks and seaweed are slippery. And be mindful of the incoming tide.

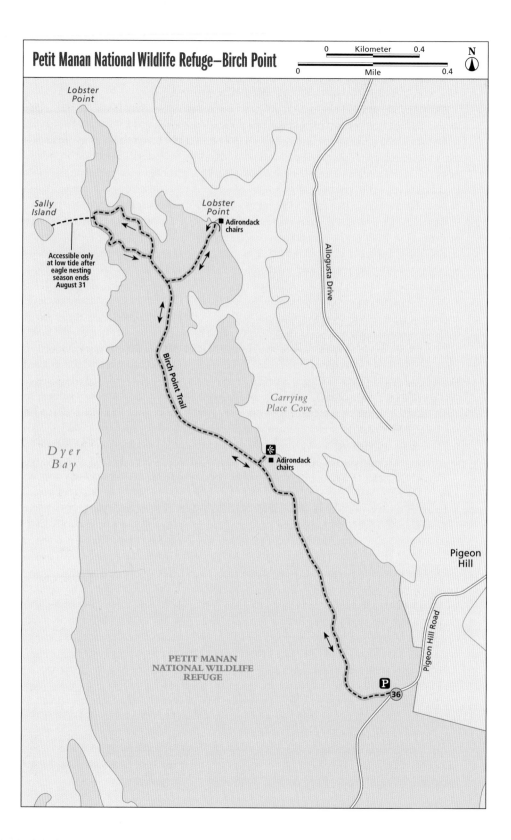

Petit Manan National Wildlife Refuge–Birch Point

0   Kilometer   0.4

0   Mile   0.4

N

Lobster
Point

Sally
Island

Lobster
Point

■ Adirondack
chairs

Accessible only
at low tide after
eagle nesting
season ends
August 31

Allogusta Drive

Birch Point Trail

Carrying
Place Cove

D y e r
B a y

■ Adirondack
chairs

Pigeon
Hill

Pigeon Hill Road

PETIT MANAN
NATIONAL WILDLIFE
REFUGE

P
36

Once across to the near eastern shore of Sally Island, we walked counterclockwise to the north shore and saw a large stick nest high in the trees. As we stood nearly under the nest just off the north shore, we watched a juvenile eagle land in the nest and then later fly away, getting a closeup view of its large wing span.

On the Birch Point Trail, as you round the point away from Sally Island, cross a cobble beach along the edge of wetlands and read about eagles at an interpretive sign at 2.4 miles, just as the trail reenters the woods. At 2.7 miles close the Birch Point loop and bear right (south) to head back on the main trail to the parking lot, bypassing the side trails to Lobster Point and the overlook on the return.

Arrive back at the parking lot at 4.2 miles.

MILES AND DIRECTIONS

0.0 Start at the Birch Point trailhead, at the southwest end of the refuge's first parking lot.

0.8 Reach a junction with a short spur to an overlook; turn right (northeast) for views of Carrying Place Cove.

0.9 Retrace your steps back to the junction; turn right (northwest) to continue on the main trail.

1.5 Reach a junction with a side trail to Lobster Point; turn right (northeast) to head toward Lobster Point.

1.7 Reach a cobble beach on the left (northwest); bear right (east) to loop around tiny Lobster Point, passing Adirondack-style chairs.

1.8 Return to the start of the Lobster Point loop; bear right (southwest) to return to the main trail.

2.0 Return to the Birch Point Trail; bear right (northwest) to continue on the main trail.

2.1 Reach a series of bogwalks that take you around the Birch Point Loop, bearing right (north) to go counterclockwise to reach the shoreline views more quickly.

2.3 The trail turns left (south) at a white arrow painted on a wooden sign. (**Option:** If it's low tide and after eagle nesting season ends on August 31, you can walk 0.1 mile west across the rocky tidal flats to reach Sally Island, where an eagle's nest can be found high in the trees on the north shore [to the right] of the island.)

2.4 Continue on the Birch Point Trail as it rounds away from Sally Island, crosses a cobble beach along the edge of wetlands, and reenters the woods.

2.7 Close the Birch Point Loop and bear right (south) to head back on the main trail to the parking lot, skipping the side trails to Lobster Point and the overlook on the return.

4.2 Arrive back at the parking lot.

37 PETIT MANAN NATIONAL WILDLIFE REFUGE— HOLLINGSWORTH

The John Hollingsworth Memorial Trail passes through a forest of jack pine, tamarack, and spruce to bring you to some king-size stretches of rocky shoreline and a little-visited beach ideal for exploring tide pools and flats at low tide. In fall the beach comes alive with migrating plovers, and black huckleberry shrubs are ablaze with red foliage. Located on the eastern side of Petit Manan Point, the trail provides views of islands amid the broad waters of Pigeon Hill Bay.

Start: Hollingsworth trailhead, on the east side of the road across from the refuge's second parking area
Elevation gain: 173 feet
Distance: 2.7-mile circuit hike
Difficulty: Moderate
Hiking time: 1.5–2.5 hours
Seasons/schedule: Open year-round during daylight hours; best spring through fall, low tide for shorebird viewing
Fees and permits: No fees or permits
Trail contact: Maine Coastal Islands National Wildlife Refuge, PO Box 1735, Rockland 04841; (207) 594-0600; fws.gov/refuge/Maine_Coastal_Islands/
Dog-friendly: Dogs permitted on a hand-held leash no longer than 10 feet
Trail surface: Gravel path, forest floor, rock ledges, boardwalks, bogwalks, cobble and sandy beach, tidal flats

Land status: 2,195-acre mainland Petit Manan refuge; part of the Maine Coastal Islands National Wildlife Refuge, owned and maintained by the US Fish and Wildlife Service
Nearest town: Steuben
Maps: USGS Petit Manan Point; Maine Coastal Islands National Wildlife Refuge trail map
Other trail users: Birders, local residents, trail runners, dog walkers
Special considerations: No facilities. No camping, fires, bicycles, horses, or motorized vehicles. Open to deer hunting during Maine's muzzleloader season in December. Interpretive exhibits along the trail are taken down for the winter, although plant identification tags remain on display. Limited parking for 8 vehicles. Benches and Adirondack-style chairs available at select viewpoints. Trail map can be downloaded at fws.gov/uploadedFiles/Region_5/NWRS/North_Zone/Maine_Coastal_Islands/Maine%20trails.pdf.

FINDING THE TRAILHEAD

From US 1 in Steuben at the refuge's brown Petit Manan Point Division sign, turn south on Pigeon Hill Road. Follow the road 5.7 miles into the refuge; pass the refuge's first parking lot and travel 0.4 mile on what is now a gravel road to the refuge's second parking area on the right (west). The Hollingsworth trailhead is on the east side of the road. **GPS:** N44 26.00' / W67 53.51'

WHAT TO SEE

The John Hollingsworth Memorial Trail is home to a tremendous variety of birds and plants and takes hikers over stunning bedrock and boulders to a quiet and isolated pocket

Black huckleberry turns scarlet in October along the Hollingsworth Trail at the Petit Manan National Wildlife Refuge.

On their migration south, eight semipalmated plovers make a stop on a beach at the Petit Manan National Wildlife Refuge.

beach with distant views of Petit Manan Island. The trail is named for photographer John Hollingsworth, who with his wife, Karen, took pictures of more than 400 national wild-life refuges, spurring support for wildlife conservation. The eponymous trail includes seasonal exhibits on wildlife, plants, and geography with viewing and photography tips from the Hollingsworths.

Totaling 2.7 miles round-trip, the hike leads to a pocket beach that alone is worth the trip because of its large spaces for walking, even at a higher tide, and opportunities for watching shorebirds such as plovers and sandpipers.

If you hike the Hollingsworth Trail in the fall, you will walk along some thick stretches of black huckleberry bushes that turn blazing red, providing some bright fall color that contrasts nicely with the green conifers and blue ocean waters. In summer the marsh near the shore is bursting with blue flag iris. Laughing gulls and terns can be spellbinding as they soar and sometimes dive into the ocean for food right in front of you. You might also get lucky, as we did, and see a spruce grouse in the conifer forest.

The Petit Manan Point peninsula includes a fascinating history of dreams of wealth gone bust and, finally, a generous transfer by a Maine family to create conservation land for public access.

Near the turn of the twentieth century, most of the peninsula was owned by a com-pany that planned to turn the land into a summer haven for the well-to-do, much like Bar Harbor, located just 12 to 14 miles away by boat, explained Sean Billings, president of the Steuben Historical Society. The company constructed tennis courts, a golf course, a saltwater swimming impoundment, a steamboat wharf, a recreational hall, and a 700-acre deer enclosure with the goal of attracting hunters at a time when the white-tailed deer population had been nearly wiped out by hunting in the United States.

The company planned a hotel and also subdivided portions of Petit Manan Point into hundreds of development lots, along with a tower for viewing the lots. The com-

pany went belly up, however, and after at least two other failed development attempts, much of the peninsula eventually was acquired by the Mague family, who turned it into a saltwater farm and used the cleared areas for sheep grazing and blueberry barrens.

In 1975, with the threat of development once again looming over the land, William R. Mague and his wife, Priscilla Hall Mague, sold 1,706 acres at "very little compared to its value" to The Nature Conservancy, according to an article in the *New York Times*. The Nature Conservancy then transferred 1,743 acres to the US Fish and Wildlife Service in 1976 and 284 acres in 1977 to create the Petit Manan National Wildlife Refuge, according to the US Department of the Interior.

A pink-edged sulphur butterfly feeds on the nectar of orange hawkweed at the Petit Manan National Wildlife Refuge.

In the *Times* article, Curtis Bohlen, then deputy assistant secretary of the Department of the Interior, said the preservation of Petit Manan, one of the largest undeveloped peninsulas remaining on the Maine coast at the time, was "an act of unselfish public spirit by a family of modest resources."

Without the refuge, Billings said, the land would have been developed and Maine would be without what has become a great public asset.

William Mague, who was 94 when he died in 2002, and his wife were married for fifty-four years and had four children. A native of Worcester, Massachusetts, he was a choir director at churches in New Haven, Connecticut, and Springfield, Massachusetts, and later became director of the old Northern Conservatory of Music in Bangor. In his later years, he became a registered surveyor and a deacon at a church in Milbridge.

The Mague family lived on Petit Manan and loved and maintained it in an unspoiled state for more than four decades before the transfer to the federal government. After the sale of their land, the Magues kept a 175-acre homestead on Petit Manan peninsula; their family farmhouse still stands on the land. When Priscilla Mague died suddenly at her home in 1987, the refuge manager noted in an annual report, "Her love for and support of the refuge will always be missed."

We hiked the Hollingsworth Trail twice, once in mid-October and again on July 4.

The trail starts across from the parking area on the east side of the gravel road, following a

A laughing gull lifts its long wings to fly above other laughing gulls off the Hollingsworth Trail at Petit Manan Point.

path through a field where we saw a pink-edged sulphur butterfly feeding on the nectar of orange hawkweed during our July hike. Enter the woods at 0.1 mile; when the trail forks at 0.2 mile, with an arrow pointing to the right (west), head left (east) to reach the shoreline faster.

Cross a bogwalk and see tamarack and jack pine, and soon reach a cedar swamp with thick bushes of black huckleberry. We paused for several minutes to listen to the beautiful whistle of a white-throated sparrow hidden in the woods. The trail starts to parallel the shore of Pigeon Hill Bay, one of two big bays that flank the peninsula, and at 0.7 mile comes to a place where you can access a small cobblestone beach. Walk over a double-plank walkway, keeping the cove to your left (east), and then cut into a small forest.

At 0.8 mile you reach an Adirondack-style bench with great views on a clear day of 1,155-acre Bois Bubert Island and Little Bois Bubert, both donated by The Nature Conservancy and owned by the national wildlife refuge. Bois Bubert is about 1 mile to the east and runs parallel to Petit Manan Point peninsula. To the north you can see 317-foot Pigeon Hill, owned by the Downeast Coastal Conservancy.

During our July hike, common terns, with black caps and orange bills, hovered over the water and sometimes dived into the surface, apparently looking for fish. Perched nearby on ledges covered by rockweed were about eight laughing gulls, a species of special concern in Maine, the northern limit for their breeding.

In the distance to the southeast are the first views of Petit Manan Island with its 1855 lighthouse. Jutting off the nearby shore is a distinctive flat-topped rock that almost looks like a small obelisk. One double-crested cormorant perched on the rock; another was next to it.

Follow the trail to a rocky point and intertidal ledges. There are some vast spaces to explore along the shore, with huge blocks of pink and black granite and two impressive tide pools. We saw a song sparrow perched on a post near here. You soon pass a stretch of marshland blooming with dozens of northern blue flag iris in early July and beach pea. Blue flag is common in Maine, but the numbers seemed immense for one small area. We also saw hedge bindweed, a wild morning glory, along the shore near here.

At 0.9 mile the trail rounds a point and heads northwest on a series of bogwalks. At 1.0 mile turn left (west) onto a spur trail to reach Adirondack-style chairs and access to the big pocket beach just to the west. Be careful of wet or moss-covered rocks while clambering down to explore the beach.

The wide beach, composed of cobblestones, pebbles, and sandy stretches, is bordered to the northwest by Chair Pond. Chair Pond, with fresh and brackish water, is isolated from the ocean by the pocket beach and is surrounded by bogs and peat.

In early October, at least twenty to thirty shorebirds, mostly semipalmated plovers, scurried on the pocket beach and fed along the shoreline and tide pools and sometimes flew low over the sand. The birds migrate great distances and were likely headed to Central and South America for the winter.

During low tide in July, two bigger black-bellied plovers rested on rocks near the beach. One was a nonbreeding adult, with a mostly brown back and white breast; the other was a juvenile, with bold streaks on its breast.

From the beach, 16-acre Petit Manan Island can be seen 3 miles to the southeast. The island was named by French explorer Samuel de Champlain in 1604 and came into the refuge's ownership following a transfer by the US Coast Guard in 1974. The island, a nesting site for eiders, laughing gulls, terns, and other seabirds, has no trees but it hosts

Petit Manan Light rises in the distance in the Gulf of Maine from the Hollingsworth Trail at Petit Manan National Wildlife Refuge.

Petit Manan Light. The closed light tower, topped by a lantern house, is Maine's second-highest lighthouse, with an automated solar light projecting 123 feet above the ocean.

Reach the far (southwestern) end of the beach at a granite ledge at 1.2 miles with tamarack growing along the beach and a black dike, evidence of ancient volcanic activity, stretching from the shore to under the ocean. Turn around and return along the beach to the junction with the main trail at 1.5 miles. Turn left (northwest) to loop back to the parking area.

Walking through a forest, including more tamarack and evergreen such as jack pine, we heard the call of a spruce grouse and then saw the bird perched on a boulder before it flew and landed on a branch. The spruce grouse displayed a bright red eyebrow with brown and black spots on its back and tail. It's also known as "fool hen," for its tameness around humans.

Cross more bogwalk and pass tamarack, mountain ash, and catberry.

At 2.4 miles you are back to the fork near the start of the trail, where we had headed east to get the shoreline views as early as possible. Stay straight (northwest) to head back to the parking lot, arriving at 2.7 miles.

MILES AND DIRECTIONS

0.0 Start at the Hollingsworth trailhead, across from the refuge's second parking area.

0.2 The trail forks, with an arrow pointing to right; head left (east) to reach shoreline views sooner.

0.7 Skirt a cobble beach.

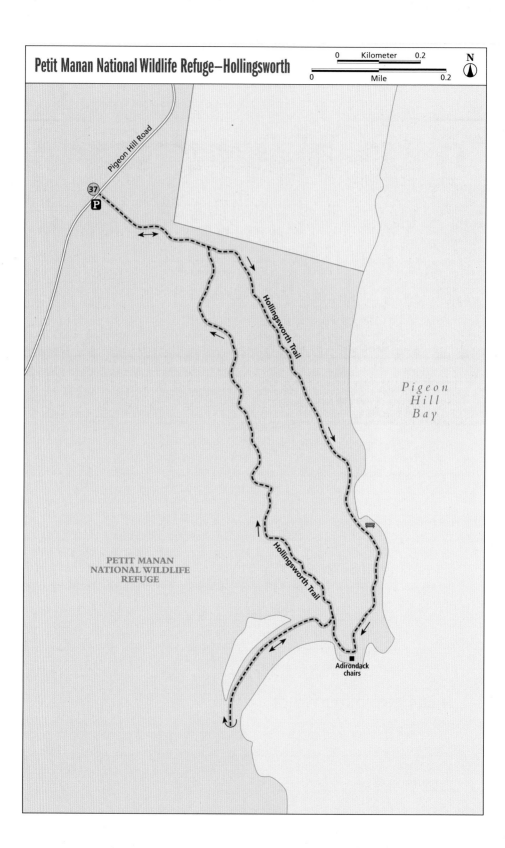

Petit Manan National Wildlife Refuge–Hollingsworth

Pigeon Hill Road

37

P

Hollingsworth Trail

Hollingsworth Trail

Pigeon Hill Bay

PETIT MANAN
NATIONAL WILDLIFE
REFUGE

Adirondack
chairs

0   Kilometer   0.2

0   Mile   0.2

N

The Hollingsworth Trail at Petit Manan offers a variety of habitats, including this long beach.

0.8 Reach an Adirondack-style bench just as Petit Manan Island with its lighthouse comes into view.

1.0 The trail rounds a point to the right (northwest) along a bogwalk.

1.1 At a junction with a spur trail to the sandy pocket beach, turn left (west) off the main trail to explore the beach. Or sit on the Adirondack-style chairs to take in the views of the beach and Chair Pond directly behind the beach.

1.3 Reach the end of the beach at a granite ledge; turn around.

1.5 Return to the junction with the main trail; turn left (northwest) on the bogwalk to loop back to the parking area.

2.4 Arrive back at the fork near start of trail; stay straight (northwest) to head back to the parking area.

2.7 Arrive back at the parking area.

38 GREAT WASS ISLAND PRESERVE

Jutting out farther to sea than any other land mass in eastern Maine and protected by The Nature Conservancy since 1978, Great Wass Island Preserve is a place unto itself, like a primeval forest or even Alice's Wonderland. Rare plants like the subarctic baked-apple berry, coastal plateau bogs that formed thousands of years ago, a microclimate created by the meeting of the waters of the Gulf of Maine and the Bay of Fundy, a dramatic shoreline, and wildlife like beaver, snowshoe hare, and black-bellied plover make this worth adventuring to.

Start: Little Cape Point trailhead, at the east end of the parking area
Elevation gain: 387 feet
Distance: 5.0-mile loop
Difficulty: Moderate
Hiking time: 4.5–6 hours
Seasons/schedule: Open year-round during daylight hours; best spring through fall
Fees and permits: No fees or permits
Trail contact: The Nature Conservancy, 14 Maine St., Ste. 401, Brunswick 04011; (207) 729-5182; nature.org; e-mail: naturemaine@tnc.org
Dog-friendly: No dogs allowed

Trail surface: Forest floor, rock ledges, bogwalks, sandy and rocky beaches
Land status: 1,576 acres owned and maintained by The Nature Conservancy, a global environmental nonprofit
Nearest town: Beals
Maps: USGS Great Wass Island; The Nature Conservancy trail map
Other trail users: Local residents, birders, trail runners
Special considerations: No facilities. There are a couple of iron rungs to navigate a rock face. Do not drive beyond the parking area onto the private road and do not park on the road if the lot is full.

FINDING THE TRAILHEAD

From US 1 take ME 187 south to Jonesport; turn south at the US Coast Guard station onto Bridge Street and cross over Moosabec Reach to Beals. Turn left (east) at the end of the bridge onto Bay View Drive; continue for 1.1 miles and go over the causeway to Great Wass Island. At the T intersection, turn right (southeast) onto Black Duck Cove Road and continue for 2 miles to the Great Wass Island Preserve parking lot, on the left (east). **GPS:** N44 28.52' / W67 35.40'

WHAT TO SEE

Like Alice entering Wonderland, visitors to the Great Wass Island Preserve may find things out of the ordinary, from jack pines that don't need fire to reproduce as they do elsewhere to a beaver grooming itself by a saltwater pool, unbothered by onlooking hikers, like the fawn who was unafraid of Alice in the forest "where things have no name."

There's even a White Rabbit, when the snowshoe hare takes on its winter coat.

It's easy to be awestruck by the wonders of this place, whether by one of the largest jack pine stands in coastal Maine, the pink and white granite and colorful cobble beaches, or harbor seals hauled out on offshore ledges. We were amazed during our late-May hike to observe up close the grooming beaver and, later, two hopping snowshoe hares. On top of that, we saw our first-ever black-bellied plover in its distinctive black-and-white breeding plumage—and no other hikers during the 5.0-mile trek.

Part of the Great Wass Archipelago, made up of more than forty islands and considered to be of statewide ecological significance, Great Wass Island is connected via causeway to Beals Island, which in turn is connected to the mainland via a bridge. More than 90 percent of the 1,700-plus-acre island is owned by The Nature Conservancy (TNC). "No doubt the Great Wass Island Preserve is a special place," said Daniel Grenier, TNC Maine Preserves manager, in an e-mail. "From an ecological perspective, it's one of Maine's crown jewels."

Nearly thirty different natural communities, from forest to bog, headlands to salt marshes, can be found here, but perhaps none is more special than the jack pine woodlands, according to a paper by University of Maine at Farmington biology professor Andrew M. Barton, "Of Bogs and Pines: The Rare Nature of Great Wass Island."

Maine is the southernmost limit for jack pine, but the jack pine found on Great Wass Island is unlike that in the rest of the state. Normally, jack pines depend on fire to open cones and release seeds. Not those on Great Wass. In addition, "on the island, jack pine is a stunted, twisted, bonsai-like tree living on thin soils where other tree species cannot compete," said Grenier.

Another special aspect of Great Wass Island is a result of sticking out "dramatically" into the Gulf of Maine, Grenier explained: "an oceanic microclimate—always wet, cool, and windy—and buffered from temperature extremes." As a result, "the preserve provides excellent habitat for several rare plants typically found much farther north," such as bird's-eye primrose and beachhead iris. "Much of the shoreline gives the impression of being in the Arctic."

Start on the Little Cape Point Trail on the east end of the parking area, turning left (northeast) at 0.1 mile onto the Mud Hole Trail to get to the coastal views sooner, starting

The landscape at Great Wass can seem otherworldly.

The sun begins to set over Great Wass Island, leaving muted shades of yellow, orange, and purple.

with the area known as The Mud Hole. At 0.7 mile follow the trail right (east) to parallel The Mud Hole. At 1.4 miles reach the open waters of Eastern Bay and Mistake Harbor, where we saw harbor seals hauled out on a ledge to the northeast, with Steele Harbor, Head Harbor, and other islands of the Great Wass Archipelago in the distance. At first the marine mammals appeared part of the ledge; it was only when one dove into the water that we were able to confirm they were seals.

As the trail rounds Mud Hole Point, see Moose Peak Light on Mistake Island across the bay.

At 1.6 miles the picturesque pink granite slabs along the shoreline suggest Acadia's Ocean Path. The shoreline gives way to colorful cobbles, sandy patches, pebble beach, and then back to granite slabs again. At 2.2 miles follow a blue blaze painted on a rock into the woods for a short stretch; if you're lucky, you may see a beaver up close like we did, first swimming in a saltwater pool and then coming ashore to groom itself. We were so fascinated by this beaver's behavior—it used its forepaws and then its webbed hind feet to groom, sat on its broad leathery tail like a cushion, and seemed as though it was enjoying the relief of scratching an itch—we watched for 20 minutes, and could have watched longer.

The trail goes back out to the shoreline and at 2.3 miles starts rounding a sandy beach along a cove before going in and out through woods and along coastal granite slabs as it makes its way around Little Cape Point. Watch for blue blazes on trees and rocks so as not to lose the trail.

At 2.7 miles walk through a field of beach peas and round a wooded knoll at the tip of Little Cape Point, with a view of offshore pink granite ledges to the southeast. Although no obvious sign marks the transition, you are now on the Little Cape Point Trail and looping northwest back toward the uplands.

The shoreline is now white granite; at 2.8 miles climb a couple of iron rungs to get up a tricky rock face, transition back to cobble beach, and follow an arrow on a wood sign to head away from the shore for a bit. It's at this point in our hike that we saw a white-tailed deer bound off into the woods and watched two snowshoe hares nibble on grass and hop off on their large hind feet, which keep them from sinking in winter's snow and propel them as fast as 25 miles per hour.

A sandy beach at Great Wass is nestled between pink and white granite ledges and colorful cobble beaches.

At 3.0 miles return to the shoreline as it alternates between cobble, sand, and pebble beach, and round a peatland. Depending on the season, you may see a black-bellied plover in breeding plumage, like we did along this stretch of wild coast, spot a territorial eastern willet, or hear the loud honks of Canada geese. At 3.3 miles reach a weathered bench and hand-painted Little Cape Point Trail sign pointing to the right (west). Head into the woods past jack pine and tamarack to complete the loop.

At 5.0 miles arrive back at the parking area.

MILES AND DIRECTIONS

0.0 Start at the Little Cape Point trailhead, at the east end of the parking area.

0.1 Turn left (northeast) onto the Mud Hole Trail.

0.7 Follow the trail sharply right (east) to parallel The Mud Hole.

1.4 Reach Mud Hole Point with views of Steele Harbor, Head Harbor, and other islands of the Great Wass Archipelago to the east and northeast, along with the more-open waters of Eastern Bay and Mistake Harbor.

2.2 Follow a blue blaze on a rock into the woods for a short stretch.

2.3 Round a small cove along a sandy beach; follow the trail in and out through woods and along granite slabs as it makes its way around Little Cape Point.

Great Wass Island Preserve

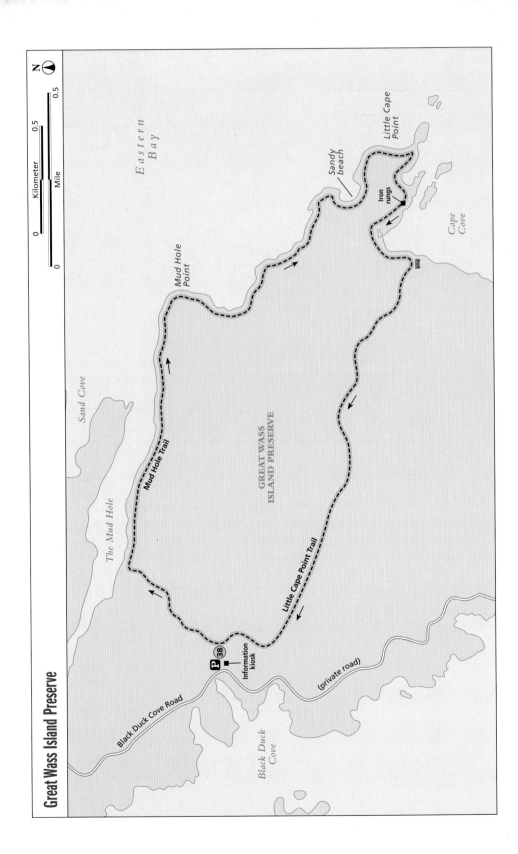

Walking along colorful cobbles demands attention on Great Wass Island.

2.7 Round a wooded knoll at the tip of Little Cape Point, where the Mud Hole Trail joins the Little Cape Point Trail.

2.8 Climb a couple iron rungs up a rock face and head away from the shore for a short stretch.

3.0 Return to the shoreline as it alternates between cobble, sand, and pebble beach and round a coastal peatland.

3.3 Reach a weathered bench; follow the sign pointing to the right (west) and head inland on the Little Cape Point Trail.

4.9 Reach the junction with the Mud Hole Trail on the right (northeast); stay straight (west) on the Little Cape Point Trail.

5.0 Arrive back at the parking area.

39 CUTLER COAST PUBLIC RESERVED LAND

The state-owned Cutler Coast Public Reserved Land offers 4.5 miles of undeveloped shoreline for hiking along sheer cliffs and cobble beaches, and shows why this Downeast stretch of Maine is called the Bold Coast.

Start: Coastal trailhead by the information kiosk, at the northwest end of the parking area

Elevation gain: 1,525 feet

Distance: 6.4 miles out and back

Difficulty: Moderate to strenuous

Hiking time: 3.5–5 hours

Seasons/schedule: Open year-round; best spring through fall, summer for chance of seeing whales offshore

Fees and permits: No fees or permits

Trail contact: Maine Bureau of Parks and Lands, Eastern Public Lands Office, 106 Hogan Rd., Ste. 5, Bangor 04401; (207) 941-4412; maine.gov/cutlercoast

Dog-friendly: Dogs must be under owner control at all times, on a leash no longer than 4 feet at campsites.

Trail surface: Forest floor, rock ledges, footbridges, bogwalks, wood and stone steps

Land status: 2,174-acre coastal reserve owned and maintained by the State of Maine

Nearest town: Cutler

Maps: USGS Cutler; Cutler Coast guide and map

Other trail users: Campers, birders, local residents, trail runners

Special considerations: Chemical toilet at the parking area and pit toilet at primitive campsites about 4 miles in, but no other facilities on the trail. Cliff tops can be dangerous, especially in wet or icy conditions. Mosquitoes and blackflies are thickest late May through early July. Wild Maine blueberries may be ripe for picking from late July through early August. If parking area with room for 20 vehicles is full, parking along ME 191 is permitted. No ATVs allowed on the coastal section of the public reserved land, only on the part of the property north of ME 191. Hunting is allowed, but loaded firearms are not permitted at campsites or on hiking trails, and discharge of weapons within 300 feet of trails, campsites, or parking area is also not permitted. Beaver activity has led to a recent reroute of the northern part of the Inland Trail, adding 1.2 miles to any hike incorporating that section, as noted at the parking area's information kiosk and on the updated trail map available for download at maine.gov/dacf/parksearch/PropertyGuides/PDF_GUIDE/cutlercoastguide.pdf.

FINDING THE TRAILHEAD

From US 1 in East Machias, head south on ME 191 for 16.9 miles, through the town of Cutler, to a parking area on the right (southeast) marked by a large Cutler Public Reserved Land sign. The Coastal trailhead is by the information kiosk, at the northwest end of the parking area. **GPS:** N44 41.55' / W67 09.29'

WHAT TO SEE

When you hike along the high, craggy cliffs towering over the Atlantic Ocean on the Cutler Coast, it's clear why it's sometimes called the Bold Coast Trail. The Cutler Coast Public Reserved Land, a signature attraction of the Bold Coast section of northern

Maine, boasts 4.5 miles of spectacular shorefront with sea arches, distinctive volcanic rock, pocket cobble beaches, and towering cliffs.

The Cutler Coast Public Reserved Land totals more than 12,000 acres, but the coastal section described in this hike comprises 2,174 acres, all south of ME 191; the rest is north of ME 191 and not included in this hike. The lands, owned and managed by the Maine Bureau of Parks and Land, were spared from development when they were purchased by the state at the rock-bottom price of $2.5 million in 1989, with some major behind-the-scenes help from Peggy and David Rockefeller and a national charity built by heirs to Mellon Bank.

"Bold Coast" is a maritime term for "a prominent landmass that rises steeply from the sea," according to the US Army Corps of Engineers. Bold Coast stuck over the years as a way to describe the coast mainly from Cutler northeast to West Quoddy Head.

The hike takes you through a thick northern forest and then up and down the coastline with views of the open sea and Grand Manan Island on the horizon. Try to hike on a clear, sunny day, as we did, because this trail is best known for the ocean and cliff views from some of the highest terrain directly on the coast in Maine. An early start also helps to avoid crowds, especially on weekends, in this area that is free to access with about twenty parking spaces.

This hike is 6.3 miles round-trip, all on the Coastal Trail. Instead of looping back on the more level Inland Trail through a sometimes wet and boggy maritime forest, return the way you came and take it easy on the ups and downs to capture the ocean views a second time.

Steve Spencer, retired outdoor recreation planner for the Maine Bureau of Public Reserved Lands, who supervised design and construction of the trails of Cutler Coast in the 1990s, said Maine is amazingly lucky to have public access to the coastal lands. "They are an absolute gem," he said.

Two hikers stand above the Bold Coast at the Cutler Coast Public Reserve Lands.

Here's a touch of pink granite in a coast dominated by black and gray rock, with Black Point in the distance.

Spencer estimates that some of the cliffs are likely in excess of 100 feet high. Hikers can also get great views from open heathlands and low rocky nubbles.

Before you hit the trail, consider that the 2,174-acre Cutler coastal property was for sale and could have easily been developed amid a building boom in the 1980s. Instead the lands were conveyed to the State of Maine by the Richard King Mellon Foundation in 1989 at the suggestion of Peggy Rockefeller. At the time, the land was believed to be the largest privately-owned mainland coastal property in Maine and maybe the Northeast.

The 2,174-acre coastal section is among 12,898 acres purchased by the Pittsburgh-based Mellon Foundation and conveyed to the State of Maine. The sale was facilitated by The Conservation Fund of Arlington, Virginia, and the Maine Coast Heritage Trust. The state purchased the coastal acreage for an incredible bargain of $2.5 million, according to the Land for Maine's Future, a program approved by voters in 1987 to buy land for conservation and recreation.

In 1997 the Mellon Foundation donated to the state the rest of the Cutler reserved lands: 10,724 acres of forest, peat bogs, and grasslands in Cutler and Whiting north of ME 191. The foundation had purchased those lands from a division of the Hearst Corp. responsible for paper procurement for Hearst-owned publications.

Maine resident Peggy Rockefeller recognized the threat of second-home development faced by the Bold Coast in the 1980s and worked to save the Cutler Coast lands. She was a founding board member of the American Farmland Trust, and her husband, David Rockefeller, was the son of Acadia National Park cofounder John D. Rockefeller Jr.

At the urging of his wife, David Rockefeller arranged a meeting between the Richard King Mellon Foundation and the Hearst Corp., which was seeking top dollar for the

A raft of black scoters, a type of sea duck, float in the ocean off the Cutler Coast.

12,898 acres. Before the request from Rockefeller, the Hearst Corp. had not responded to the foundation's requests for a meeting.

David Rockefeller, who died in 2017 and was CEO of the old Chase Manhattan Corp., and his wife, who died in 1996, had a home on Mount Desert Island in Maine for many years. Richard King Mellon, president of Mellon Bank and once among the wealthiest people in the United States, was a passionate conservationist like the Rockefellers and was an heir to the Mellon family fortune.

The Richard King Mellon Foundation, working with Maine Coast Heritage Trust and other land trusts, has purchased millions of acres of wildlands across the United States and has played a significant role in preserving big sections of the Bold Coast and other parts of Maine.

The hike starts from the parking lot on the south side of ME 191 in Cutler, which is part of the 125-mile Bold Coast Scenic Byway from Milbridge to Eastport. Hike along the Coastal Trail and go through a shady forest of evergreens such as spruce and balsam, as well as deciduous trees like gray birch and mountain ash. We hiked in late May; the woods were packed with warblers, and the distinctive call of the black-throated green warbler filled the air.

Pass a junction with the Inland Trail at 0.4 mile and stay straight (southeast) on the Coastal Trail, stepping on stones to cross a brook. Hike along some new wood planks and walkway, ascend along roots and up and down some rocks and then walk along multiple sections of bogwalk.

The forest is wet ground and delicate in many spots, with a lot of sphagnum moss, bogs, and heath. To protect the habitat, a lot of cedar walkway was built during trail construction before there was a lot of use. A helicopter crew from the Army National Guard in Bangor airlifted some 40,000 pounds of cedar planks for construction of the bogwalks. The trails were built over three years in the 1990s, after a planning process involving the town of Cutler and others. The trails were first scouted, flagged, and then constructed with assistance from the Maine Conservation Corps.

At 1.3 miles in the hike, you start hearing the ocean; at 1.5 miles you reach the coast and get your first good view of the ocean with an overlook into a narrow ravine. Climb up the Coastal Trail to the right (southwest) and you soon can get ocean views from the cliffs.

Ascend steeply at 1.7 miles and reach a height of land at 1.8 mile. Head down the cliffs, including some stone steps, with a dark granite cliff to the left (east). At 1.9 miles you get a close view of a cobble beach in a cove that is a mini version of Monument Cove off Ocean Path in Acadia National Park. Look back to the northeast, where some jagged bedrock cliffs rise over the cove.

Begin a descent from the view of the cove, with the ocean visible through trees. At 2.0 miles you get an alluring view of dark rocky ledges to the south and the ocean crashing on the ledges and smaller ledges farther out to sea.

At 2.1 miles there is a small, open grassy area near the coast and then a waterfall splashing down the cliffs to the ocean from a creek. At 2.3 miles we watched a raft of five black scoters splashing and diving in the ocean. At least some of the birds were males because of the bright butter color at the base of their bills.

Come to a grassy meadow with tamarack on the edge of the meadow at 2.4 miles. This tall-grass meadow may have persisted since the 1800s, when farmers burned forest to clear land for sheep or cattle, and shows how much more resilient such meadows

are than earlier thought, according to a Natural Heritage Hikes brochure about Cutler Coast, a project of the Maine Natural Areas Program.

Look back to the northeast at 2.6 miles and you can see the dark rocky cliffs jutting into the sea. Soon you see some pink cliffs and Black Point looming to the southeast. Cross a cascade at 2.9 miles; look south and you can see the Little River Lighthouse on Little River Island in the distance. We also saw a female eider and a common loon here.

Walk over a powerful creek at a cobble beach cove with some grassy slopes to the north off the trail and some difficult stepping along jagged rock at the coast. At 3.1 miles reach a junction with the Black Point Brook Cutoff on the right (west) and stairs on the left (east) down to a cobble beach along Black Point Cove. Descend the stairs and at 3.2 miles explore the beach with large cobbles and boulders tossed ashore by the open ocean; admire the surrounding granite cliffs, some of them a dark pink.

A rope at the far end of the beach allows you to climb the cliff and continue farther on the Coastal Trail to the campsites at Fairy Head. Fairy Head should probably be spelled "Ferry Head," because ferryboats on the Grand Manan Channel used the headland as a landmark to navigate into Cutler Harbor.

Return the way you came, for a 6.4-mile round-trip.

Option: Hike southeast another 2.0 miles on the Coastal Trail to Long Point Cove and finally Fairy Head, where there are several backcountry campsites. If you do this, you can loop back on the Inland Trail (but remember to factor in a trail reroute that has added 1.2 miles through what can be boggy territory) or return to the parking area by doubling back on the Coastal Trail.

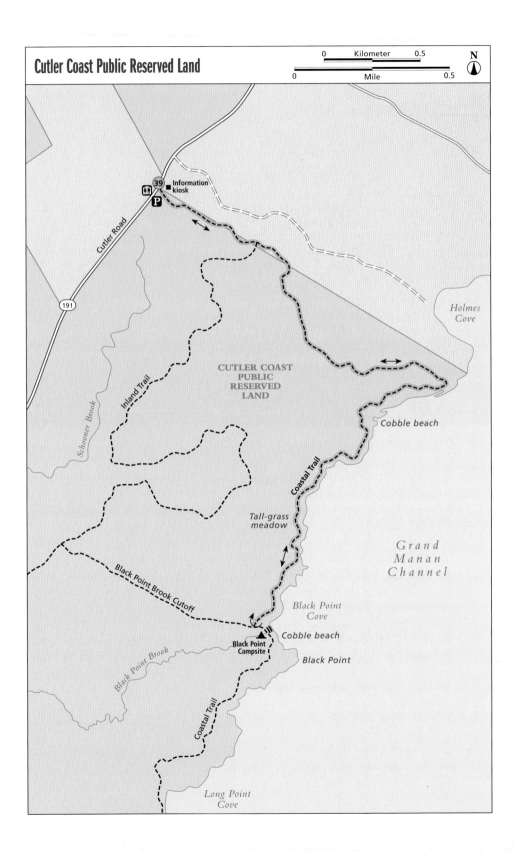

Cutler Coast Public Reserved Land

0   Kilometer   0.5

0   Mile   0.5

N

39

Information kiosk

Cutler Road

191

Schooner Brook

Inland Trail

CUTLER COAST
PUBLIC
RESERVED
LAND

Holmes
Cove

Cobble beach

Coastal Trail

Tall-grass
meadow

Grand
Manan
Channel

Black Point Brook Cutoff

Black Point
Cove

Black Point
Campsite

Cobble beach

Black Point

Black Point Brook

Coastal Trail

Long Point
Cove

This cobble beach on Black Point Cove is the turnaround point for the hike on the Bold Coast Trail.

MILES AND DIRECTIONS

0.0 Start at the Coastal trailhead, by the information kiosk at the northwest end of the parking area.

0.4 Reach the junction with the Inland Trail on the right; stay straight (southeast) on the Coastal Trail.

1.5 Reach the coast and follow the Coastal Trail to the right (southwest) as it parallels the shore.

1.9 Reach cliff top view of a cove with cobble beach below.

2.4 Cross a tall-grass meadow.

2.9 Cross a cascade.

3.1 Reach a junction with the Black Point Brook Cutoff on the right (west) and stairs on the left (east) down to a cobble beach along Black Point Cove.

3.2 Take the stairs and explore the beach; turn around and return the way you came.

6.4 Arrive back at the parking area.

40 QUODDY HEAD STATE PARK

This hike starts at the easternmost point of the US mainland, at the historic West Quoddy Head Light, noted for its red and white stripes. The Coastal Trail then takes you along rocky headlands to a long sandy beach backed by a rare coastal raised-plateau bog, and a series of inland trails leads you to an "arctic bogwalk" with insect-eating pitcher plants and sundews. In summer there's a good chance you could see whales swimming offshore at the mouth of the Bay of Fundy. Come on Saturday in July and August for a public lighthouse tour.

Start: Coastal trailhead, to the right (southwest) of the lighthouse visitor center and service building
Elevation gain: 503 feet
Distance: 4.0-mile circuit loop
Difficulty: Easy to moderate
Hiking time: 2.5–3.5 hours
Seasons/schedule: Open 9 a.m. to sunset May 15 through Oct 15; off-season visitors can walk past the locked gate during daylight hours. Best spring through fall, summer for chance of seeing whales offshore.
Fees and permits: Day-use fee
Trail contact: Quoddy Head State Park, 973 South Lubec Rd., Lubec 04652; (207) 733-0911, May 15–Oct 15
  Maine Bureau of Parks and Lands, 106 Hogan Rd., Ste. 7, Bangor 04401; (2017) 941-4014, Oct 16–May 14; maine.gov/quoddyhead
Dog-friendly: Leashed dogs permitted
Trail surface: Forest floor, rock ledges, footbridges, boardwalk, bogwalks, graded gravel, wooden steps, sand and gravel beach
Land status: 541-acre park owned and maintained by the State of Maine
Nearest town: Lubec
Maps: USGS Lubec; Quoddy Head State Park trail map

Other trail users: Lighthouse visitors, beachgoers, local residents, dog walkers, trail runners
Special considerations: Facilities include picnic area, grills, and chemical toilets. No camping or alcohol. Hunting is permitted in season, but not within 1,000 feet of the lighthouse. The self-service fee station, cash or check only, is at the main picnic area parking lot, on the right as you enter the park. The lighthouse visitor center is open 10 a.m. to 4 p.m. Memorial Day weekend through mid-Oct. The first 0.4 mile of the Coastal Trail, from the lighthouse to a series of memorial benches, is over graded gravel and may be accessible with assistance for visitors with wheelchairs or baby strollers. There are interpretive exhibits at the start of the Coastal Trail, at the picnic area, and along the Arctic Bog Walk. Be careful on cliffs, especially when they are wet. If exploring the beach at the base of the stairs by the picnic area or at Carrying Place Cove, watch for the incoming tide, as there can be a 20-foot difference between low and high tides. Mosquitoes and blackflies can be a problem in late spring and summer.

FINDING THE TRAILHEAD

From ME 189 in Lubec, head south on South Lubec Road for 2 miles to a fork in the road; bear left and continue another 2 miles to the park entrance. If you park at the main parking lot on the right as you enter, walk back to the lighthouse to start at the Coastal trailhead to the right (southwest) of the visitor center and service building. **GPS:** N44 48.54' / W66 57.03'

WHAT TO SEE

The Coastal Trail is 2.0 miles one way, but it is the longest of Quoddy Head State Park's five hiking trails. The Coastal Trail is also the most dramatic, with cliffs that are up to 150 feet high providing outstanding views of Sail Rock and into the waters of Canada to Grand Manan Island. The cliffs, rising 90 to 150 feet above the sea, stem from ocean volcanoes that blew their tops more than 400 million years ago and now constitute the bedrock of northern Maine. Glaciers and pounding surf helped create the cliffs.

The hike starts at the park's centerpiece, West Quoddy Head Light, located on the peninsula of West Quoddy Head, the easternmost point on the US mainland. During a quiet late afternoon in May, we were lucky to receive an impromptu tour of the lighthouse by Shawn Goggin, manager of Quoddy Head State Park. While many of Maine's sixty-six lighthouses are offshore, West Quoddy Head is among those more accessible to the public. Weather permitting, the lighthouse is open 1:30 to 3:30 p.m. for tours on Saturdays during July and August, or during special Maine open lighthouse days in September.

Goggin led the way up the narrow spiral cast-iron staircase to an observation area in the lantern room. The current brick tower was built in 1857, following a stone lighthouse in 1830 and the original lighthouse made out of wood in 1808. "From the ground to the top, the tower is 49 feet high," Goggin said while pointing out islands in the ocean outside the deck. "From the water to the light, it is 83 feet high."

The lighthouse's massive, 1,000-watt Fresnel lens from Paris, France, is in an enclosed, protected space at the top of the tower. The lens was installed in 1857, the same year as the stairs, and is still maintained and used as an aid to navigation by the US Coast Guard, which transferred ownership of the tower to the State of Maine in 1998.

West Quoddy Head Light peeks above the last rocky ledge, with the distinctive Sail Rock offshore to the right at Quoddy Head State Park.

Goggin said he is sometimes mistaken for a lighthouse keeper, but keeper duties are not included in his job as park manager. The last Coast Guard keeper left when the light was automated in 1988. "The lens still flashes 24 hours a day in a pattern, 2 seconds on, 2 off, 2 on and 9 seconds off," he noted. "The light is visible for 15 to 18 miles." Goggin's experience is somewhat similar to a keeper's, however; he, his wife, Kate, and two sons, Michael and Matthew, live year-round in the old keeper's house.

The West Quoddy Head Lightkeeper's Association operates the park's visitor center, located in another part of the old keeper's dwelling.

The top of the lighthouse affords 360-degree views of islands in the distance, while the Coastal Trail offers a more limited but still beautiful perspective. Looking south from West Quoddy Head Light, the second ledge in front of the lighthouse is Sail Rock, shaped like a sail. Look 10 miles to the southeast over Grand Manan Channel and you see the big cliffs and forested shores of 21-mile-long Grand Manan Island in Canada, first settled by British loyalists who opposed the American Revolution.

The southern end of Campobello Island, site of the Franklin D. Roosevelt summer home and Roosevelt Campobello International Park in New Brunswick, Canada, is to the northeast over the Quoddy Narrows and can be seen partially from the lawn of the lighthouse. The Wolves Islands, a cluster of three islands including the Southern Wolf Island Nature Preserve, can be seen about 12 miles farther out to sea to the east of Campobello in Canadian waters.

The waters off West Quoddy Head are also prime for whale watching—right from shore. Goggin was standing on the lawn near the lighthouse during the middle of the day in 2018 when he saw a humpback whale breach, exposing about two thirds of its back before it dived. Goggin said he has watched a lot of minke whales swim off the park's shores and has also seen finback whales.

From July to September, whales migrate off West Quoddy Head from their winter habitat in the US South and South America and can be seen following the tides here, which are among the most dramatic in Maine, located as it is at the mouth of the Bay of Fundy, according to a Maine Natural Heritage Hikes brochure about Quoddy Head State Park.

Taking our cue from Goggin, we sat on a picnic table on the lawn next to the light when the seas were calm and placid on a sunny early September day and black guillemots floated easily atop the mild waters. After staring at the ocean for a while, we spotted a couple of minke whales and a pod of harbor porpoises. It took patience to see the whales surface, and the mammals vanished quickly after showing their dorsal fins. It was easier to follow a gray seal that often poked its pointed nose and horselike head above the water while swimming near shore. Kimberly Ashby, executive director of the visitor center, said that September day we chose was one of the park's "magical days" for whale watching, when she herself saw whales from a window inside the center and numerous other hikers reported being thrilled by sightings of finbacks and minkes.

To start the hike, bear right (southwest) by a service building near the lighthouse along a gravel path that parallels the shore to pick up the Coastal Trail. Reach the picnic area parking lot, with some excellent exhibits at the edge of the lot. At a little more than 0.1 mile on the hike, come to a set of forty-one stairs that lead to a pebble beach and a small boulder beach that you might want to explore if the tide is right. The Coastal Trail is classified as easy to moderate, but it includes some challenging terrain.

A stone monument declares the easternmost point in the United States on the lawn around West Quoddy Head Light.

Visitors who don't go beyond West Quoddy Head Light miss out on views of steep cliffs and dramatic coastline.

A huge rocky head, covered with spruce and other conifers, looms to the southwest along the Coastal Trail as you hike by the first of a series of memorial benches with great views over the ocean out to Grand Manan Island. At 0.3 mile you can look down the cliffs to a chasm with big springtime cascades flowing down the rock face onto a rocky beach at the foot of cliffs. At 0.4 mile bear left (southwest); the trail changes from a gravel path to a narrow, rooted, and sometimes boggy path. Reach a bench before a cliff, with a cable for safety.

See a sign at 0.5 mile that points left (east) for a viewpoint of Gulliver's Hole, located at the foot of very steep volcanic cliffs. From the cliffs you can look over a vast blue sea and see the top of the lighthouse to the northeast, as well as part of Campobello Island and the Wolves Islands. Looking down the almost vertical cliffs to Gulliver's Hole, you can see a narrow chasm with waves crashing, but be careful around the edges of the cliffside. You get a better look at the precipitous sheer cliffs and rock formations that jut out above Gulliver's Hole.

The trail soon ascends wood steps with a view below to the left (south) of High Ledge, a 150-foot-high bluff. High Ledge has a sign and open area with views to the northeast of the lighthouse, Campobello Island, and the Wolves. High Ledge was matted in spots with black crowberry, a common low-growing evergreen shrub in north coastal Maine with purple flowers and dark berries.

Continue left (southwest) on the Coastal Trail when you reach a junction with the Inland Trail at 0.6 mile, which heads right back to the parking lot.

In a boggy area, cross a footbridge and at 0.9 mile reach the sign for a short side trail on the left (south) to Green Point, a sprawling ledge with views of a cobble beach to the north and a different perspective on Sail Rock. The lighthouse and Campobello are no longer in view at Green Point.

You can step along the rocks and climb to the top of Green Point, where you get tremendous views several miles to the southwest of aptly-named Boot Head, a giant headland kept in conservation by the Maine Coastal Heritage Trust, and of the pink granite of High Ledge to the northeast. As we stood on the pinnacle of Green Point, we saw a great blue heron glide in the sky and then land on rocks below the point, while three other great blue herons stood like sentries in the distance on the ledges of the southern shoreline. A solitary common loon floated offshore.

Continuing on the main trail, complete some rugged hiking and at 1.0 mile you get views of a rocky head stretching out into the ocean; then you see springtime cascades tumbling onto a beach off the trail. Cross some more bogwalk and then see a calm, quiet cove, similar to coves on Isle au Haut, an island off Stonington that is part of Acadia National Park. Look out to sea between the granite walls surrounding the cove for a great view of Grand Manan Island.

Pass an astonishing black-and-rust-colored cliff, with spruce on the sides of rock created more than 400 million years ago when volcanic magma jutted up from beneath the ocean floor and busted between existing rock layers.

The trail bears right (northwest) at 1.7 miles and parallels the shore as it starts rounding huge Carrying Place Cove. Descend steeply along sixteen steps on a stairway and reach a view over the ocean. Pass a cobble beach and continue the descent. Climb some wooden stairs and hike away from the shore.

At 1.8 miles you can see shacks and houses across the cove and hear vehicles on nearby South Lubec Road. The cove includes 1,200 feet of sandy, muddy beach at low tide, ideal for walking or watching migrating shorebirds in late summer and early fall.

At 2.0 miles reach a rocky beach and a bench at the cove and the junction with the Thompson Trail, the inland route back to the parking lot and a side trip to West Quoddy Head Bog and the Arctic Bog Walk. To the west and north of the beach is 40-acre Car-

rying Place Cove Bog, owned by the state and named a National Natural Landmark by the National Park Service for its coastal raised-plateau bog, one of only six such fully-featured peatlands in the United States. You can see the bog on either side of South Lubec Road, the access road for the park, but the distinctive raised wall of peat is only visible on the other side to the north. The bog is stop #42 on Maine's Ice Age Trail, a project of the University of Maine's Climate Change Institute founded by Harold Borns, professor emeritus. You can download a map to learn more about how the last ice age shaped the coast of Downeast Maine, from Bar Harbor

A sundew plant, growing at West Quoddy Head Bog, can trap and digest insects.

to Lubec, at iceagetrail.umaine.edu and explore the bog on your way out of the park on South Lubec Road.

Take a right (northeast) on the Thompson Trail and ascend slightly along rocks and roots on this inland route.

Walk along a series of bogwalks, cross some wet areas, and reach a junction with the Bog Trail at 3.1 miles. Turn left (northwest) to head to the Arctic Bog Walk for the not-to-be-missed West Quoddy Head Bog, created by glaciers some 8,000 years ago. At 3.2 miles take the short boardwalk that loops around the bog with some exhibits about these open peatlands, which are the farthest east of their kind in the United States.

Some of these exhibits are showing their age, but they are written clearly and are some of the best around in using plain English to explain the plants and formation of a big bog. The exhibits are also posted strategically to point out pitcher plants, which use their leaves to trap insects for food. Look out over the bog to see a virtual forest of colorful pitcher plants, or photograph the plants next to the walkway, but please remain on the boardwalk to conserve the delicate peatlands.

The bogwalk also includes stops for sundew, with gummy hairs that can glitter in the sun like dewdrops, giving the plant its name, and allowing it to catch and digest insects, as well as baked-apple berry, sphagnum moss, and the hummocks and hollows that distinguish this magnificent bog.

After spending some time at the bog, return to the junction with the Thompson Trail at 3.4 miles and bear left (southeast) to head toward the Inland Trail. At 3.5 miles turn left (northeast) onto the Inland Trail and stay straight on it as it overlaps with the Coastal Trail. At 3.7 miles, as the Inland Trail veers left, back inland, bear right to continue following the Coastal Trail along the oceanside cliffs.

Reach the picnic parking lot at 3.9 miles and the lighthouse at 4.0 miles.

MILES AND DIRECTIONS

0.0   Start at the Coastal trailhead to the right (southwest) of the lighthouse visitor center and service building and follow the gravel path along the shore.

0.1   Reach the picnic area parking lot; bear left on the gravel path to continue on the Coastal Trail, passing stairs that lead down to a small gravel beach.

0.4   Reach a junction and bear left (southwest) to Green Point. The trail changes from a gravel path to a rugged and sometimes boggy trail.

0.5   A sign points left (east) to the Gulliver's Hole viewpoint.

0.6   Reach a junction with the Inland Trail, which heads right, back to the parking lot. Go left (southwest) to continue on the Coastal Trail.

0.9   Reach a short side trail on the left (south) to Green Point.

1.0   Enjoy views of a rocky head along this stretch of trail, which can be wet here.

1.7   The trail bears right (northwest), paralleling the shore as it starts rounding Carrying Place Cove.

2.0   Reach a rocky beach and a bench at Carrying Place Cove and the junction with the Thompson Trail. Turn right (northeast) on the Thompson Trail to loop back toward the parking lot and the side trail to the Arctic Bog Walk.

3.1   Reach a junction with the Bog Trail and turn left (northwest) to head to the Arctic Bog Walk that takes you over West Quoddy Head Bog.

Quoddy Head State Park

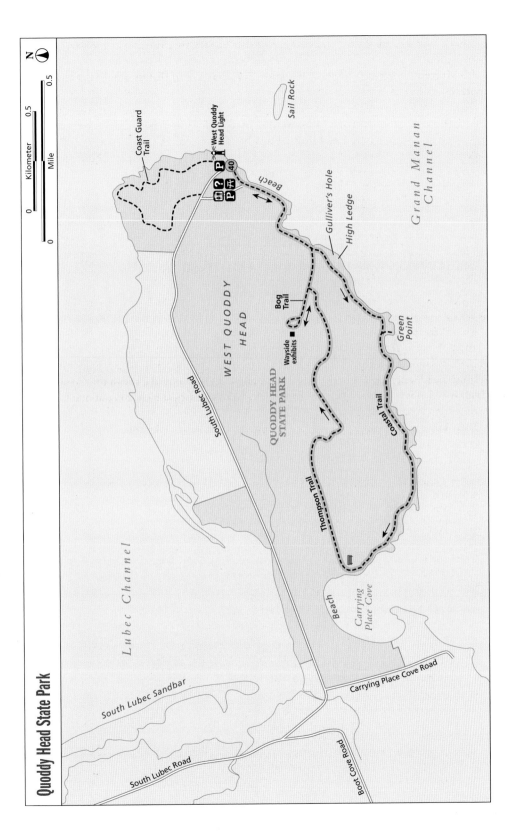

3.2 Take the short boardwalk that loops around the bog, and read the exhibits explaining the unique environment and plant life.

3.4 Return to the junction where the Thompson Trail came in; bear left (southeast) to head toward the Inland Trail.

3.5 Turn left (northeast) onto the Inland Trail, staying straight as it overlaps the Coastal Trail.

3.7 As the Inland Trail veers left, back inland, continue following the Coastal Trail along the oceanside cliff tops.

3.9 Reach the picnic area parking lot.

4.0 Arrive back at the lighthouse.

WATCHING FOR MARINE MAMMALS AND OTHER WILDLIFE

The coastal trails of Maine offer an exciting opportunity to spot some of the thousands of seals, harbor porpoises, and whales that feed and migrate in the Gulf of Maine.

Harbor and gray seals were once devastated by bounty programs in Maine and Massachusetts, but the resilient animals have recovered with the help of federal protection.

Samantha Wilkinson, manager of Reid State Park, says to keep your eye out for "our flippered friends," which are a common sight on the beaches, rocks, and water year-round at Reid. "You are likely to encounter a seal at Reid basically anywhere, at any time," she said. Carry binoculars or a camera with a zoom lens to best see seals and other marine mammals.

Numbering about 75,000 in the North Atlantic, harbor seals occur year-round in eastern Canada and Maine and are found farther south to New Jersey September through to May, reports the National Oceanic and Atmospheric Administration's National Marine Fisheries Service (NOAA Fisheries). About 27,000 to 40,000 of the much larger gray seals live in US waters, with pupping colonies on Green Island and Seal Island off Maine. Harbor seals are often seen hauled out on tidal ledges off the coast, especially during pupping season, the middle of May through June along the Maine coast.

With binoculars, you can watch harbor seals on ledges off Indian Point Blagden Preserve on Mount Desert Island or Great Wass Island Preserve. If you're patient, you can spot migrating minke whales and porpoises in August or early September at Quoddy Head State Park. Shawn Goggin, manager at Quoddy Head State Park, said people can fairly regularly see harbor seals swimming near shore off the Coastal Trail or off the lawn near the visitor center from about June until late September or early October.

From the shore at Wolfe's Neck Woods State Park in Freeport, people can see seals on the ledges in front of Little Bustins Island in Casco Bay. In 2019 there was a colony of

Three harbor seals and two pups are hauled out on a ledge off Great Wass Island during late spring.

about fifteen or more harbor seals, with a larger colony of closer to twenty-five seals in 2018, said Andy Hutchinson, park manager.

Maine and Massachusetts once paid a small bounty for the killing of harbor and gray seals. Seals were believed to hurt commercial fishing because they eat salmon, other fish, and lobsters. In 1973 Maine estimated that only thirty gray seals remained off the coast. Seal populations bounced back after the passage of the Marine

A pod of harbor porpoises surfaces at Schoodic Point in Acadia National Park.

Mammal Protection Act in 1972, which banned the killing and harassment of all marine mammals in American waters.

Over the years, viruses also have been fatal for seals. In an unusual event starting in July 2018 and through September 2019, more than 2,600 dead or stranded harbor and gray seals washed up on New England beaches, including more than 1,450 in Maine, according to NOAA statistics. The deaths were attributed to the phocine distemper virus. Anyone who sees a sick or injured seal, porpoise, or whale can report it on a NOAA hotline at (866) 755-NOAA (6622).

A couple of animals you are unlikely to see near the coast are moose and black bear, although they may wander to protected coastal lands such as in Acadia National Park or Petit Manan National Wildlife Refuge. Moose and black bear are more prevalent in the forests of western and northern Maine.

Deer are common in coastal Maine; porcupines, coyotes, and snowshoe hares can also be found. Saltwater beaver are seldom seen, but at least one beaver was thriving in a brackish pool near the ocean on Great Wass Island during a June visit.

You could potentially see bobcats in the coastal region, especially around the 2,174-acre Cutler Coast Public Reserved Land. "There have been sightings there in the past and plenty of signs that they are in the area on a somewhat frequent basis," said Carl Tugend, assistant regional wildlife biologist for the Maine Department of Inland Fisheries and Wildlife.

41 MOWRY BEACH PRESERVE

The chance to see a green heron or bald eagle, witness 20-foot tides, and learn why this area is a stop on Maine's Ice Age Trail are among the highlights of this Downeast Coastal Conservancy trail. The hike also features a 2,100-foot boardwalk, a sandy beach along what's usually a rockbound stretch of Maine coast, and nearby views of Canada, West Quoddy Head, and one of only three "sparkplug" lighthouses in the state.

Start: Mowry Beach Preserve trailhead, at the southwest end of the rear parking lot of Lubec Consolidated School
Elevation gain: 14 feet
Distance: 3.2 miles out and back
Difficulty: Easy
Hiking time: 1.5–2 hours
Seasons/schedule: Open year-round; best spring through fall and at low tide
Fees and permits: No fees or permits
Trail contact: Downeast Coastal Conservancy, PO Box 760, Lubec 04654; (207) 255-4500; downeastcoastalconservancy.org
Dog-friendly: Leashed dogs permitted
Trail surface: Boardwalk, sandy beach, tidal flats
Land status: 48 acres, including 1,800 feet of shorefront on Mowry Beach, owned and maintained by the nonprofit Downeast Coastal Conservancy. Remaining stretches of shoreline described in this hike are open to the public below the mean high-tide mark.
Nearest town: Lubec
Maps: USGS Lubec; Downeast Coastal Conservancy trail map

Other trail users: Birders, local residents, dog walkers, beachcombers
Special considerations: Chemical toilet available seasonally at a second parking lot at the end of Pleasant Street. Boardwalk and viewing platforms accessible for visitors with wheelchairs or strollers. If hiking out on the flats at low tide, be mindful of incoming 20-foot tide. It's generally safe only within 1.5 hours on either side of low tide. Check a tide chart in local newspapers or at usharbors.com/harbor/maine/lubec-me/tides/. Respect private property. Maine's law regarding public access to the coast is complicated; some private oceanfront owners have deeded rights to the mean low-tide mark, but the public has rights to "fish, fowl, and navigate" in the intertidal zone, as interpreted by the courts. The latest edition of a Maine citizen's guide says the public is permitted to use privately owned coastal areas below the mean high-tide mark, unless an owner explicitly restricts access. To stay updated on evolving Maine coastal law, visit accessingthemainecoast.com, a project based at the University of Maine.

FINDING THE TRAILHEAD

From US 1 in Whiting, take ME 189 toward Lubec, following signs to the Franklin D. Roosevelt International Memorial Bridge and Campobello Island in Canada. After passing the Lubec Historical Society on your left and the cemetery on your right, turn right (southeast) onto South Street to head toward Lubec Consolidated School. Park at the southwest end of the school's rear lot near the Mowry Beach Preserve boardwalk. **GPS:** N44 51.16' / W66 59.19'

WHAT TO SEE

Mowry Beach has a special edge-of-the-continent feel, located as it is in Lubec, the easternmost town in the United States. And like so many locations at the edge, it's a place of diversity, extremes, and juxtapositions, drawing artists and others seeking inspiration, or escape.

Mowry is an important spot for migratory, nesting, and wintering birds and is featured on the Downeast & Acadia Birding Trail. It lets you see an extreme 20-foot tide appear to strand the sparkplug-shaped Lubec Channel Light on vast tidal flats. It's a stop on Maine's Ice Age Trail, where you can look for a "drowned" or "drowning" forest—a sign of climate change and rising sea level—and for evidence of glacially deposited rocks, as Lubec was at the edge of the last ice age's ice sheet. It's also a largely sandy beach in a part of Maine where the coastline is usually made up of cobbles, boulders, or jagged cliffs.

The 48 acres that make up the Downeast Coastal Conservancy's Mowry Beach Preserve were purchased at a "bargain sale" price in 2004 from the family that had owned the land since the early 1800s with the help of the state's Land for Maine's Future Program. Though a relatively small parcel, the preserve provides important public access to

Lubec Light, known locally as the "sparkplug" lighthouse, seems stranded by the 20-foot tides off Mowry Beach.

Mowry Beach is a dog-friendly destination.

the 1.2-mile long Mowry Beach, as well as insights into what makes this area so rich and dynamic.

For more than thirty years, Ted CoConis, an artist in the Society of Illustrators Hall of Fame, has combed Mowry Beach at low tide with Kristen, his wife, model, and muse, looking for inspiration and stones. We ran into them one early-July morning, and they sang the praises of Mowry, noting that in certain zones it is layered with stones of all shapes, patterns, colors, and sizes. "Some of these rocks are utterly amazing. They are fantastic," said CoConis, whose illustrations have graced movie posters for *Hair* and *Fiddler on the Roof* and covers of books by Vladimir Nabokov, Jerzy Kosinski, and James Michener. He and Kristen have a home in nearby Cutler, and they maintain a website: tedcoconis.com.

For longtime Lubec resident Charles Legris, it's not the rocks but the wildlife that attracts him. We ran into the retired boatbuilder on a late-May visit. Among the wildlife he particularly appreciates seeing are bald eagles, which he said can put on "very spectacular" shows, often flying in twos or threes at different altitudes in the sky over Mowry.

As if on cue, a bald eagle flew high to the west and then another appeared in the sky overhead.

Bald eagles aren't the only birds on display at Mowry Beach. We've seen a green heron land on a log at the edge of a small brackish pond in front of us, common yellow warblers flitting from branch to branch, a red-winged blackbird, a song sparrow, a female American redstart, a catbird, and a black-capped chickadee.

As rich as the bird life is the plant life, especially along the 2,100-foot-long boardwalk through the wetlands behind Lubec Consolidated School. On visits in late May and early June, we saw along the boardwalk big-toothed aspens, alders, a cattail swamp, and the blooming white petals of shadbush, perhaps as thick a concentration of the shrub as we have ever encountered in one small area.

Shadbush only bloom for a couple of weeks, about the time of the spring shad run, before they shed their petals and then fruit, attracting cedar waxwings. Shadbush can freely hybridize and blend, even with a peach, noted botanist Jill E. Weber. They possess such complicated genetics that they can set seed without pollination. A single shadbush can display the shape of one species of the plant, the hairs of another, and the flowers of a third. "Shadbush are amazing," Weber said. "A lot of what you see is species in the process of becoming. They are neither one species nor the other, but a blending of several."

The botany of Mowry Beach is so dynamic, Downeast Coastal Conservancy is working on an interpretive guide to the plants with Carol Goodwillie, an East Carolina University

The Franklin Delano Roosevelt Bridge crosses a narrows to connect Lubec in Maine to Campobello Island in Canada.

associate professor who specializes in plant evolutionary genetics and ecology, said Jennifer Multhopp, a member of the nonprofit and Town of Lubec librarian.

But perhaps the most dynamic forces in evidence on Mowry are the ocean and the greatest tidal range on the East Coast of the United States, positioned as Lubec is at the mouth of the Bay of Fundy. A few years ago, a storm breached the sand dunes that once separated Mowry Beach from a freshwater pond and wetlands, and a section of the boardwalk that had once been protected is now vulnerable to the ocean's force, said Multhopp, who was among the volunteers spending a total of 800 hours building the boardwalk after the land was first acquired by the nonprofit. "Each winter, more and more water gets in," flooding underneath the boardwalk, she said. "I've always wondered in the spring what it's going to look like."

Saltwater intrusion is leading to a "drowning forest," as Multhopp termed it, with dead and dying trees now dotting the landscape at the edge of what had once been protected pond and wetlands. There's no need to search for a "drowned forest" of old rooted stumps along the expansive tidal flats off Mowry Beach, as Maine's Ice Age Trail map suggests, to understand the impact of climate change and sea level rise. Multhopp sees fresh evidence of it every time she walks the beach and boardwalk.

From the trailhead at the edge of the Lubec Consolidated School parking lot, head east on a gravel path at first and then pick up the wide, well-maintained boardwalk. At 0.2 mile reach a viewing platform with four wooden benches. Here you'll see the buildings of Lubec in the distance to your left (north) and hear the sounds of warblers in springtime.

At 0.3 mile reach a small brackish pond and another viewing platform, where you get your first glimpse of Lubec Channel Light and Mowry Beach through the sand dunes that have been breached here. Look for evidence of salt-intolerant trees, which are dead or dying as a result of the sea's intrusion. Multhopp said that before the dunes were breached, the pond had been a popular place to ice-skate in winter.

The boardwalk turns left (northeast) to parallel the shore and transitions to a gravel path that takes you a short distance to the second parking lot for Mowry Beach, at the foot of Pleasant Street. Upon reaching this lot, turn right (southeast) on a sandy path

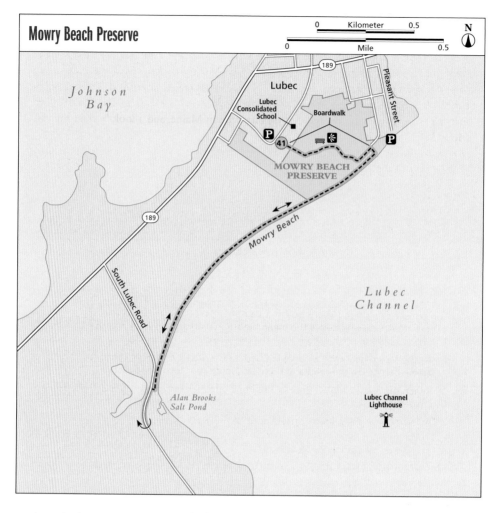

through the rugosa rose to reach the beach at 0.4 mile. Take in the expansive views of nearby Campobello Island to the left (east); Lubec Channel Light, known locally as the "sparkplug" lighthouse, straight ahead (south); and West Quoddy Head and Grand Manan Island farther south.

If you arrive at dead low tide, the tidal flats seemingly stretch forever and the lighthouse appears stranded. Be mindful of the incoming tide if you explore the flats—there is about a 20-foot swing between low and high tides. The tide is so powerful here that in 2014, it exposed the bones of a 54-foot finback whale that had washed ashore on Mowry Beach and been buried in a 15-foot trench twenty years earlier. A local business, Turtle Totem Cooperative, and volunteers unearthed the whale with permission from Downeast Coastal Conservancy and the help of researchers from the University of Maine at Machias and the College of the Atlantic in Bar Harbor. The plan is to reassemble the bones and display the skeleton somewhere in Lubec.

Turn right (southwest) to explore the 1.2-mile beach. Once beyond the first 1,800 feet of shoreline, which is owned by the Downeast Coastal Conservancy, be careful to stay below the mean high-tide mark in accordance with Maine law regarding public access to the coast, and respect private property owners' rights.

As the beach nears the S curve in South Lubec Road at 1.4 miles, turn right (northwest) on a gravel path up to the road; then turn left (southwest) along the road, being careful to watch out for oncoming traffic. At 1.6 miles reach the roadside 4.4-acre Alan Brooks Salt Pond, another Downeast Coastal Conservancy property, for a view of its spartina salt marsh, a rare natural community type in Maine, and a look back at the vast Mowry Beach you just walked.

Return the way you came.

MILES AND DIRECTIONS

0.0 Start at the Mowry Beach Preserve trailhead, at the southwest end of the rear parking lot of Lubec Consolidated School.

0.2 Reach a viewing platform with four wooden benches.

0.3 Reach a viewing platform near a brackish pond; follow the boardwalk as it turns left (northeast).

0.4 Reach a second parking lot at the end of Pleasant Street. Turn right (southeast) on a sandy path to Mowry Beach then right again (southwest) to walk the 1.2-mile beach, staying below the mean high-tide mark in accordance with Maine law regarding public access to privately owned stretches of the coast.

1.4 As the beach nears the S curve in South Lubec Road, turn right (northwest) on a gravel path up to the road and then left (southwest) along the road.

1.6 Reach the roadside Alan Brooks Salt Pond, another Downeast Coastal Conservancy property.

3.2 Arrive back at the Lubec Consolidated School parking lot.

MORE IN DOWNEAST

BREWERIES, EATS, AND SLEEPS

Strong Brewing Co., 7 Rope Ferry Rd., Sedgwick 04676; (207) 359-8722; strong brewing.com. Located on the Blue Hill Peninsula, the family-operated brewery has taproom hours Wed through Sun. Beers include a hybrid lager ale called Localmotive, Maineiac double IPA, and seasonally available Bluff Head brown ale, named for a hiking trail overlooking the Bagaduce River within walking distance of the brewery, with 5 percent of sales proceeds donated to the Blue Hill Heritage Trust. There are no formal tours, but ask and you likely will receive. Near Witherle Woods Preserve and Holbrook Island Sanctuary. Open year-round.

The Bluebird Ranch Family Restaurant, 78 Main St., Machias 04654; (207) 255-3351; bluebirdranchrestaurant.com. Family-owned since 1996, the restaurant is noted for its homemade donuts on Sundays, daily dinner specials, breads and jams, cocktails, fresh seafood like blackened haddock with crabcake, prime rib, cheesecakes, and pies. Near Great Wass Island Preserve, Cutler Coast Public Reserved Land, Quoddy Head State Park, and Mowry Beach Preserve. Open year-round.

Lubec Brewing Company, 41 Water St., Lubec 04652; (207) 733-4355; facebook .com/Lubec-Brewing-Company-1406990739591377/. On-site brewery offers daily tastings. Beers with distinctive names like Quoddy Head Red and Bailey's Mistake. The restaurant menu includes sourdough pizzas, soups, salad, seafood, and vegan dishes. *Saturday Night Live* founder Lorne Michaels and *The Tonight Show* host Jimmy Fallon have been spotted here, as have many of the participants in the Bay of Fundy International Marathon, held the fourth Sunday in June. Near Cutler Coast Public Reserved Land, Quoddy Head State Park, and Mowry Beach Preserve. Open year-round.

Helen's Restaurant, 111 Main St., Machias 04654; (207) 255-8423; helensrestaurantmachias .com. Known for its wild Maine blueberry pie and "Famous Fish Chowder," Helen's is a Downeast tradition, established in 1950. With "Death by Pie" as a motto emblazoned along with the restaurant's name on baseball caps and other souvenirs, Helen's has a Downeast sense of humor, displaying sayings like "Did you say exercise or extra fries?" by the dessert case. Near Cutler Coast Public Reserved Land, Quoddy Head State Park, and Mowry Beach Preserve. Open year-round.

Helen's Restaurant is a must stop for blueberry pie and seafood in Machias.

Frank's Dockside Restaurant and Take-Out, 20 Water St., Lubec 04652; (207) 733-4484; facebook.com/FranksDocksideRestaurantTakeOut/. Soups, chowders, and stews made from scratch every day, seafood, prime rib, and other fare. If you see wildlife—whether a loon or a gray seal—while dining on the deck overlooking Lubec Narrows, tell the waitress and she'll put your sighting on the daily chalkboard. Near Quoddy Head State Park and Mowry Beach Preserve. Open seasonally.

The Castine Inn, 33 Main St., Castine 04421; (207) 326-4365; castineinn.com. Historic inn overlooking Castine Harbor, featuring 19 guest rooms, including 3 suites; breakfast at discounted price for guests. On-site pub, notable garden open to the public, and locally made strawberry and blueberry jam. Near Witherle Woods Preserve and Holbrook Island Sanctuary. Open seasonally.

The Inn at Schoppee Farm, 21 Schoppee Dairy Rd., Machias 04654; (207) 263-8817; schoppeefarm.com. An 1800s farmhouse converted into an inn, it's set up on a hill overlooking the Machias River and the Down East Sunrise Trail, a multiuse trail open to runners, walkers, ATVs, and, in winter, snowmobilers, cross-country skiers, and the occasional dogsled. Currently offers 3 rooms, including a 2-bedroom suite, and has plans for expansion. Not a bed-and-breakfast, but a short distance from Helen's Restaurant. Near Great Wass Island Preserve, Cutler Coast Public Reserved Land, Quoddy Head State Park, and Mowry Beach Preserve. Open year-round.

The Eastland Motel, 385 County Rd., Lubec 04652; (207) 733-5501; eastlandmotel .com. Billing itself as "Your Eco-Adventure Destination," this motel offers complimentary snowshoes in winter to guests, homemade continental breakfast in season; offers several MP3 audio interpretive tours of the Lubec and Cobscook region for rent to the public. Near Cutler Coast Public Reserved Land, Quoddy Head State Park, and Mowry Beach Preserve. Open year-round.

CAMPING

Oceanfront Camping @ Reach Knolls, 666 Reach Rd., Brooklin 04616; (207) 359-5555; reachknolls.com. About 40 sites, some for RVs. Dogs allowed on-leash. Stairway to beautiful beach and shoreline on Eggemoggin Reach. Near Witherle Woods Preserve and Holbrook Island Sanctuary. Open Memorial Day to mid-Oct.

McClellan Park Camping and Picnic Ground, Wyman Road, Milbridge 04658; (207) 546-2688. Owned by the Town of Milbridge, offering wilderness camping on 12 sites for tents only. Campground is about 200 feet from oceanfront picnic area on Narraguagus Bay. Dogs allowed and must be under control of owner. Call the town for information at (207) 546-2422. Near Petit Manan National Wildlife Refuge and Great Wass Island Preserve. Open Memorial Day to the second Monday in Oct.

Cobscook Bay State Park, 40 South Edmunds Rd., Edmunds Township 04628; (207) 726-4412; maine.gov/cobscookbay. A total of 106 sites for tents and RVs. Dogs allowed on-leash. Starting in early February, reservations at Maine State Park campgrounds may be made online at maine.gov/dacf/parks/camping/reservations/ or by calling (207) 624-9950. Near Cutler Coast Public Reserved Land, Quoddy Head State Park, and Mowry Beach Preserve. Open May 15 to Oct. 15.

Sunset Point RV Park, 37 Sunset Rd., Lubec 04652; (207) 733-2272 in season, (401) 932-9011 off-season; sunsetpointrvpark.com. Billed as the "Easternmost Campground" and 1 mile from downtown Lubec, the park offers 37 sites, 29 for RVs and 8 for tents, all with water view on Johnson Bay. Near Cutler Coast Public Reserved Land, Quoddy Head State Park, and Mowry Beach Preserve. Open Memorial Day week to Oct. 1.

LIGHTHOUSES, MUSEUMS, AND HISTORIC SITES

Fort Point Light Station, 207 Lighthouse Rd., Stockton Springs 04981; (207) 941-4014; maine.gov/fortpoint. Located in Fort Point State Park, the 31-foot brick Fort Point Light was constructed as the first river light in Maine. Automated in 1988, the light beams above the Penobscot River between Stockton Springs and Castine. It was built in 1836 to aid ships that sailed the river to Bangor, once one of the world's most prosperous lumber ports. The tower and keeper's house, rebuilt in 1857 to replace the originals, are not open to the public, but the grounds and more than a mile of shoreline and a tidal sandbar are accessible. The 120-acre Fort Point State Park also includes the remains of Fort Pownall, the site of a Revolutionary War battle in 1775. Near Witherle Woods Preserve and Holbrook Island Sanctuary. Open Memorial Day through Labor Day.

Little River Light Station, Little River Island, Cutler 04626; (877) 276-4682; littleriverlight.org. If you want to channel the life of a lighthouse keeper, consider a stay at the historic Little River Light, named for its 15-acre island home at the entrance of Cutler Harbor and billed as the most northeastern island light station in the United States. (Nearby West Quoddy Head Light is on the easternmost point of the US mainland.) The Friends of Little River Lighthouse, a chapter of the American Lighthouse Foundation, which owns the lighthouse, offers 3 historic-style rooms for rent in the restored 1888 Keeper's House. Volunteers will meet you at the Cutler boat ramp and take you on a 12-minute boat ride to the lighthouse. The volunteers also provide special open houses at the lighthouse. Near Cutler Coast Public Reserved Land, Quoddy Head State Park, and Mowry Beach. Overnight stays are available June 15 to Sept. 15.

Burnham Tavern, 14 Colonial Way, Machias 04654; (207) 255-6930; burnhamtavern .com. Visit the place where Machias settlers met and hatched plans to win the first naval battle of the American Revolution. Called the Battle of Margaretta, the fight took place on June 12, 1775, when a group of patriots, some battle-tested from the French and Indian Wars, defeated the British schooner *Margaretta*. Today the tavern, built in 1770, is called the Burnham Tavern Museum and is a National Historic Site. Learn the history of the battle and see memorabilia from the family of Jeremiah O'Brien, who led the patriots to victory. Near Great Wass Island Preserve, Cutler Coast Public Reserved Land, Quoddy Head State Park, and Mowry Beach. Open seasonally.

COASTAL ATTRACTIONS

Machias Wild Blueberry Festival, 9 Center St. and other locations in Machias; (207) 255-6665; machiasblueberry.com. Held annually for more than forty years to coincide with the Maine wild blueberry harvest, the festival includes craft booths, food courts, a pie-eating contest, kids' activities, and fresh wild blueberries, good for freezing year-round. Sponsored by Centre Street Congregational Church, United Church of Christ, and held the third weekend of Aug. Near Great Wass Island Preserve, Cutler Coast Public Reserved Land, Quoddy Head State Park, and Mowry Beach.

Eastern Knubble Preserve, ME 191, Cutler 04626; (207) 729-7366; mcht.org/pre-serve/eastern-knubble/. Accessed from the village center of Cutler, this 31-acre Maine Coast Heritage Trust property, although small, includes cobble beaches, sheer cliffs, a low-tide walk to a small island known as Eastern Ear, and a spur trail to an old mine. Near Cutler Coast Public Reserved Land, Quoddy Head State Park, and Mowry Beach Preserve. Open year-round.

Lost Fishermen's Memorial Park in downtown Lubec is a somber shrine to the dangers of a life at sea.

Walking tour of Lubec, Lubec Memorial Library, 55 Water St., Lubec 04652; (207) 733-2491; lubec.lib.me.us. Start at the library, a valuable community resource with maps and information, and make your way north along Water Street, passing such sites as Lubec Landmarks and the McCurdy Smokehouse Museum, to the town pier and Lost Fishermen's Memorial Park overlooking Lubec Narrows, where you might spot a gray seal and other marine mammals coming in or out with the big tides. Not to be missed is the old Lubec Jail on Ferry Street, built in the

The old Lubec jail, a brick building nearly one hundred years old, is a site on the downtown walking tour.

1930s and one of the first brick buildings in town, located just west of the memorial park. At the intersection with Pleasant Street, bear left on what looks like a gravel driveway then left onto Ferry Street, now a little-used gravel road still marked by a street sign. Other sources for walking tours include toursoflubecandcobscook.com, with links to information about locally narrated MP3 audio tours available for rent. Near Cutler Coast Public Reserved Land, Quoddy Head State Park, and Mowry Beach Preserve. Walking tours possible year-round, weather permitting.

HIKE INDEX